Imagine an evening. The stars are high in an ink-black sky, and you are sitting, watching logs burn slowly on a campfire. You feel nothing, except warmth. Suddenly, a young woman casually begins setting fire to a thick wad of twenty pound notes above it, one-by-one. Emotions, like the spring sap, surge through you. Indignation. An uncontrollable urge to physically stop her. Utter bewilderment. The thought of all the useful things you could have done with those thin paper sheets, perhaps. Burning logs, burning paper. Why do the two acts invoke such vastly different emotional reactions, when, on a fundamental level, we are incinerating the same thing? The only significant distinction is that one wears a symbol. Because of a little symbol, and the cultural stories underlying it, people either live luxuriously or starve; forests stand proud or are clear-cut; oceans are left abundant with life or have their bottoms trawled. For reasons that have long since become obsolete, this is the power we have granted the story of money.

THE MONEYLESS MANIFESTO

MARK BOYLE

PERMANENT PUBLICATIONS

Published by
Permanent Publications
Hyden House Ltd
The Sustainability Centre
East Meon
Hampshire GU32 1HR
United Kingdom
Tel: 01730 823 311
Fax: 01730 823 322
Overseas: (international code +44 - 1730)
Email: info@permaculture.co.uk
Web: www.permaculture.co.uk

Design by Tim Harland
Cover design by Jacob Stow, www.jacobstow.com

Printed in the UK by CPI Antony Rowe, Chippenham, Wiltshire

Printed on paper from mixed sources certified by the Forest Stewardship Council
The Forest Stewardship Council (FSC) is a non-profit international organisation established to promote the responsible management of the world's forests. Products carrying the FSC label are independently certified to assure consumers that they come from forests that are managed to meet the social, economic and ecological needs of present and future generations.

British Library Cataloguing-in-Publication Data
A catalogue record for this book is available from the British Library

ISBN 978 1 85623 101 5

"Written with passion and outstanding integrity, Mark Boyle's latest book breaks new ground in the field of genuine sustainability – one without money. It's not as if we haven't done this before. The Romans brought us money along with marriage (the ownership of a woman by her husband) and nuclear families. Boyle is living proof that it's not only possible to live without money, but that life is more heart-ful, more real, and infinitely more sustainable."

Manda Scott, *Sunday Times* bestselling author of *Boudica* and *Rome*

"The revolution before us is only worth joining if it goes to the depths that Mark has explored ... it is my hope that this book will deepen its readers' belief in the possibility of such a world."

Charles Eisenstein, (from the Foreword)
author of *Sacred Economics* and *The Ascent of Humanity*

"In this timely and deeply thought-provoking book, Mark Boyle gently dissolves and rethinks the ultimate quantity that so preoccupies us in our measurement-obsessed culture: *money*. Read this book to discover how your life can be transformed by a world of qualities where the central values are reciprocity, community and the growth of our humanity and compassion."

Dr Stephan Harding, author of *Animate Earth: Science, Intuition and Gaia*
and Head of Holistic Science at Schumacher College.

"Our culture has lost its way and our love affair with money has led us to exploit people and our planetary resources to such an extent that we are now threatening our very existence and committing Ecocide. By reframing our reliance on money and demonstrating that we can even live without it in a modern society, Mark delivers a powerful message that we can build a saner, more ecologically balanced and just culture."

Polly Higgins, international barrister
and award-winning author of *Eradicating Ecocide*

"An inspiring meditation on the divisive power of money, which also offers excellent practical suggestions for escaping its grip."

Tom Hodgkinson, *Sunday Times* bestselling author of *How to be Idle*

"Mark Boyle is a brave man. *The Moneyless Manifesto* explodes the myth about money and brings the reader nearer to the truth that money is not true wealth. It is the land, the forests, the animals, the people, the community and the human hands that creates true wealth. I hope the Chancellor of the Exchequer reads this book. This book will open the eyes of bankers, hedge fund managers and financiers who live in the world of make believe. *The Moneyless Manifesto* shatters the illusion that we cannot live without money."

Satish Kumar, Editor-in-Chief of *Resurgence & Ecologist*

"This book will make you think – make you wonder, make you ponder, maybe make you change. It's remarkably important."

Bill McKibben, author of *Deep Economy* and *The End of Nature*

"*The Moneyless Manifesto* is a must read for anyone who wants to reassess their relationship with money. Whatever your circumstances, this book will provide you with the tools and strategies to rewrite your own personal story and will empower you to begin making the transition towards a 100% local gift economy. In this book, Boyle has drawn upon his background in economics, his experience of living both inside and outside the monetary system and the deep insights afforded to him through his reconnection with the natural world. It is a unique and important book for these unique and important times."

Brigit Strawbridge, star of BBC's 'It's Not Easy Being Green'

"*The Moneyless Manifesto* combines a practical guide to reducing or eliminating dependence on money with potent reflections on why we might want to. Both are born of solid experience. Writing with his natural humour and everyman accessibility, Mark Boyle reminds us of the urgency of living well and escaping the madness of money-led living, not only as a positive lifestyle choice, but as a direct response to the ongoing devastation of our only life-support system, Nature. Boyle's rarely-trodden path seems to me a key element in our collective groping towards a better way to live. I suspect he will soon have a whole lot more company."

Shaun Chamberlin, author of *The Transition Timeline*
and founder of Dark Optimism

Money is no longer a method of trade and exchange, it has become the control mechanism of 21st century post-industrial society that holds us all in its sway. Mark Boyle's example of living without money, whilst living a satisfying and full life, explodes the myth that we need money to survive modern life. Quite the opposite, he proves that less money can mean more personal freedom. This is a liberating concept and it paves the way for strategically developing a human-scale gift economy that will set us free.

Maddy Harland, editor of *Permaculture* magazine
and co-founder of The Sustainability Centre

"In *The Moneyless Manifesto*, Mark Boyle invites us to develop a different kind of wealth, one based not on money but on the quality of our relationships, connectedness with community and sense of purpose in life. At a time when social, economic and ecological systems might be on the verge of collapse, this book offers an essential pathway to recovery."

Dr Chris Johnstone, author of *Find Your Power*
and (with Joanna Macy) *Active Hope*

"I'm not related to Mark Boyle (as far as I know), but I wish I was – not because I have the courage to follow him down all the logical paths he is taking, but because he is a true heretic, in the very best sense of the word: someone who questions everything and comes to dangerous and exciting conclusions about life and the future."

David Boyle, author of *Money Matters, Authenticity*
and *The Human Element*

"I've heard Mark speak in public and I can tell you it's a moving experience. His deep compassion, his refusal to shy away from hard truths, his vision of a better future and the power of his personality combine to make it so. I imagine Old Testament prophets must have had the same quality as Mark. In as much as the written word can ever express such passionate communication, it's here in this book. *The Moneyless Manifesto* is both a practical guide to creating a gift economy in place of our present money economy and the testament of a truly inspired man."

Patrick Whitefield, author of *The Earth Care Manual*

"This is the time to ask questions that challenge fundamental assumptions hidden beneath our day to day preoccupation with 'earning a living'. Mark Boyle's book does just this. It is courageous, vibrant, and alive with possibility. *The Moneyless Manifesto* is a call to action, a paean to our beautiful Earth, an invitation to freedom. We would be wise to listen, and remember that inaction is a choice."

Tim 'Mac' Macartney, author of *Finding Earth, Finding Soul* and founder of Embercombe

"Mark has taken some of the leading thinkers from the present day and the past to write a manifesto for the Occupy generation."

Andy Hamilton, author of *Booze for Free*

"Mark Boyle really makes you think. If this is a pursuit you enjoy, this is the book for you."

Tristram Stuart, author of *Waste: Uncovering the Global Food Scandal*

"Part manual and part philosophy, Mark's book promises to change the way you look at money."

Dave Hamilton, author of *Grow your Food for Free (well almost)*

CONTENTS

WHY THIS BOOK IS ALSO AVAILABLE FREE

I wanted to make this book as free as possible for three reasons. First, the ideas and practical tools contained within it should be free to whoever may find them useful, and not made falsely scarce by the mechanisms of the monetary economy. Second, just as actions display our beliefs more honestly than our words, the ways in which ideas and practical tools are shared are at least as important as the words themselves. I wanted the medium to be fully aligned with the message. Third, I wanted to release it under a Creative Commons licence because it felt fraudulent to have my name on the front of this book. As I said in the acknowledgements page of my last book, what are my words but "an accumulation of all that has come before them – the people I have met, the books I have read, the songs I grew up with, the rivers I've swam in, the girls I've kissed, the movies I've watched, the traditions I've learned, the philosophers I've studied, the mistakes I've made, the violence I've seen, the love I've witnessed." The ideas in this book could be no more truly mine than the piece of the Earth I inhabit.

If you have bought a hard copy of this book, your money is going towards two things – the cost of printing a book in a money-based economy, which is a reality of our Age; and supporting some other work – that of Permanent Publications in the field of permaculture, and that of myself and others in our efforts to create a fully localised gift economy. We aim for this to be a resource for others to draw upon, and an example of another way of living on this planet – one in intimate connection with the land under our feet, the myriad forms of life we share it with, and the people of our communities. Thank you for your kindness in supporting these endeavours.

For more information, or to contribute your own thoughts and practical solutions to the forum accompanying this book, go to:
www.moneylessmanifesto.org

ABOUT THE AUTHOR

Mark Boyle has lived completely without money in England for two and a half years, an experience which formed the basis for his first book, *The Moneyless Man*. He is also the founder of Freeconomy (*justfortheloveofit.org*), an alternative economy with local groups across 160 countries. He holds a degree in Business and for most of his professional career was involved in the management of organic food companies.

ACKNOWLEDGEMENTS

Recognising and celebrating our interconnection and interdependency with all of life is a prominent theme of this book, so I ought to start by saying thank you to some of those who don't get much appreciation in The Age of The Machine. To the algae and the trees for filling my lungs full of fresh air, the soil for the nourishment it gives me each day, the Sun for both its warmth and its reflection on our planet's waterbodies, whom themselves deserve thanks for hydrating me so generously and for gifting me innumerable swims. To the earthworms for digging, the bees for pollinating, and the bluebells for bluebelling. Instead of writing words they'll never read and which will be of little use to them if not acted upon, the best way I can acknowledge their unquantifiable contribution to my life and this work is to defend and protect their health to the fullest of my ability from this day forth, something I haven't done a very good job of up to now.

There are a number of humans that have made invaluable gifts of their time, thoughts and talents to this book, too. Top of that list are Jess Pasteiner and Shaun Chamberlin. Jess, thank you for reminding me that life is a wonderful adventure, for loving me unconditionally and for wanting to share your life with me. Not to mention the small matter of your marvellous work on this book. I love you. Shaun, you're a brother to me and I cannot thank you enough for the days you spent going through each line painstakingly. Most importantly, for your friendship. On top of that, I want to say a heartfelt thanks to Tom Smith and Zoe Wangler, for your feedback, support and growing friendship.

I want to say a special thanks to the inspirational Maddy and Tim Harland (and the rest of the team) at Permanent Publications for their courage, integrity and enthusiasm in bringing this book into the world in the way they have. I hope their bravery will inspire other publishers to follow suit. Most of all, thank you for your friendship. A huge thanks to Jacob Stow for his fantastic work and generosity designing the accompanying website for this book, to Dan Knowlson at Lightbeing Creations for very kindly offering to host it for free, and to James Light for making such a wonderful film in the spirit of the book.

Then there are those who weren't directly involved in creating this book, but whose influence has had an invaluable impact on my life. Mum and Dad, I will never be able to thank you enough for your unconditional love and support throughout my life. To Mari, I'll always hold you very dear in my heart, you're a beautiful spirit. To Fergus, it is a pleasure just knowing your feet are gravitated to the same planet as mine. To Adeline, I wish you all the courage in the world for your journey, and thank you for all your care, kindness and mousse over the last year. And to others such as Dawn, Chris, Suzie, Markus and Paradox, thank you for the time we've spent together. To my oldest friends: Marty, Stephen, Fergie, Bernard, Hoey, Ronnie, Paddy and the rest of the crew for the lifetime of friendship. To my sister Jean and all her family. My community – near and far – thank you for your support.

If I have forgotten anyone I shouldn't have, sue me for a pint of cider the next time I see you.

THANKS TO THE CONTRIBUTORS

I would like to say a heartfelt thanks to David Holmgren, Charles Eisenstein, Martin Crawford, Zoe Hawes, Charles Dowding, Fergus Drennan, Tim 'Mac' Macartney, Kath Kelly, Jess Pasteiner, Chris Johnstone, Dave Hamilton, Andy Hamilton, Steph Hafferty, Nicky Scott, Ross Mountney, Malcolm Handoll, Will Lord and Richard Andersen for contributing your time, energy and knowledge to this book, and especially for the many years of graft and study that enabled you to be able to make such valuable contributions to begin with. The results of your labours are a huge benefit to us all and they will prove essential to whatever type of economy comes next.

To the day that Humanity walks with humility, connection and great heart amongst the Wild again, and that little inch of each of us that knows there is a story more sublime, more dignified, more glorious, than numbers.

FOREWORD

by Charles Eisenstein

Going into my first conversation with Mark Boyle a year ago, I was feeling a little bit defensive. "He probably thinks he is better than the rest of us," I thought. "More ethical, more pure, less complicit in the sins of civilization." His very lifestyle was an implied accusation.

When we actually began talking, though, I found Mark to be free of sanctimoniousness or self-congratulation. That is why his message resonates with so many people. His evident goodwill, care and compassion disarms us so that we can take in what he has discovered: going moneyless is a gateway to connection, intimacy, adventure, and an authentic experience of life. Far from being a path of sacrifice to qualify oneself as good, it is a path of joy and – dare I say it? – a path of wealth.

One contribution of this book is to open that path to others. Often I hear people preface their thoughts on right livelihood with, "Of course, we all have to make money..." We have mortgages to service, bills to pay; there is, after all, a 'cost of living'. We take it for granted that we have to pay merely to be alive. What Mark shows is that this assumption is part of an illusion. While we might for very good reasons choose to use money, we may not actually have to.

To break free of that illusion requires a profound shift in our perceptions, habits, and core beliefs; a shift in our way of being in the world, even in our sense of self. The monetized life is a life that separates people from community and from Nature, channeling our interdependency through an anonymous medium. Money promises that, if only we acquire enough of it, we can be independent. We can be independent of the people around us: "I don't need their help – I can pay for whatever I need." We can be independent of the nature around us: "If the water is polluted, I can buy it in bottles.

If the soil is toxic, I can buy organic food from afar. In the worst case I can afford to move away."

Here, then, is another illusion: we cannot actually achieve independence via money. All we can do is transfer our dependence from one place to another: from the people and places around us, to money and the distant institutions it associates us with. In fact, we are connected beings, utterly dependent on the rest of life to sustain us. Civilized humanity has denied that dependency for a long time, seeking lordship over Nature, transcendence of Nature. Money has been part of that illusion of mastery. But today we are moving into an ecological age, seeking to rejoin the circle of life in all its dimensions – ecological and social.

Mark Boyle offers us one way to do this. The circle of life is the circle of the gift. Except in those rare instances of barter, living moneylessly reconnects a person to the immediate experience of giving and receiving, and to the ties that result from that experience. Receiving a gift, one feels gratitude toward the giver, toward the giver's community, or even toward the universe, and with it the desire to give in turn. Giving a gift, one feels a connection as well: a freedom to ask something of, and receive from, that person, community, or planet. Whereas a money transaction is a closed relationship, over as soon as the money is paid, a gift-relationship is open-ended. Gifts create bonds, connections. This, and not some imagined exculpation from the sins of industrial society, is the best reason to live moneylessly.

None of this means that living moneyless is the only way to enter the spirit of the gift. After all, money itself can be given as a gift. However, money as we know it is fraught with noxious, disconnecting states of consciousness that are contrary to that spirit: scarcity, anxiety, grasping, competition. Going moneyless is therefore a short-cut to the spirit of the gift.

What about the collective level? Can we build a society on the spirit of the gift? And would this necessarily be a moneyless society? Perhaps so, in the long run, but even then we will need some way to circulate various forms of wealth, to coordinate labor over vast social distances, and to direct human creativity toward a common purpose. Money, although increasingly dysfunctional today, is supposed to perform these functions. In a more enlightened society, money would do so while evoking a whole new set of intuitions about wealth, security, and the nature of work, and a different way of being in and relating to the world. Indeed, I and many other theorists are working on how to transform money so that it is no longer the enemy of ecology, sustainability, justice and abundance.

That is why I believe Mark's work has a significance beyond merely describing a more joyful, connected way of living. He is also contributing to the psychic groundwork of a new system – even if that system includes something we might call money. The revolution before us is only worth joining if it goes to the depths that Mark has explored: the surrender to the flow of life, the recognition of generosity as a core principle of human nature, the trust that as I give, so shall I receive. It is my hope that this book will deepen its readers' belief in the possibility of such a world.

Charles Eisenstein
August 2012
author of
Sacred Economics – Money, Gift & Society in the Age of Transition

INTRODUCTION

Rather than love, than money, than fame, give me truth.
Henry David Thoreau

We were crunching our way through the fresh January snow one blue-skied afternoon, my little hand in hers, when my mum gently told me that Santa Claus wasn't real. She was being kind of course, a pinch of tough love to save me the ignominy of telling the more streetwise kids what he had brought me that Christmas. But I was seven and a half, and I had already begun questioning the credibility of this rather portly *gift economist* for myself. My suspicions kicked in when I was about four.

Up until then, Santa gave to me unconditionally, just like my own mother's breast had once done, regardless of whether I was naughty or nice. As my fifth Christmas approached, I remember being told that things weren't so easy with the big guy after all, and that I wasn't deserving of his kindness any longer unless I was a good boy. Santa's love, and life with him, seemed to be slowly turning conditional. But us little kids knew that conditionality was not the way of Nature (the bramble never asked me if I was naughty before giving me its blackberries, nor the stream its water), so I smelt a rat. Yet voicing such doubts, I feared, could have resulted in a sudden drought of new toys, so for two and a half years I blanked out the thoughts, shut up and went along with the fanciful story. Little kids can be cunning too.

Despite my strong suspicions, I remember experiencing various emotions as mum confirmed my doubts. Most of these feelings manifested as questions. If Santa wasn't real, but just a myth that all us kids believed – or chose to go along with because we perceived some benefit from it – then where on Earth did all the toys under our noble fir tree come from? Who made them if not his little helpers?

Feelings of hurt quickly abounded. Why did those I loved lie to me for so many years? Why did they believe that telling me that some strange, fictional entity had brought me the toys would serve me better than telling me the truth: that those I loved had given them to me? Was it a case of my parents wanting to give me what many religions believe to be the purest of all gifts: the gift which seeks no gratitude or recognition, in the mindset "that the only true charity is anonymous"?[1] Or had our culture long since twisted this most life-affirming of stories into a gradual lesson in conditionality, an incremental acclimatisation to the economic sphere my schooling was already preparing me for? Was it now being used to accompany me on that lonesome modern journey from the unconditional to the conditional, a precursor to a life where everything I received would be conditional on what I gave in return? A life where I would only give, or behave in a certain way, if I received something else. Or was it more simple than that: a society of people mindlessly passing down and reliving an old story, one long since manipulated by corporate marketing departments, with little thought about whether this revamped myth was actually serving them well or not any longer?

Like all big girls and boys, deep down I wanted to know the truth, as disconcerting as it was. The truth is always better than a story, which is partially why I felt compelled to write this book. The truth I needed to face back then was that Santa Claus wasn't real. He was just a myth we made up, passed down from one generation to another, just like leprechauns, the concepts of good and evil, and the belief that licking goats' testicles is a remedy for impotence.

Just like money.

It was this last truth I wanted to face up to in my late twenties. Believe it or not, the concept of money – that modern numerical manifestation of our ideas about credit and debt – is no less of a story than that of Santa Claus and his previous incarnations. When questioned about the extremity of his decision to live moneylessly, Daniel Suelo,[2] who has been living for over twelve years in the US without a dime, once said:

> *... to say that I live without money isn't saying anything, really. That's like saying I live without belief in Santa Claus. Now,*

> *if we lived in a world where everyone believed in Santa Claus, you might think I am stepping out on a limb to live without Santa Claus.*

Why is the need for money a myth? Take a minute to look around you. Try to find one thing you believe hasn't been provided by money. My guess is you can't. Even if you've grown your own food, I would imagine you'd be thinking 'well, I paid for the seeds, and I paid for my tools'. And that is the power we have granted money – we have come to believe that we need it, that we depend on it to survive. The fact we've designed this impersonal and destructive economy of ours around it only serves to perpetuate such delusions. The cultural narrative that is money has such a powerful grip on our minds today that we have come to believe that we could not possibly ever live without it. Through observing humanity's actions, it would appear that living without clean air, fresh water and fertile soil is considered a more moderate challenge in comparison.

We grown-ups strangely believe that money provides for us when it is actually Nature (which includes humans) that does so. That we must rely on money is simply another delusion, given power only by the fact that we collectively agree to believe in it. Even Adam Smith, the father of modern economics, said that "all money is a matter of belief".[3] We believe in it because experience has taught us that we can get things in return for it, and every time we enact the various rituals (cheque signing, credit card purchasing) of this story, we strengthen that belief and its grip on our minds.

Fiat currency,[4] money's most common form today, has no intrinsic value to set alongside its use as a medium of exchange, meaning that unless we believe the socio-political, cultural and economic stories that go with it, it can become almost worthless overnight, as countries who have suffered hyper-inflation have miserably realised. If our culture stopped believing the myths that back money – and the converging ecological, social and financial crises are forcing us to do so – the notes in the bank (which in a fractional reserve system, aren't many) would have no more worth than their value as a fire-starter. Which, believe me, is much less than a piece of birch bark.

One myth that backs money is that our bank balances will always be redeemable for goods and services *with* intrinsic value, such as vegetables or a table. However, in a world where almost all of our natural and social capital has been melted down into numbers, with increasingly less of our physical and cultural 'assets' left to be liquidated, such beliefs must soon be questioned. When the rivers are devoid of salmon and full of pollutants, when the invasion of our forests and oceans is complete, when our topsoil is fully depleted and we've laid desert to much of the Earth, "all that will be left is cold, dead money, as forewarned by the myth of King Midas so many centuries ago. We will be dead – but very, very rich."[5]

Another such myth is that you and I are separate. When the illusion of this myth also fades (and one of the aims of this book is the dissolution of this myth), me charging you for the gifts I bring to the world (gifts, remember, that I have originally been given), is no less daft than me charging a tree for the nitrogen in my urine when I pee under it, and it then invoicing me for the oxygen it produces and supplies to my lungs. Nature, like me, abhors bureaucracy and administration, so it simply gives unconditionally, wastes no energy on accounting and surveillance, and instead gets on with doing what it was born to do. In fact, its monumental efficiency is down to the fact that nothing – not the bacteria, not the birds, not the algae – is keeping count. And we should be thankful for that reality – there are so many million interactions going on in every square inch of soil alone, at any given moment, that our entire world would collapse if it ever tried to.

There is absolutely nothing wrong with stories in themselves as long as they continue to serve us and our habitat well and we can remember one thing: they are just stories, and we can create better ones if we feel they'd be more appropriate for the world we are confronted with. If believing in the myths of Santa Claus or money or licking goats' testicles helps us live more fulfilling, free and healthy lives in a way that affords the rest of the community of life the same opportunities, then I'm all for it. But if not, would we not be a little wiser to start creating new cultural stories that serve us better?

At this point you're probably thinking that money has actually served us well thus far. It has facilitated the 'civilisation' we have before us today – the televisions, the cars, the World Wide Web. Yet how many of us feel utterly enslaved by it, always feeling that we need a little more of it to survive, be happy or feel successful? As I once read on the back of a toilet door, freedom disappears under the dominance of a bad habit.

What if the cultural stories (such as the narrative of the separate self, which I'll be exploring throughout this book) that gave rise to money in the first place turned out to be based on nothing less than the destructive delusions of humanity? What if you realised that the very concept of money, despite its supposedly functional beginnings, would inevitably lead to the Earth and its biosphere becoming uninhabitable for humans and many other life forms in the process? Would you continue to go along with such a destructive story, or would you want to create a new one, a story that worked for your Age and for the unique challenges that your people faced?

Throughout this book, I am going to question the myths that laid the foundations to the birth of money, to highlight the damaging consequences that were inevitable since its very creation but which only hindsight has made evident, and – most importantly – to ask you to help humanity come up with new stories, different ways of doing things that makes sense for the world we're all faced with today.

A reluctant author

I've found that the more I learn in life, the less I know, or could ever know. It feels arrogant to write a book that could, inadvertently, give the impression that I – a man only beginning to fully understand even the most basic parts of himself – have any of the answers to humanity's current conundrums. So it is with a certain degree of reluctance that I write this book.

We live in a world of many human cultures, despite the fact that they are being relentlessly homogenised by the cultural hegemony and imperialism that has replaced its more traditional forms and which has become synonymous with globalisation. Amongst these there are myriad subcultures, all existing in relationship with ecologies and social conventions too complex to ever intellectually grasp. We're a collection of ancestries, with different spiritual and religious faiths and the deep-rooted stories that come with them. Over millennia our planet has been sliced up into nations with borders, who have developed their own laws, levels of development, social etiquette, cultural myths, material expectations, gender and sex issues, physical and emotional addictions, microclimates and financial complexities. Even within such diverse demographic groups, personalities vary widely. The same nation homes both Noam Chomsky and Rupert Murdoch.

Yet despite such vast differences, there is much to unite every one of us. We live on one planet, within one biosphere, and our fates are interdependent. Together we face a smörgåsbord of social, ecological and economic challenges of a truly epic scale, and we hold in common some of the stories that originated them. These converging crises – which provide us with the most exciting opportunity to reappraise and fundamentally change the way we (in the global West) live for the benefit of all life – have no panacea, with one possible exception: the cultivation of a new attitude and spirit in which to live our lives, a simple changing of the lens through which we perceive the world.

While collectively taking off the lens called *how much can I get?* and putting on another labelled *how much can I give?*, *how many people can I make smile today?* or *how can we work together to nourish and sustain the life around us?* wouldn't by itself cut the Gordian Knots of climate chaos, resource depletion and TV-generated boy bands, it would make for a crucial starting point. Take a moment and think about it. Imagine how our days would feel if we lived our lives with such a fresh outlook and focus. None of us fully understand what lies ahead, but fostering an unconditional commitment to help each other through it all, come what may, is a rather useful prerequisite to any of the more technical solutions. If we can't find a more caring, respectful, fulfilling and meaningful way to live together, what is the point of existing here anyway?

Aside from suggesting such a new and radical life perspective, I certainly lay no claim to having any, let alone all, of the answers to humanity's monumental challenges. It is true that I have a rather peculiar and unique perspective on the world, having made an odd journey from being an overtly consumerist business graduate to someone who lived completely without money for almost three years, allowing me the opportunity to experience both perspectives and to see which story most fulfilled me. It turned out to be a life-altering endeavour,[6] yet it made me realise that there is no one global answer, and the logic behind thinking that there might be is precisely the same logic that got us into this mess in the first place. The answers to the challenges we face must be localised, and stories must be tailored to meet the needs of the people in each unique landbase.

That said, in the coming chapters I would like to do two things. I aim to dive deep into what I believe to be one of the root causes of many of our seemingly unsolvable predicaments and explore one of the myths that have led us to this pivotal point in human history. A myth that almost the entirety of the world's cultures, nations and faiths now buy into, perhaps the most omnipresent tale in the history of our species.

By suggesting possible solutions to the challenges that await us I aim only to encourage you to recognise that the monetary economy is not the only type of economy we can choose, and to consider whether or not other economic models are needed for the unique period of human history we are facing. This is no longer 16,000 B.C. after all, so why should we continue mindlessly perpetuating rituals which grew from cultural myths that were relevant and useful for that stage in our evolution, but arguably are not so appropriate for us now?

Regardless of whether you love money or hate it, its benefits are widely recognised and it is undoubtedly one of the most revolutionary concepts we've ever devised, having provided a framework for all the subsequent revolutionary change that has shaped today's world. What I feel is entirely lacking, however, is a deeper awareness and understanding of what the full consequences of money are on us personally, socially and ecologically. One of my aims will be to explain why I believe humanity needs to move beyond the tale of money, and its underlying mindset of formal exchange, if we are to have a long-term future worth having on this planet.

This book's *raison d'être* certainly isn't just to explain the reasons I believe we need to reexamine our relationship with money. Its ultimate goal is to provide you with a comprehensive menu of ways through which you can meet your needs without money (or at least become less dependent on it); ways that allow you a lot more control over your life and as much creativity as you can handle; how you can limit your negative – and increase your positive – impact on the rest of Nature and your own community; how to free yourself up from a job you are not enjoying any more; or simply pathways to parts of yourself you didn't even know existed.

We all have our own reasons for wanting to reduce our dependency on money, or to simply spend less of it. My own initial, and very personal, reason was to reconnect with my landbase and the people and creatures I share it with, as I strongly believe that until we reconnect in those ways, true sustainability and non-exploitative ways of living will simply remain something we talk about at posh conferences over coffee. Now my reasons for moving beyond the monetary economy seem to grow by the day, and I will explore these in the next chapter. I also realised I wanted to live in freedom, in a way that afforded the rest of life I share the planet with that same simple opportunity. Freedom and happiness won at the expense of that of another is not the freedom and happiness I want.

For many people I know, their reason is more urgent and less highfalutin': they no longer have a job. The large negative equity on their mortgaged homes means that they're unable to move somewhere that has available employment. Others simply want to live outside of the system and take back some of the freedom they feel is being incrementally stolen from them. More still are outraged at the privatisation of the money-creation process, whilst some are getting ready for both financial and ecological apocalyptic scenarios. These are all mostly practical reasons, but just as many people tell me they strive towards moneylessness for their own private spiritual reasons.

None of these reasons for questioning our relationship with money are more right or wrong than the others, and they are all valid. This liquid tool, one that ought to exist to serve us, has stealthily become our master instead, harming us on many levels, each of us in different ways. It is my opinion that it may have already served its useful time here, having already brought us to a point in our collective evolution where we can now decide to start moving beyond the monetary economy, and into a *localised gift economy*, which I will describe in chapter two.

All art is propaganda

When reading this book, there are a couple of things I'd ask you to keep in mind. The more practical part of this book – chapter five onwards – describes the range of building blocks that you, often unknowingly, already have at your disposal for the new design of human society. Pioneers have long since been dedicating their lives to the various parts of the localised gift economy; therefore many of the potential solutions have already been tried and tested, waiting for us to design them into a new holistic way of living and, most importantly, to enact them.

Where it's possible to describe how to do something fully, such as growing your own shampoo or foraging your own wild sexual lubricant, I do. However, some of the moneyless solutions throughout the following chapters, such as forest gardening in small back gardens in the city, are books in themselves, and when that is the case my only aim is to give you a glimpse of its potential to see if it catches the corner of your eye. If it does, you'll find that I've referenced the books and other sources (often as a footnote) that, from my experience, will give you the most accurate and complete information on the element of the moneyless economy I've just touched on. Whether the solution is big or small, they are all important components.

Here and there I will describe some of the parts of this vast practical toolkit as *transitionary tools*, elements which require us to use what we have now (whether it be waste materials from skips, the internet or money) as one-off acts that will help us put in place sustainable livelihoods for the future. I have tried to find a balance between idealism and realism throughout, but it can oft be a tricky thing to do, so forgive my judgement if I don't always get it right.

Once you start exploring this path, you'll quickly realise that you have even more tools available to you than you will find in this book, as many of them will be localised, specific to your land, your people, your life. My hope is that this book will provide you with the foundations and the confidence to co-create your own moneyless economy (or at least a less monetised economy) with others from your local community. And there is good reason to be confident – if I have been able to live without need for money, then trust me, anyone can, for I am at best of average ability and intelligence, and I personally know many people who would be much more capable than myself of doing so. This is not false humility or self-deprecation, but fact.

This is not a one-rule-fits-all book, and is not meant to be prescriptive. Whether you are a full-time volunteer, salesperson, activist or a hedge fund manager, whether you want to help protect the planet's ecological systems or your own dwindling savings, this book is simply an offer of help to anyone who finds it useful.

Most importantly, take everything I say with a pinch of salt. George Orwell once said that "all art is propaganda". Whilst I will make every effort to speak only the truth, as I interpret it, I cannot guarantee you that some of my own bias will not be in here too. Therefore if you recognise the chaff of propaganda within these pages, shake it off and keep whatever grains of truth you find left.

CHAPTER 1

THE MONEY DELUSION

Either you repeat the same conventional doctrines everybody is saying, or else you say something true, and it will sound like it's from Neptune.

Noam Chomsky

Recently I was at a dinner party where the paper napkins were printed with the image of a ten pound note. Oddly serene, disturbingly familiar, the Queen's face stared back at all of us, daring us to wipe our grubby faces on what has become the most sacred of symbols. Not one person did; each napkin lay as smooth and undisturbed as it was when it was laid out. There is something that feels very wrong about using a ten pound note, even its image, to wipe icing off your mouth.

Take a minute to think about that paragraph, and you'll begin to see how absolutely stark raving mad the concept of money is turning us. Had those napkins been the plain white kind that we're force-fed with every coffee, burger, cocktail and slice of lemon drizzle at your nan's cake sale, the kind that float in the background of every outdoor culinary experience, then I would wager that we wouldn't have thought twice about using it once, before throwing it *away*. We're only too happy to churn a countless number of trees through our convenience food sector, yet we hesitate at wiping our face with something with the mere image of a ten pound note.

Money – that soulless, empty, arbitrary concept, subject to the fickle whims of markets and inflation, in itself good for neither feeding us, sheltering us nor loving us – has become more meaningful, more valued and more sacred in our lives than trees – providers of oxygen, water, food, shade, shelter and soil structure. We are in Alice's wonderland, where nothing is what it seems, and nothing is as it should be. We are completely delusional about what we need in order to live nourished, meaningful lives, and our delusion is destroying not only our ability to do that, but the ability of every other species on the planet to do so too. As the Cree Indian proverb goes, it seems that "only when the last tree has died, the last river been poisoned and the last fish been caught, will we realise we cannot eat money".

Considering its power over us, you would wonder why in 2008 I decided to abandon that course of action and try something different. When I originally decided to start living without money – or as I prefer to call it, to start living *with* the types of local gift economy that I will examine in chapter two – I did so on the basis of one major realisation: much of the suffering and destruction in the world – factory farms, sweatshops, deforestation, species extinction, resource depletion, annihilation of indigenous peoples and their cultures – were symptoms of a much deeper issue. From what I could see, only a people desperately unaware of their own intimate connection with the rest of life on this planet could behave in the ways we do, and only a people surrounded by powerful distractions could not feel the deep scars that this behaviour was causing. Not only was money enabling us to remain shielded from the horrors resulting directly from our consumption habits, it was also the most powerful distraction of all.

As time afforded me ever more experiences and lessons in living beyond money, the reasons for doing so took on an almost infinite scale. Embedded in the use of money are distractions and disconnections that I could not have imagined. The list is endless, and I could not include them all here. In the following pages I have picked out what I feel are the most important points, looking at the consequences of money on our physical, mental, emotional and spiritual selves, and the subsequent effects on the state of our society and our planet. What it all seemed to boil down to, however, was one simple point: *living without money changed my way of being*. Existing outside the monetary economy enabled me to sit inside the organic flow of life and recognise the interconnected oneness; it enabled me to experience a different sense of self.

We are here to awaken from our illusion of separateness.

Thich Nhat Hanh

MONEYLESS PHILOSOPHY AND THE DELUSION OF SELF

> *Humankind has not woven the web of life. We are but one thread within it. Whatever we do to the web, we do to ourselves. All things are bound together. All things connect.*
>
> Chief Seattle

Regardless of whether you believe that the story of money serves us well or not – whether you're a capitalist or a socialist, hippie or yuppie, Christian or Buddhist – you probably spent most of your life wanting a bit more of it. Considering that everyone pays lip service to the old adage that money doesn't bring you happiness, and that it is not exactly famous for improving the character of those who get their hands on increasing amounts of it, you'd wonder what the hell everyone finds so attractive about it. But we do. We love it, and envy those who have lots of it. We even give up our time – those precious, finite moments that make up the totality of our lives – in return for it, regardless of how much we already have, and how hideous or soul-destroying the task. Everyone, it seems, wants more money. We're all Spike Milligan, when he quipped "all I ask for is a chance to prove that money can't make me happy".

What is it about money that makes it so attractive? The ease of life it promises, perhaps – a nice home, a car, good schools for the kids; nice clothes, holidays, eating out once or twice a week. These are all understandable aspirations in themselves, but it doesn't take Buddha to realise that these are merely things that *we can have.* Money can certainly play a crucial role in changing the material world around us, but can it really change the way *we can be?* And what is it that we *want to be*?

There is no 'natural' way of being human. We are not inherently greedy, nor inevitably destructive. A sweeping glance around the cultures dying on our periphery will quickly tell you that there are infinite ways of living as a human being, and the way *we are* influences the way we behave.

Who are you? You are a mother, perhaps, a teacher or a lawyer. You are your ego, your memories, and your imagination. You are your desires, your fears and your joys. You are a range of expressions from moment to moment. Compassion. Love. Creativity. Care. A pain in the ass.

Spontaneity. Honesty, integrity, truth. The human spirit is potent.

Does it stop there though? Where does your perception of self end? Is it at the limits of the human spirit, or the human body? You probably acknowledge that your leg is part of you. But what about the bacteria in your intestines or colon, which are life-forms supposedly *independent of you* in themselves, but which are also a hugely important, interdependent *part of you*? Not so clear-cut, right? Consider the water you drink from the stream (or these days, the tap) – do you believe that it is part of you? It makes up between 30-90% of your body, once it is inside you, so you probably ought to. But what about that split second before you cupped it in your hands and drank it, when it was still labelled a stream – is it still separate from you then? Or when you swill it around in your mouth? Or when it lies in your intestine before being absorbed into your bloodstream? How about if you spit into a glass of water – would you then hesitate to drink it, because that spit no longer seems a part of you, despite that you certainly swallow that same saliva every time you drink?

My point is that the boundaries of our sense of self seem to be fuzzy and ill-defined. We might think of ourselves as a discrete 'object', bounded by our skin (what Alan Watts describes as "the skin-encapsulated ego"),[7] but it's hard to justify that when even skin itself is constantly exchanging atoms and energy with the wider environment. No person is an island, we are instead part of a flow of energy, food, water, minerals, radiation and so on, constantly passing in, out and through us, much of which has no respect for the boundary of the skin at all. We are no more a bounded 'object' than a wave on the ocean is. Like a wave, we are a form through which many objects (in that case, water molecules) are passing. To identify one's self with the molecules that are within your skin right now is no more appropriate than to identify an ocean with the molecules that are within its form at a given moment.

But what is real is interdependence. It is clear that if the stream I cup my water from is poisoned, I will die. If the soil under my feet is stripped bare, I will eventually starve. And so in a real, clear, practical sense I am one with them – like the bacteria in my colon, they are part of what is necessary for my form as a living human being to continue.

Shamans and mystics, free thinkers and tribes people have been banging on about 'oneness' since the dawn of humanity, but it is only since the 1960s, with Lovelock's Gaia theory, that the idea has had any credence in the modern world. We are not, as contemporary culture would have us believe, glorious beings separate from the savagery of Nature. Instead, it would appear, we are glorious beings inherently part of glorious Nature, an interconnectedness which makes that stream as much a part of you as the flesh, blood and bones that you consist of at this precise moment. At a fundamental, particle level we are all the same – different assortments of the same basic elements (such as oxygen, carbon and nitrogen). Should our sense of self not stretch to encompass all life? Albert Einstein put it beautifully,

> *... a human being is part of the whole called by us universe, a part limited in time and space. We experience ourselves, our thoughts and feelings as something separate from the rest. A kind of optical delusion of consciousness. This delusion is a kind of prison for us, restricting us to our personal desires and to affection for a few persons nearest to us. Our task must be to free ourselves from the prison by widening our circle of compassion to embrace all living creatures and the whole of nature in its beauty. The true value of a human being is determined by the measure and the sense in which they have obtained liberation from the self. We shall require a substantially new manner of thinking if humanity is to survive.*

The human sense of self is integral to our behaviour, and to the way we decide to build our lives. It is reflected in our institutions, our social values, and our power structures. If we do not see ourselves as connected to, or dependent on, our community, why would we bother nourishing it? If we do not see ourselves as connected to, or dependent on Nature, why would we bother preserving its splendour and bounty? Modern culture has developed and encouraged a sense of self which implicitly denies these integral connections and dependencies – implicitly denies oneness – and the results of this have never been clearer: deforestation, desertification, species extinction, air and water toxification; rising rates of cancer, asthma, diabetes, heart disease and obesity; increasing incidents of suicide, depression, drugs and violence; cults of celebrity, obsessions with physical beauty, fear of death. All of these are immensely unhealthy, and, I would argue, stem directly from a nature-illiterate people lost in their understanding of themselves, disconnected from their communities and stores of knowledge, and terribly misguided about their place in the world.

This is not a book about the self, it's about money, but questioning where the boundaries of self lie is a crucial foundation to understanding the call to move beyond monetary economics. People assume that I would agree with the old misquoted adage, *money is the root of all evil.* I don't. Instead I propose that it is *our deluded sense of self which is the root of many of our current personal, social and ecological crises.* Money is instrumental to maintaining and affirming this delusion.

Money is both chicken and egg in relation to this delusional sense of self. Whilst it originated as a mere symptom itself of the illusion of separation between ourselves and all other life, and the consciousness of concepts such as debt and credit which stem from that, it has in turn perpetuated and greatly intensified the extent to which we feel disconnected from the rest of life by increasing the degrees of separation between us and what we consume. This creates an even stronger delusion and more severe symptoms. Therefore it plays a major role in contributing to the destructive acts which each of us undertake when we put the narrow interests of our own skin-encapsulated ego over the interests of the whole, our holistic self.

Why is this important? Where we draw the boundaries between our-*selves* and *other* has huge implications for the personal, social and ecological problems we face. Our current monetary economic model works partially on the basis that we will act in what Ayn Rand,[8] and those such as Adam Smith before her, describes as our rational self-interest. But what if the boundaries of the self are not as clear as Rand and the rest of us first assumed? The terms rational self-interest and selfishness take on a much different understanding under a more expansive, holistic sense of self. If a person perceives their self to be the entire whole, then to act in your own self-interest would involve making decisions where looking after yourself would mean protecting the rivers, atmosphere, soil and forests that provide the hydrogen, oxygen and minerals that make up the physical elements of what you presently define as 'I'. Redefining and expanding the boundaries of the self would also make charging other humans for the gifts you bring into the world, which you yourself have been gifted, become no less ludicrous than your penis or clitoris charging your knees for the experience of an orgasm.

Can you imagine such a world?

THE MONETARY CULTURE

Contrary to the linear time frame our present cultural narrative forces us to inhabit, life is a series of cycles. What's more, unlike a linear system, which starts one place and ends up in another, cycles feed into each other. We reap what we sow what we reap what we sow. Of course, this means that a certain amount of care and thoughtfulness are needed in order to make sure that you reap something worthwhile, as well as a heavy degree of self-restraint in order to ensure the cycles have enough energy to sustain themselves.

Western civilisation, however, has decided to champion the linear, a framework which requires an arbitrary input which eventually gets transformed and spat out as an output into 'nowhere'. From within those ecological cycles operating quietly all around us, we pluck out what takes our fancy, process it through our factory lines, and enjoy, for a while, what comes out the other side. Then we throw it away, and start again. We are constantly taking energy, and putting none back. At some point, these cycles will collapse. Many already have.

This behaviour is not incidental; nor, as defenders of the status quo would have us believe, is it human nature. It is simply the mindset born of a culture in which disconnection and separation are built into its infrastructure; a mindset which we absolutely have to move on from if we are to have any hope of surviving, let alone reversing, the ecological meltdown we are faced with. If, as the 19th century naturalist Henry David Thoreau said, "In wilderness is the preservation of the world," then Wendell Berry's remark has never been more poignant: "In human culture is the preservation of wilderness."

You might well ask how this fear of the wild has emerged. The answer, unsurprisingly, isn't crystal clear. Charles Eisenstein[9] has produced a fascinating theory of separation, detailing our transition from bacteria immersed in oneness to the disconnected suburban yuppies we find ourselves today. The metamorphosis, of course, did not happen overnight. We did not wake up in the forest one day, gather some berries for our breakfast, then decide "to hell with oneness! I want an electric toothbrush!" and march out of the trees to build a factory. The process was far more subtle than that – a journey, a long, incremental passage of separation. The cultivation of fire, language, linear time, and measurement, leading to the development of agriculture, technologies, centralised politics and the mass media, all contributed, over thousands of years, to the gradual separation of human beings from Nature, our communities and, ultimately ourselves, until we end up with what we have today – beings utterly swept up in the illusion of our own independence and separation.[10] Born of this illusion is our modern culture.

At the moment, our culture is not preserving the wilderness. It is, in fact, destroying it – obliterating it from the face of the Earth. This is not something new – the war against Nature began in Genesis, and since then a passionate fear and hatred of that uncontrollable, animal nature of ours has manifested itself amongst us, especially amongst those in power. The beast, the wildman, the heath-an, the un-civilized, the savage – all of these images lie deep within our psyche as dark, uncertain forms where danger undoubtedly lurks. The battles to tame our wilderness have raged throughout the centuries, often consciously and deliberately, sometimes simply a natural reflection of the social mentality. The Church waged war on sexuality, animism, witchcraft and herbalism; the aristocracy fenced us off from our commons; the industrialists forced us from our land into the factories; the rise of rationality and science drove emotion and subjective experience out of the land of the respected, and men everywhere have done everything in their power to repress that wild, organic female nature. Some would look out into the world and argue that today our incessant need to conquer Nature is hastening – in genetic modification, nano technology, and the criminalisation of substances which take us to altered states of consciousness. Is it really outside the realms of possibility then that our entire monetary economic system requires us to feel divided and separate from all else in order to function as it does? *Divide et impera. Divide and rule.* It is the oldest trick in the book. When we're divided from each other and Nature, we're easily conquered.

How successful has it been? Let me ask you this. How many of you see yourselves as a spirited and wondrous being, a magnificent encapsulation of the entire universe? How many of you feel that you live in a world that forever affirms and celebrates the beauty, care, compassion and spontaneity that we are all capable of? How many of you feel you live in a world in which integrity and creativity are considered more important than clocking hours, or paying bills? Not many, I would think. Yet who would doubt that living in such a world would make us happier, and more fulfilled?

Wilderness runs much deeper than physical spaces; wilderness – wildness – is an essence, one present in all of us. We cannot put our finger on it, but we know when it is there; we know when we feel it. I would argue that *wildness is a state of experiencing and participating in oneness,* and that the use of money, as a tool of separation, fundamentally prevents us from experiencing this.

Let me ask you some more questions. Beneath the roar of the machines, do you feel the dying pain of an ancient forest when it is razed to the ground, its songs and aromas and glory gone forever? Beyond the glare of the new developments, do you feel the loss when a species disappears, its own unique perspective and understanding of life irretrievably gone? And underneath the rumble of the gold mine, can you hear the echoes of the dying cries of sadness of an entire culture that once was?

For hundreds of thousands of human beings – billions, if you count those who no longer walk the Earth – the answer is a plaintive, pain-filled 'yes'. Yet for us citizens of the 'developed' world, I would imagine that the answer would be a sheepish, shame-faced 'no'. We cannot hear the cries, cannot feel the pain, because we – all of us – have been programmed not to. Our deafness and our numbness is essential to maintaining the globalised monetary system, and in a beautiful, sordid dance of chicken and egg, we have enveloped ourselves in a culture which affirms and reinforces it. Standing at the centre of this dance, its arms raised triumphantly, its waistcoat shimmering, is money.

TIME ISN'T MONEY

> *Man ... sacrifices his health in order to make money. Then he sacrifices money to recuperate his health. And then he is so anxious about the future that he does not enjoy the present; the result being that he does not live in the present or the future; he lives as if he is never going to die, and then he dies having never really lived.*
>
> Dalai Lama

Nestled neatly in humanity's journey of separation, embodying all that came before it and adding its own tart, intangible flavour, is money. Building on the illusion of linear time and the development of language, measurement and quantification – reducing unique, irreplaceable creatures and plants to just another word, just another number, and eroding "place-distinctiveness to [the homogeneity of] a global suburbia"[11] – money sits high enough up the chain to blind us to all that came before it. Nowhere is this more clear than in the relationship it forces us to have with time.

Money is little more than the consciousness of credit and debt made exact. If you owe money you're partially stuck in the past, like it or not, and if you've stored some in a bank or under the mattress then you're at least subconsciously thinking ahead into the future. If you've fooled yourself into thinking you're not, then give every penny you have away right now and start to live day by day. Undoubtedly this is due to a need for security: we have been taught that to save is to provide a guarantee, a safety net for our future. What does this do to our sense of trust though?

Anthropological studies have shown time and time again that many tribal people, regardless of how much food they gather or successfully hunt, will never store food. Daniel Everett, a renowned linguist who has spent years amongst the Pirahã – a Brazilian tribe who have no concept of numerical systems, let alone money – writes in *Don't Sleep, There are Snakes*[12] that when asked why they didn't store any food, the Pirahã replied "I store meat in the belly of my brother". Implicit in this is a deep trust in Nature to provide, and an acknowledgement in the interdependency of the community. The very odd day they go hungry, but mostly they feast. They never worry. From Everett's accounts they are a much happier and more content people for it too, and understandably so: like an unconcerned child, wouldn't you be happier assuming that tomorrow you will be provided for?

Contrast that with how we live in civilisation today, always worried about things from the past and planning ahead for the future, never being in the moment. How much of life do we miss out on because our minds are time travelling?

The concept of money plays a grossly underestimated role in our historically unrivalled inability to live in the present moment. It is not just anthropological studies which show a link between the use of money and a decreased sense of living for the day – my own limited experience taught me exactly the same. Counter-intuitively, and to my own surprise, I slowly began to worry *less* – not *more* – about everything after three to four months of living without money. Admittedly, in those first few months I worried much more, due in a large part to the fact that money had for so long provided me with a sense of security, and I was concerned that if I was hungry or got into a bit of bother I had zero to fall back on.

As the wheel of time slowly turned I found myself voluntarily surrendering to life and started living for the moment, something I had never done in the days when I was much more conscious of concepts such as credit and debt. Every day seemed to provide for me, and with that repeated experience you slowly stop worrying about the next day. Somewhere in your psyche you realise that it'll all be fine, and that the worst that can happen to you is that you return to the whole, which is my understanding of what your true self is anyway. Orwell once said that "happiness only exists in acceptance", and that has been my experience in life, and the experience of people like the Pirahã. Accept what life brings to you every day, regret nothing and don't worry about the future. And have fun – none of it is that serious.

REAL COMMUNITY REQUIRES INTERDEPENDENCY

I babysat my friend's kid recently. She was stuck and I was free, so I was happy to look after little Elijah for a few hours. We went to the park, we did some painting, he kicked my ass at a game called *animal memory*;

we had fun. Imagine the difference in experience – for my friend, Elijah and myself – if she had put him in paid childcare instead. She would probably have felt a little guilty, leaving him in the care of strangers, for whom Elijah may have been just another face; she also would have undoubtedly felt a little isolated, not having the support of a community she could depend on. It certainly would have cost her money (which she would have had to work extra hours at her job to pay for, meaning yet more need for paid childcare). Elijah wouldn't have felt as comfortable, spending his time with people with whom he didn't have an ongoing, trusting relationship, and he wouldn't have been able to spend the time outdoors, playing in his neighbourhood. And I wouldn't have spent my morning remembering that three year olds can teach us much about the beauty of the world. What's more, by entering into that spirit and understanding of mutual dependency, all three of us got to strengthen our relationships to each other – relationships which reinforce and affirm that spirit. Next time I'm in a jam, those relationships will kick in and let me know that I've got a friend who will support me.

The conversion of those relationships into paid services – a process which is encroaching into more and more aspects of our lives – leads to the destruction of communities, just as the translation of our natural wealth into 'resources' to be exploited leads to the destruction of our ecosystems. To pay for something, to assign a value to it, is to quantify it. It becomes just another number, its uniqueness and relationships and interdependence with all other things swept aside. It is not a five hundred year old tree, provider of food, shade, shelter and soil structure, but £10,000 worth of wood products; she is not a person needing care, with her own hopes, dreams, desires, sorrows, joys and circumstances, she is a 'client', or 'service user' – costing the taxpayer £30,000 a year. We do not see things for what they *are,* we see them for what they're financially worth. Price tags blind us to real worth. In seeing childcare only in terms of money, we lose a wonderful chance to learn from, support and nourish each other; in seeing a forest only in terms of money, we will eventually lose the ability to live on this planet – and prevent countless others from doing so too.

Charles Eisenstein, in *The Ascent of Humanity*, sums it up nicely: "We find in our culture a loneliness and hunger for authenticity that may well be unsurpassed in history. We try to 'build community', not realising that mere intention is not enough when separation is built into the very social and physical infrastructure of our society. To the extent that this infrastructure is intact in our lives, we will never experience community."[13] In *Sacred Economics* he adds that "community is not some add-on to our other needs, not a separate ingredient for happiness along with food, shelter, music, touch, intellectual stimulation, and other forms of physical and spiritual nourishment. Community arises from the meeting of those needs. There is no community possible among a people who do not need each other." With money, especially in a globalised economy, we certainly do not need each other.

The implications of this stretch further, breaking off sections of what were once community into their own separate markets. Most notably in the realms of art and music our relationships have immeasurably changed, so that in the space of one hundred years the vast majority of us have moved from being participants and creators to being consumers. In Ireland, my native land, in the 1920s, people gathered around each other's fires every evening and played music. Most people could contribute something – whether a jig on a fiddle or the stamping of their foot – and all involved intrinsically knew and felt the value of creative, communal play.

That was before the advent of the radio, then the television, quickly followed by the tape, the compact disc and the ipod, with a brief appearance by something called a mini-disc if my memory serves me correctly. Each new technological development – itself only made possible through the increasingly larger economies of scale and finer divisions of labour that I talk about later in this chapter – takes away one nugget of creativity and community, until we are left with fifty people in a room absorbed by fifty different pieces of music – none of them creating, and none of them sharing. The same process has infiltrated almost every aspect of our lives, to the point that we are now just consumers of life, and not participants in it.

All this is the result of the monetisation of life. Everything has come to have an intrinsic financial value, so that it can be bought and sold. What we now term 'economic growth' is simply the conversion of our natural, social, cultural and spiritual commons into money.[14] Soil, art, music, education, hospitality, health – we are even having debates about the financial value of motherhood and the planet. The commodification of all these things takes away their meaning and their authenticity and they become just another service, to be purchased from any stranger with the qualifications to provide it. How is community possible when everyone is as replaceable as interchangeable cogs in The Machine, and how is it possible not to feel isolated, when everyone you deal with is a stranger?

This is a precarious position to adopt. Money has come to replace community as our primary source of security, and as countries who have suffered financial collapse will attest to, this is no real security.

In contrast to the monetary economy of today, within which most of our relationships are of a purely utilitarian nature, Lewis Hyde[15] and others argue that within the gift economy (a model of economy I will describe in chapter two) the economic is merely a subset of the social, whose primary goal is to strengthen relationships and connect us to each other, as opposed to profiteering from one another. Ran Prieur has said that in many tribes "purely utilitarian relationships were forbidden",[16] which juxtaposes itself to the monetary economy we've developed today, where we're told we shouldn't mix business with pleasure (surely one of the most absurd pieces of 'wisdom' we've ever invented). What a horrid way to live, where what we do everyday isn't brimming with pleasure and laced with the people we love to spend our time with. The result is a world where all our economic activity is impersonal and all of our so-called community is based on superficiality without any real interdependency.

In *Debt: The First 5,000 Years*, anthropologist David Graeber makes a further important point when he notes that by paying off your debts immediately (which is what money, in its more exact forms, allows us to do) we can perceive ourselves as having no further obligations to the other person. We have settled our debt with them, and therefore can in all good conscience sever that relationship, given the moral framework we live within. He uses an example from Margaret Atwood's book, *Payback: Debt and the Shadow Side of Wealth*,[17] detailing the curious case of a nature writer called Ernest Thompson Seton, who on his twenty first birthday received a bill from his father for every expense connected to Ernest's childhood, "including the fee charged by the doctor for delivering him". As Graeber points out, to most of us this behaviour "seems monstrous, inhuman".

But young Seton paid his father the bill, and never spoke to him again. Graeber adds that "this is precisely why the presentation of [the] bill seems so outrageous. Squaring accounts means that the two parties have the ability to walk away from each other. By presenting it, his father suggested he'd just as soon have nothing further to do with him."[18] I would suggest that by simply paying it, Seton junior was expressing exactly the same sentiment. Money allowed twenty one years of emotional connection and history to be wiped out with the handing over of some cold, hard cash.

Even to those within our *money-driven* culture, a son paying off such a debt to his father seems absurd; yet in other *connection-driven* cultures, paying off your debts to those in your wider community is equally absurd, and can only serve to diminish connection and the collective sense of interdependency. By asking for a debt to be paid, and then paying it, the relationship can be considered over.

There are other points to be made here. When you have money, it doesn't matter whether you act like a cretin every day, especially if you derive your income from outside the community you live in. The cashier at the supermarket will still sell you your food, as they probably won't know your name let alone how kind (or otherwise) you are. Your reputation is no longer your currency. Not that I am suggesting reputation being currency is the ideal to strive for, but there has to be some social merit in everyone taking responsibility for their character – something which feels like a million miles from where we are today.

To illustrate this last point in real life, I'll share a story with you, the video of which went viral on *Sina Weibo*, a Chinese hybrid of Facebook and Twitter. A little two year old girl, named Yueyue, got hit by a car. The driver drove over her with the front wheel, stopped briefly, and then continued driving, going over her again with the back wheel, crushing her body. Over the coming seven minutes, over a dozen people walked by her, looked at her, and walked on. Many cars and motorbikes drove past, some of them swerving around her broken little body – one of them even drove over here again, crushing her further. After seven minutes, someone finally dragged her off the road and got her help. A week later she died. When some of the people who came onto the scene were questioned about it later, they claimed that the reason they didn't dare help was (citing a similar incident in 2006) because they risked getting sued by the person whose life they would have been trying to save, which could in turn push their own family into poverty.

This is a logical consequence of a society based on money and competition, and in hindsight such consequences were inevitable from its inception. In a society based on a gift economy, in which your character and your actions are intimately linked with your livelihood, such a depressing tale couldn't even be imagined.

OUR DISCONNECTION FROM WHAT WE CONSUME

The reduction of life and all its expressions to an empty statement of financial worth is only made possible through the use of such an abstract, objective, meaningless thing as money. Cold, hard cash. It changes hands so easily, so thoughtlessly – numbers entered on a screen. It makes life so easy, because we don't have to think. We don't have to question where the endless rows of Ikea furniture come from, or how we can have strawberries in February; we just hand over the money. Simple.

The real costs of these luxuries are not internalised in the price because they can't be. How do you quantify the loss of a rainforest – the death of a hundred thousand trees, the extinction of plant and animal species, the loss of homes, cultures, languages, knowledge and ways of being human? How do you figure in the costs of climate change, of soil depletion, of depriving a people's land of its water, and then forcing them to work in effective slavery, doing soulless jobs growing monocrops for faraway people whose eyes they'll never look into?

You can't. So we don't. And money is the only way we can do that, because it is so completely, utterly abstract that it can embody all that harm and sadness and tragedy and not be the slightest bit affected. Cold, hard cash. Numbers on a screen.

Once again, it is not only our biosphere that is negatively affected by the use of money; our selves and our community suffer greatly too. Because of the disconnection today's monetary economy causes us, few people even know the person who baked their bread, let alone the farmer who grew the grain or the miller who ground it into flour. To us, the loaf is just a product on a shelf, and there is usually no real connection between producer and consumer.

In pre-monetary economies the degrees of separation between producer and user ranged from zero to two – if you didn't make what you used yourself, either your neighbour Henry or his wife Anne did. This meant that you were intimately connected to everything in the process. In today's context, if Anne was abusing animals or spraying the crops you ate with biological weapons, you'd know about it and probably have a discussion with her over it if you had your wits about you. If Henry's health was suffering because of the processes in which he made you a pair of shoes as his gift, you'd probably want to help him come up with a solution that was beneficial to him.

If you grow your own food, you don't waste it. If you have to take responsibility for your own water supply, you're probably not going to shit in it. I was speaking with a journalist recently about a report from the Department for Environment Food, and Rural Affairs (DEFRA)[19] which states that bread is now the number one food item that we waste, and he asked me why I thought that was so. I told him it is simply because we no longer have to knead and bake our own bread. If we had to put thirty minutes of love and elbow grease into it, we wouldn't waste a slice.[20]

The less intimately connected we are with our food, the more of it we waste. The more we stay disconnected from what we consume, the less hope we have of ever understanding that we are not all independent separate beings, but an interdependent part of a larger whole. In turn, we will continue to make decisions we think are good for our egocentric sense of self (the skin-encapsulated ego, I) at the cost of our holistic self (the whole).

Some people will argue here that this is where ethical consumerism comes in – allowing money to reflect people's consideration for destructive processes. I would counter that there is no such thing as ethical consumerism, in much the same way as I would argue that there is no such thing as ethical rape. Ted Trainer concurs, stating that "a sustainable and just society cannot be a consumer society".[21] Consumerism is the insistent and endless purchase of ever increasing amounts of goods, resources and services. It is inherently linear, as it presupposes – and depends on – an infinite supply of inputs, which does not exist, and does not take into consideration what happens to the outputs when their designed obsolescence runs its course. How can such a system be ethical, let alone smart? What's more, ethical consumerism cannot take into account the full spectrum of human and biological relationships affected by a product or service. Its considerations of 'ethical' or even 'environmental' are inevitably extremely narrow. The idea that we can shop our way to sustainability is no more ludicrous than thinking we can shag our way to virginity.

But more, much more than that, ethical consumerism reinforces the status quo – it reinforces what all of us know to be false, that money is meaningful, and in reinforcing this, it reinforces and affirms our separation from ourselves, our community and Nature. This is not to say that buying your groceries from your local organic farmers market instead of the supermarket is not beneficial. Of course it is. Eating isn't an act of consumerism, it is an act of living, and supporting those who grow food with respect for the health of the biosphere is crucially important right now. All I am saying is that such acts themselves will not bring about the level of change that we desperately need. Some forms of consumerism can obviously be *more* sustainable and *less* exploitative and polluting than others, but can never be in absolute terms. A rapist who cares to use a Fairtrade condom could be said to be marginally *more* ethical, but would anybody, regardless of their definition of 'ethical', this most vague of terms, dare to call it absolutely ethical?

Until we understand that our own health, our own lives, are dependent on the health of the whole, we will not adequately resist a culture that seems hell-bent on looting every fish, tree and mineral from the planet, polluting our air and rivers and streams along the way. Derrick Jensen, an American author and environmental activist, points out that "if your experience is that your food comes from the grocery store and your water comes from the tap, then you are going to defend to the death the system that brings those to you because your life depends on them. If your experience, however, is that your food comes from a landbase and that your water comes from a stream, well, then you will defend to the death that landbase and that stream."[22] Nothing stops us understanding our interdependency with our landbases better than money.

* * *

Oneness, wildness, community, and self-hood – ideas floating free in the wonderfully languid land of philosophy. Who am I to say whether they are wrong or right – they are only a hunch, a strong hunch at that, because it all seems to fit, but it is just a hunch. So, what if I'm wrong? Is there anything we can point to that says, despite the philosophy, despite the mystical musings on the nature of self, is there anything concrete, anything 'real', which suggests that the use of money is inherently harmful?

Plenty. Enough to fill three of these books. But I only have one, and only a small chapter at that. So I'll pick the best in the hope that some of it may be useful to you as you help us all create the stories of the future, stories that will make sense for our Age.

THE PERSONAL, SOCIAL, ECOLOGICAL AND ECONOMIC CONSEQUENCES OF MONEY

We all know the benefits of money. We're bombarded by them every day. Economists, politicians, journalists, CEOs of corporations and charities, advertisers, tabloids, everyone from Adam Smith to Katie Price and other celebrities famous for the inhaling and exhaling of atmospheric gases – they've all extolled the virtues of money, repetitiously, every day. The world certainly doesn't need me to add to its considerable applause. Therefore "as time is short", I will do as Thoreau and "I will leave out all the flattery and retain all the criticism".[23]

The Economies of Scale (EOS) married to money

The concept of money is central to the mechanisms of modern economics, especially the dominant capitalist model of our time. Two of economics most basic principles, the *economies of scale* and the *division of labour*, are of particular importance to the scope of this book. Both have always existed to some extent, as any couple who has made dinner for ten people, and any wife who chopped the carrots as the husband washed the potatoes for it, will testify to. But the advent of money, married to these principles, introduced an unharmonious element, creating an extremity our forebears could never have imagined.

My goal is to show you how both these economic principles, once married to the idea of money, consummated their relationship by giving birth to forces that would lead to the pillaging of the planet, the exploitation of both human and non-human life on it, and the transforming of traditional crafts and sustainable livelihoods into boring jobs on the assembly line of industrialised society, jobs that offer little in the way of freedom, creativity or autonomy. But most importantly of all, I aim to show you why such extreme consequences are only possible because of – and an inevitable product of – this tool we call money.

The economies of scale principle is powerful, yet extremely simple. It basically means that as one entity, be it a corporation, a farmer or the State, produces increasingly larger quantities of something, they can potentially benefit from increasing cost and/or labour efficiencies as the scale of the operation increases, up to a point. For example, lets say it cost £1 million to construct a factory that produces one of Adam Smith's little pins. If they were to produce just one pin it would have to be sold for over £1 million just to break even. However, if it produces 100 million pins, which it probably would like to do, then each pin only costs one pence. The more it produces, the cheaper it can become, theoretically meaning increased sales and even cheaper pins until that factory hits its maximum output. This same idea is also responsible for the fact that I can post a package from England to Ireland at the cost of only a couple of pounds, and that the tiny population of Cuckoo's Knob can have a car, a BlackBerry (not the fruit, that other phoney thing) and a liposuction treatment to remove the fat they accumulated from sitting on an assembly line producing BlackBerrys and from driving cars.

What's the problem with that? I hear you demand! Nothing, at first glance. That is until you realise that the economies of scale, taken to their logical conclusion, lead to what I call the *ecologies of industrialisation*. Yes, it is a very efficient economic model, and that's precisely the problem. Our realisation that efficiencies can increase with scale, (and this is the important point) coupled with the ability of money to logistically allow humanity to reach such incredible scales, means that cost-efficiency *demands* production on vast scales, which requires both vast material inputs and vast monocultures of consumers demanding identical products. This has led us to the brutally efficient looting of the Earth, the death of its fertility, the puncturing of its lungs, the stripping of everything else that we humans would classify as a *resource* (which other species would call a part of their home) and the impersonalisation and homogenisation of entire cultures. If you want to see an example of this, go to a clear-cut of an ancient forest and inhale the deep sadness that the machines have left behind. There is no denying this economic model is efficient – too efficient for the dry eyes of any person that has retained any connection to the rest of the community of life.

Without money, the maximum scale we could reach is one where real relationships based on trust were possible, most likely a village with a population of approximately one hundred and fifty people or fewer (give or take eighty), which is the famous number of people that research by anthropologist Robin Dunbar[24] suggests we can have a meaningful relationship with. Money acts as a proxy for trust in economic transactions where the consumer never gets to meet the producer. Without money nobody from Italy is going to spend all day producing tins of beans destined for some village in the south-west of England, in the trust that they're off working in the same spirit producing cider to be shipped to Rome. It's a nice thought, but it's just never going to happen. Money enables you to trade with people you'll never get to know or meet. Why we would ever want to is a deeper question.

This most basic of economic ideas tempts us into a world where we can make almost anything we want, as long as we can then convince enough people to buy them with the money they, in turn, get from working in jobs we increasingly find devoid of meaning, creativity and autonomy.

This is why I believe that the environmental and counter-culture movements, in particular, are grossly misguided when they claim that simply consuming less will make any significant difference whilst they still live lifestyles that require complex technologies, some of which the people involved in them – often my friends – tell me they "just couldn't give up". How they propose to have a clean, healthy planet *and* products requiring mass industrialisation, I have no idea, and when questioned on it, neither do they. The higher the level of technology, the larger the economies of scale that are needed to justify them (with a few exceptions, such as very expensive technologies like jet fighters, nuclear warheads and public surveillance systems, most of which we pay for collectively through our taxes, and which none of us need directly in our daily lives). Large economies of scale mean that large numbers of people must buy them and (again, this point is crucial) it fundamentally requires as few of us as possible to share the ones we've bought. Everyone needing to buy one means that every hill is mined, every ocean floor bottom-trawled, every forest flat-packed. Every forest flat-packed and ocean floor bottom-trawled means no oxygen for you and me. No oxygen means death.

That's the complicated version, and it is not even that complicated. The simple version is this: our age old desire to benefit from the economies of scale – a very natural thing in itself – married with the invasive species money (the common weed, *Pecunia*), is making our biosphere uninhabitable for increasing numbers of species.

This is one of the major reasons that I argue for full localisation of our economies (I will explain what I exactly mean by this in chapter two) using small-scale, appropriate technology. By this I mean any technology that any human being could produce for themselves and their local community without its existence being dependent on many other people owning one independently also, or on all communities around the world (who sit on the copper, oil, etc. that our high tech products require) being forced, covertly or otherwise, into adopting the same economic and political ideologies. Such low impact technologies can be shared with the entire community, saving everyone time and effort and materials, as their existence isn't based on the economic imperative that everyone needs to have one in order for the initial outlay in capital infrastructure to be covered. The economies of scale principle is the reason that, even in times of so-called austerity, you'll never hear a politician say we should share more; the Prime Minister can only have a nice new washing machine, after all, if enough of his voters wants to own one of their own too.

Having said all that, far be it from me to be even remotely critical of anyone attempting to minimise their impact on the biosphere. It all makes a difference and it is highly admirable in a world that doesn't make it easy. It is also a great personal policy to adopt in these transitionary phases. Yet in the long term we must wake up to the fact that we need to design ways of life that don't require these economies of scale in order to prosper, so that it is possible to share the fruits of our labour without our entire economic model, which demands we don't share resources, crashing in on us.

In order for the economies of scale theory to be scaled up to the level it is today, it must be married not only to the concept of money, but also to the idea of specialised division of labour.

The Division of Labour (DOL) married to money

This is another simple principle, dating back to the first time humans ever cooperated. The only element that has changed is the precision with which it occurs. Labour has never been as specialised, and its division more clinical, as it is today. This increasing specialisation and complexity is closely associated with the rise of industrialised society and capitalism. The benefits are much the same as those you get from increased economies of scale: more efficiencies, more miraculous technologies, more labour savings per dollar produced. Yet there are huge, hidden costs to pay, costs that any sane, healthy society would not deem worth paying.

One of these opportunity costs is our need to live happy, varied, creatively free lives, where what we do every day is what we love to do. There are, of course, still people who love what they do, but they are increasingly the exception that makes the rule. Most of us, whose labours support these fortunate few (those who get to design the latest Google doodle or strum acoustic solos to 50,000 adoring fans), hate Monday morning and love Friday evening for a reason. Through little fault of our own, the jobs available to us are repetitive, boring, unfulfilling, and a waste of the precious gift which is our lives. Worse still, we're starting to realise it. Hence the antidepressants, the clinics, the suicides, the crime and the turning to all sorts of things in an attempt to fill the existentialist void that is created through doing work that doesn't nourish our souls or our bodies.

If this was the only problem, I wouldn't be so concerned. At least it would only be harmful to those of us who also perceive ourselves to benefit from it. But when a person spends forty plus hours a week in an office shuffling electronic paper from one inbox to the next, they have almost no connection to the rest of Nature, or to the stuff they consume. Such disconnection leads to voids that are plugged by escapisms such as consumerism.

Disconnection also leads to a lack of knowledge about, or empathy and caring for, everything and everyone involved in the supply chains of products which we fill our voids with. How many people think of the war in Iraq when they fill up at the service station? Do you think of what happens in order to get that oil to your tank? If not, may I ask why not? I am sure you care intellectually, but the disconnect means that such caring doesn't penetrate into your heart, a penetration that can only fully impact when you see the tears of pain run down the face of an Iraqi father who has lost four members of his immediate family, just so that we can drive to the countryside and be a nature tourist for a day.

Again, you may query what this has got to do with money. Once you create a tool like money you start walking down the path to specialised division of labour. Economists such as Adam Smith claim that this was the very reason money came into creation in the first place – to allow Mary to brew the ale and Mike to bake the bread, and for them both to be able to exchange the fruits of their labour more easily than having to work out how many pints equalled one loaf every time. According to Graeber, there is a great deal of anthropological evidence contradicting this "fantasy land of barter",[25] a place that can only be described as an economic myth, but it is easy to see why this claim of Smith's benefits economists' claims that the way things are is just a natural product of humanity's development and progress. Regardless of whether you agree with Graeber or Smith (though there isn't a shred of anthropological evidence to agree with Smith), create a concept as liquid as money and increasing economies of scale and division of labour come soon after. Keep combining them in ever increasing complexity, and all hell breaks loose.

Division of labour is a great idea, by itself. As with the economies of scale principle, it only becomes a social and ecological problem when it is married to the idea of money, creating disharmony in an ecologically based economy, similar to the manner in which a newly introduced invasive species can play havoc in a geographical region of the Earth. Without money, the division of labour in any small community would find its optimum level, instead of its maximum level. *The difference between optimum and maximum is crucial; efficiency, like everything else, has its optimal level.* So while everyone wouldn't start doing every single thing for themselves again – that would be to go to the other ridiculous extreme – communities would become sufficient as a unit, and life could be much more varied, more connected, more autonomous and free.

Money causes waste

When I was living moneylessly for two and a half years, I wasted nothing, because everything was precious. Whenever I left the caravan for a pee under a fruiting tree in the cold, dark winter evenings, I blew out the beeswax candle to save what to me was a finite resource. Whenever I stumbled upon some dead wood lying around in the summer, I gathered and stored it for winter burning. If I found a lighter on the street, I picked it up and used it, as that would save me twenty minutes working a bow drill. Every scrap of food I had was eaten, and other people's waste food too. Newspapers lying in the ditch became easy tinder. If I had eight bottles of cider to last me the entire winter, I drank them sparingly when the situation cried out for it, and not the eight in one sitting. I didn't have a bin, not even a recycling one. Everything was either used, or reused, including the waste that came from my own body. Life was cyclical, not linear.

At the time of writing I've been back in the monetary economy for over five months as I plan and organise the next stage of the experiment. I've slowly found myself doing things I would never do when I was moneyless. I now sometimes leave the lights on when I leave the room, as the energy behind the switch feels infinite. I don't make use of waste food to anywhere near the extent I used to. If I see a pen on the street, I don't bother to pick it up – a new clean one is only 20p at the corner store. I don't chop wood anymore as I've got gas shipped into my bedroom all the way from Norway. The list goes on, *ad infinitum*.

When we are connected to what we use, or when getting or making something new isn't so simple as going to the shop, we appreciate it and we certainly don't waste it. You understand how much time or energy you or someone you know put into it. Money disconnects us from our goods and services through the massive economies of scale and the highly specialised division of labour it facilitates. This disconnect leads to large levels of waste in our daily lives.

This is certainly not conventional economic logic, which argues the opposite to this, claiming that charging people monetarily for energy and resources, whether by price increases or taxes, regulates and potentially caps their use of it. On appearance, this would seem a valid argument; but its a sleight of hand, focusing your attention away from where the con is going on.

Let me explain myself if you will. The difference is one of perspective. When economists see, for example, one of the 13 billion litres of oil being (through the mechanics of the economic marriage from hell) over-efficiently turned into plastics, pesticides, fuel and toys every day, they don't perceive this as waste, as it has had an efficient use and in turn has transformed a part of the Earth into financial and material wealth for us humans. In terms of waste, their main concern is that 'our' resources, extracted and transformed at levels far beyond the optimum for sustainability and the health of both our egocentric and holistic selves, get used efficiently and turned into marketable produce. Within that context, controlling this with a monetary price can work, theoretically at least.

However, I have a different perspective, and I believe this is key. When I see men and women slaving on oil rigs, sucking out a part of the Earth that was best left where it was, just so that we can make ready meals, mobile phones and plastic toys for our kids at Christmas, I see nothing but waste: waste of habitat for other species, clean air and water, and of the lives of the workers who spend parts of their precious life extracting oil so that we can then efficiently waste it. If we had to take responsibility for producing all our own energy in truly sustainable ways, and were therefore more intimately connected with the processes involved, there is no way we would use our time, resources, health (mental, emotional, spiritual and physical), clean rivers or acreage to produce megatons of merchandise for kids or electronic tranquilisers for adults.

The economies of scale required for high technologies also demands that we don't share, and that we all have one of everything, resulting in the situation we have now where all of us are hoarding stuff in our cupboards and attics that we may only use once a year, if that. Rest assured, your neighbour is also hoarding the same stuff. If we were all to share these things, and have five high technology lawnmowers (instead of five hundred) per suburb, such a lawnmower could never viably be produced, and therefore the monetary economic model as we know it would collapse, given that the same logic applies to all other high technology products also. *It is an economy where sharing means collapse.* If that isn't the definition of waste built in to an uneconomic model, I don't know what is.

We're living in the marriage from hell. This *ménage à trois* of money, economies of scale and division of labour isn't working for the Earth, or us, any longer. It all looked very exciting to begin with, as a *ménage à trois* will, but it has got complicated, as a *ménage à trois* will, and it is going to end in tears, as a *ménage à trois* so often will. They were all much more fun when they were single. And if all involved want a future worth having, someone has got to leave.

Gross inequality through the storing of value

Money is not just a medium of exchange; amongst other things, its current form is also a store of value. Married to an economic model such as capitalism, this can only lead to gross inequality. I don't feel this needs much qualification, we all know that the saying "the rich get rich, whilst the poor get poorer" is a truism. You only have to look at a report in 2006 by the World Institute for Development Economics Research of the United Nations, which states that 1% of the world's adults now own 40% of its wealth.

Some will claim that because of the monetary capitalist system, all have been risen up, even if a few have done much better than others. This never comes from the mouths of the 3 billion people living in absolute poverty, or the 25,000-50,000 parents who lose a child to starvation every day. Absolute poverty aside, just as many social issues can stem from relative poverty, that perceived sense of injustice that people who struggle through life, on a daily basis, feel towards what many describe as 'the elite', those who hoard the wealth the working classes created, and whom then use that very wealth to tighten the grip of power on those below that little bit harder. A report by the *Guardian* newspaper and the London School of Economics (LSE)[26] highlighted that this perceived inequality was a major reason behind the riots in Tottenham and the rest of the UK in 2011.

What struck me most about the self-righteous outrage after the riots and looting in Tottenham was the fact that those voicing most disgust live lives that are only possible because of our government's looting of foreign lands, and our corporations' looting of the oceans, the rainforests, and the hills that home the minerals that we need to produce the landfill of things that we base our everyday lives around. Of course the hypocrisy and absurdity of this was wasted on us all, for little other reason than the looting of the Earth has been culturally normalised, whilst the looting of JJB Sports and Top Man has been culturally deamed a crime.

Without money as a store of wealth – and here I mean all forms of money, whether it be private property, gold, dollar or the Bristol pound – these unnecessary inequalities don't occur to anywhere near the same extent, and therefore there are less of the social problems that go with it. Some prominent economists, from Gesell to Keynes, have tied themselves up in all sorts of complex knots discussing negative interest forms of money, such as demurrage, that they claim could offer the potential to keep money as a medium of exchange and neutralise its function as a store of wealth. But such monetary systems, even if they could work (and I don't believe they can), are only necessary if we want high technologies. And as I have argued, it is such technologies that are making the planet uninhabitable.

In many of the small societies of the past, where everyone had access to all which was held for the benefit of the collective, theft was unheard of. If you had access to all the wealth of a community, why would you loot?

Prostitution is to sex what buying and selling is to giving and receiving

People often remark to me how they believe that paying for something is just another way of giving. There is truth in this to a small extent, especially as we all live in a monetary economy with bills to pay. But there is a crucial difference, and that is in relation to the spirit in which the act is done. When we freely share all that we ourselves have been given – whether it be material goods, our time, knowledge or skills – for no other reason than we can help someone, the difference in effect is both positive and huge. Unconditional kindness uplifts people, creates bonds and is life-affirming in a way that conditional monetary transactions could never be. Of course, the other person could unconditionally give back immediately using money, paying off the debt exactly, but as I pointed out using Graeber and Atwood's example earlier, this is effectively saying I no longer want to feel that I have to be in an ongoing relationship with you. It would be much more beneficial for your community if you simply just gave whatever it is you give to the world when your time comes around, unconditionally.

I believe that prostitution is to sex what buying and selling is to giving and receiving. Think about the contrast between making love to your partner – and I mean really making love and not just 'having sex' – and paying for sex with a prostitute. The difference is palpable. One is an act where two supposedly separate beings merge in the most glorious of unions, one of our few remaining pathways to experiencing oneness with all of life. The other is an orgasm, for the punter that is. Physically, there can be little difference in the two acts, but the post-coital feeling of two lovers embraced tightly in each other's arms in blissful oneness is polarised to that experience which the buyer of sex feels as he walks out into the cold of the night, having turned love-sharing into just another service to be consumed, in a similar way that we've turned the care of our young and elderly into services. If you stopped paying your child carer, would he or she still continue to care for your child? Is the care that is conditional, really care? I suspect that, at our very cores, we consciously or subconsciously know it's not, and the psychological and emotional trauma from that deep understanding is unquantifiable.

This, I must add, isn't a philosophical discussion about whether prostitution is 'good' or 'evil'. On appearance it doesn't seem a particularly healthy or fulfilling way to live, but who am I to judge and, regardless, the same could be said about almost all livelihoods today. Every day we all sell our bodies for money in one way or another. We charge people to prepare food for them, to accommodate them, to heal them, to mind their children or elderly parents – things that some previous societies couldn't even conceive of asking for something in return for. How many of us would still go into work every day if we had no financial or economic imperative to? Not many. Of course we have to pay the bills, but then again, so does the prostitute.

It may be that the prostitute really is the only honest one amongst us.

TIME TO CHOOSE A NEW STORY?

What I've been trying to show in this chapter is that it is *our deluded sense of self which is the root of many of our current personal, social and ecological crises,* and that *money is instrumental to maintaining and affirming this delusion.*

In order to have any hope of adequately dealing with the problems we are faced with, we need to fundamentally address the delusion of separation that has permeated and infiltrated our sense of self. In order to better take care of our land, our communities and, ultimately, our egocentric selves, we need to reconnect with an understanding of the interdependent whole. In order to do this we need to question and challenge the stories which support our delusions. The biggest enemy we face in doing so is that mechanism of separation, money.

Money is creeping into and informing all of our cultural information: our relationships, our food, our education, our health, our play, our media. Through all of these interactions we are rewarded for our independence and our conformity. We are encouraged to see nothing but price, and to disconnect from all other meanings. Consider the battles that take place in our daily lives – battles between integrity and convenience, passion and conformity, compassion and comfort. In how many of these is money often the deciding factor? It is all part of an ongoing war against an experience of oneness, against an experience of our wildness. We are taught to domesticate ourselves in order to better serve the institutions we have built – institutions themselves in service to money.

And the result? Consider the difference between a wild buffalo and a dairy cow. Consider the look in their eyes, the patterns of their lives, the choices they have to make. Consider their states of being, and what they would implicitly *know* about the world. *Consider what each would deem important for their survival.* Then consider what you know of the remaining peoples around the world who still live on the periphery of our culture – societies which have changed little for thousands of years simply because they had no need to.

As your entire life so far has probably confirmed to you, we *are* different. 'Civilisation' – the culture of the city-state – stands by itself, mighty and proud, and it is no accident, none whatsoever, that we are the people defiantly thundering towards ecological collapse, deaf to the cries of those whom we slaughter, oblivious to the pain we pierce in the hearts of our kin. Money is just a tool, one weapon amongst many in the war on wild. But it is a potent one, probably the most potent one we possess. It is fundamental to ensuring we do not experience our wildness, fundamental to preserving our disconnection from our actions, fundamental to ensuring our communities remain a collection of strangers to us. Just by using money we exhibit an awareness that oneness does not exist; just by using money we affirm and maintain the illusion of separation. It makes us ignorant of the state of being our own survival depends on.

Of course this entire chapter is also just a story, not necessarily more real than the story of money itself. It is up to you to decide whether or not it makes more sense to you than the current story we tell, and whether it would lead to rituals that would benefit us all, instead of harming us all on every conceivable level, which the current monetary system is undoubtedly doing.

Your choice.

CHAPTER 2

THE MONEYLESS MENU

> *In the traditional culture, villagers provided for their basic needs without money. They had developed skills that enabled them to grow barley at 12,000 feet ... People knew how to build houses with their own hands from the materials of the immediate surroundings ... Now, suddenly, as part of the international money economy, Ladakhis find themselves ever more dependent – even for vital needs – on a system that is controlled by faraway forces. They are vulnerable to decisions made by people who do not even know that Ladakh exists ... For two thousand years in Ladakh, a kilo of barley has been a kilo of barley, but now you cannot be sure of its value.*
>
> Helena Norberg-Hodge[27]

Whenever some of the concepts that make up moneyless living arise in conversation, different things tend to spring into people's minds depending on a number of factors: their unique situation, philosophical beliefs, what they believe to be an appropriate or sustainable level of technology, their conscious or unconscious addictions to the comforts that come with industrial civilisation, and whether they live in an urban or rural setting. That's a very positive thing, as a moneyless economy should be diverse, driven by factors such as local needs, land, culture and microclimate. But it's also important that we can communicate the ideas behind it accurately.

Therefore in this chapter I will outline the big ideas involved in moneyless living, including some perspectives on the concept which I don't personally subscribe to but which I include to highlight the range of options open to everyone with different philosophical beliefs to mine. In the second part of this book, from chapter five onwards, I will then describe the myriad practical ways in which you can apply these over-arching ideas to as many parts of your life as you like, regardless of your circumstances. It may be that you want to be moneyless just for food, transport or booze for now, taking on other aspects as they become appropriate for you. Or it may be that you want to go the whole hog as soon as you can. Whatever your situation, urban or rural, there will be plenty of options in the following chapters for you to choose from. Some will to a greater degree be useful to an urban setting, others to a rural setting, but almost all will be able to be applied to some extent wherever you find yourself.

WHAT IS A MONEYLESS ECONOMY?

Despite a recent renaissance of interest in alternative economics (due to a dramatic decline in confidence in the dominant economy), the vast majority of which seems to revolve around various types of exchange systems, there seems to be little clarity or unity on what a moneyless economy could look like. From anthropological studies we know quite a bit about how such economies worked in the past and these are critical for informing our future paths, but this is a book that is looking ahead, instead of backwards. We're evolving beings, and our ways of living ought to evolve to reflect that.

The moneyless economy defined

When looking at how we define the essence of the economies of the future, it is vital that we do not look at it through the same anthropocentric lens the current economic model was built with, one where humans are on top and everything else is considered solely in relation to its usefulness to us. Such a lens is responsible for reducing the Earth's splendour and bounty – its salmon, its magnificent ancient redwoods, its rolling hills, its generous soil, its gushing rivers, its gloriously wild creatures – and the pageantry of life into things labelled 'resources', assigned meaningless price tags with no intrinsic worth.

With this is mind, the following is how I define a moneyless economy that respects all life on Earth – from humans to the microbes in the soil to wild animals – and not solely human life:

> *The moneyless economy is a model of economy that enables its participants to meet their physical, emotional, psychological and spiritual needs, both collectively and individually, on the basis of materials and services being shared unconditionally (i.e. no explicit/formal exchange). Ideally (but not necessarily) these materials would be procured within walking distance of the people who benefit from them. Such an economy would be carried out in a way that considers the needs of all life (and future generations of life) in that geographical region, giving equal consideration to all, and seeing it as an interdependent whole whose overall health is inextricably linked to that of its component parts, and vice versa.*

A pure moneyless economy, in my definition, is the meeting point of the gift economy and the 100% local economy, and I believe that the physical and spiritual benefits of combining both are huge. Until the day that such an economy is either desirable or possible for you, just apply the aspects of it that work for you and your unique situation, keeping one eye on the converging crises that we will all have to face, together.

The gift economy

> *Even after all this time, the sun never says to the Earth, 'You owe Me'. Look what happens with a love like that, it lights the Whole Sky.*
>
> Hafiz

I sometimes call this the nature economy, as this is the basis of what large swaths of the rest of Nature works on. This is a hotly debated point, as many argue that Nature is based on exchange. The honeybee, after all, in collecting nectar spreads pollen around the flowers – that's exchange, right? And in the soil under our feet, in one inch of which there are more life forms than there are human beings on the entire planet, a ceaselessly complex dance is taking place between the plants and the microbes, each feeding each other, nourishing each other and sustaining each other, ensuring that both always have all they need. Again, on the surface, this certainly does look like exchange of some sort.

But I beg to differ. Such a way of viewing this flow of life and transformation of matter is nothing more than the projection of humanity's narrow sense of self onto the rest of Gaia.[28] Because we've deluded ourselves into thinking that we're nothing more than the skin-encapsulated ego, where there is a clearly defined 'me' and 'you', we therefore assume that the rest of life has the same perception of reality. Imagine, for a moment, that there was no 'me' and 'you', and that the border known as the skin that we have used to define *I* and *Other* by since early childhood was no less arbitrary than the border between the lands known as France and Germany. How would that change the way you perceive the world, and interact with all that makes it up?

The fact that we perceive reality, and our role amongst it, in a certain manner is no basis for assuming that the rest of life does the same. For if you view all life as one whole and consider that, physically (not spiritually) speaking, you're a collection of elements (such as carbon, nitrogen and oxygen) coalescing out of, interacting with and dissolving back into the rest of Earth and its biosphere, then how could you charge another part of the whole for some goods or services you offer? As Daniel Suelo once pointed out, it would be akin to your finger charging your head for scratching it, as if the finger's entire wellbeing wasn't based on the health and happiness of the head.

Charles Eisenstein notes how "nitrogen fixing bacteria don't directly benefit from doing so [fixing nitrogen, that is], except that the nitrogen they give to the soil grows plants that grow roots that grow fungi, which ultimately provide nutrients to the bacteria. Pioneer species pave the way for keystone species, which provide microniches for other species, which feed yet other species in a web of gifts that, eventually, circle back to benefit the pioneer species."[29] All just do what they do, in the organic flow of life, without any sense of debt or credit which, eventually, manifests physically in the form of money. So it could be with us, in a gift economy.

Believing that we are all completely interdependent, and part of a whole organism in the same way that *your* intestinal bacteria is part of *you*, certainly isn't imperative for anyone wanting to engage in the gift economy, as there are many good reasons to do so even from an egocentric and anthropocentric point of view. A gift economy, in my definition, is simply a society within which people share their skills, time, knowledge, information or material goods with each other without any formal, explicit, or precise exchange. The forms that gift-based societies have taken historically vary widely. But there are a few constants. No money changes hands, no bartering takes place (despite what ill-informed economists would have you believe), and no credits or IOUs are accurately noted in little books, ready to be cashed in like a £20 note. In the type of gift economy I advocate, giving and receiving is done on a largely unconditional basis, which stands in stark contrast to the rather ironically named 'free-market' economy, which has very successfully managed to turn every aspect of our beautiful little planet, whose bounty was once indeed *free* to all, into an inherently meaningless set of financial valuations.

Gifts may be given in return at some point down the line (and in most historic gift-based economies, almost always were), and they can strengthen such a society if they are. The key to this is that they are not a condition on the original gift, that they are not immediately returned, and that they are never exact. Otherwise, as we saw earlier, you are effectively saying "my relationship with you can now be ended". Gifts create bonds, and it is these bonds which create real community, not the superficial type we try to recreate today in a desperate response to our tangible lack of any authentic sense of community.

In its ideal form, there would be no emotional or psychological 'credit' in the gift economy either, though given the state of our mental landscape today, this is admittedly very unlikely, initially at least. Whether or not the increased reputation – such as sexual brownie points with your partner for giving her a massage, or Cory Doctorow's *Whuffies*[30] – conferred on the seemingly altruistic giver could be perceived as currency is the subject of much anthropological debate. It could be argued that such debates are simply more revealing about the ubiquity of the mindsets of separation, exchange and cynicism that dominate our current human culture, and their subsequent projection onto other previous societies, who – *perish the thought!* – may have simply enjoyed nurturing each other through unconditional giving. Others will argue that the joy that participants within such economies felt through giving was what they got 'in return', but again, this may reveal more about our culture then theirs. Either way, what is so terribly wrong with feeling good about helping our fellow beings? Not to mention the many social benefits of a system where those who are most generous with their gifts inherit the highest social status – today we reserve such accolades to those who take, accumulate and destroy the most, a fact that only perpetuates the culture and encourages others to do the same.

Eisenstein, in his seminal work *The Ascent of Humanity*, sheds a lot of insightful light on the matter. His writings suggest that the seemingly altruistic acts of previous gift economy societies may in fact be selfish acts, but that the key difference is that those who undertook these acts had a far more holistic, and less egocentric and anthropocentric sense of self. In short, they viewed themselves as being a part of the whole organism we now call Gaia, and that whole was their self. Therefore a selfish act is an altruistic act, as the self within this mindset is the whole and everything and everyone which makes it up. To 'look after yourself', within a more expansive understanding of self, would mean you would do what is best for the whole and not the illusory skin-encapsulated ego that you currently define yourself as.

The theory, and in many examples the practical experience, behind gift economies is that when everyone operates in the spirit that underlies it, everything that is required to be done to meet people's needs still gets done and, counter-intuitively, people end up with greater access to all the resources they need to live healthy, fulfilling lives that are also healthy to the whole that sustains them. This is in part due to the fact that the desires of people within gift economies, both historically and presently, are more minimal with less complex levels of technology, but also because their worldviews were often based on the idea of collective abundance, and not the mentality of scarcity that is central to the philosophy of monetary economics.

It is undoubtedly true that, thus far, the monetary economy has been the best economic form for creating complex products which require specialised division of labour, large economies of scale and materials from all over the world. The only thing it seems better at doing than this is convincing us that we actually need all the stuff it produces in the first place. We never felt we were missing out on the benefits of modern gadgetry before we knew about them. I don't miss my old mobile phone even now, but I certainly didn't miss it before they were invented. I was perfectly happy not being able to be contacted at all hours of the day or night. Are our lives better for having mobile phones? Indisputably many would say yes, otherwise they wouldn't buy them, but given an objective appraisal of all the ecological and social issues involved in their manufacturing, distribution and use, by someone who fully understands the inherent oneness of all life and the effects of these products on everything along the supply chain, I would think the answer would be a resounding no. The problem is, the consumer is so disconnected from the processes involved in their manufacture today that few have any idea how destructive and exploitative these consumer goods are. Central to creating and maintaining that disconnection, as we saw in chapter one, is money.

The gift economy can seem, at first glance, a very idealistic and unrealistic economic model for those of us in the West; a nice thought, but not something that could ever work in *the real world*. Most of us would associate it with lifestyles such as the Native American Indians, some far-flung uncontacted tribe in the Peruvian rainforest, or other indigenous peoples and ancient cultures throughout the world. It is true – such economies were much more prevalent before the agricultural and industrial revolutions.

Few of us would believe that there are people in the world still living in the spirit of the gift economy today, albeit some to only partial degrees now. Take one example – Anuta, one of the Solomon islands. Whilst the market economy has slowly been imposed upon the cultures of the Pacific Islands, a gift economy called *aropa* still exists there that would seem utopian to the Western mind, and peoples from these islands who have emigrated abroad still engage in this to a degree that many of us could also benefit from. Similarly, the inhabitants of Tokelau still engage in a practice called *inati*. There are many others who have resisted moving away from similar type 'human economies'[31] into the market economy that is, contrary to popular understanding, a recent phenomenon for much of the world. Anarchist communities across the globe, despite their reputations as violent, lawless thugs (a reputation created in large by the media and the agendas of those who control it), are to this day often founded on the principle of the gift economy, although the practice is getting increasingly difficult due to the infiltration of the monetary economy into every aspect of our lives, meaning that there is an increasing lack of free space and land to enable them to do so.

Even fewer of us see the operation of the gift economy in our own lives on a daily basis, which is understandable, given the success of the current model at turning every single aspect of our days into a commodity or service to be sold. We pay people to look after our kids and our ageing parents, to cook for us, to produce our food, and house us when we have to be away from home. We even pay people to come and clean our houses, which we have already paid some landlord or bank to live in. Despite this gradual but relentless erosion, the gift economy still holds strong in a few aspects of our lives. When we cook dinner for our partners, or help a friend with some task, or care for our elderly parents three days a week, we are enacting the fragments of the gift economy that haven't as yet been fully turned into *services to be consumed* by the prevalent economic model. Therefore it is obvious that we in the global West are still capable of viewing life in a very similar way to the people of Anuta, and that it is only our cultural stories that are limiting our potential to do so now.

What advocates of the gift economy are asking is *why not just extend the spirit in which we give to our close family and friends to the wider community?* If it would feel abhorrent to charge your mother or friend for dinner, then why is it so socially normalised to charge others in your local community for doing so, given that one day that stranger you charge may become one of your best friends? I'd even argue that there is a much greater likelihood that the stranger would become a friend if you did something for them in the spirit of the gift, as opposed to the mechanism of exchange. In fact, I'd go much further and say that once you start living in the spirit of the gift again, you will slowly begin to realise that the boundary between *I* and *other* isn't as solid as you've been conditioned to think it is, and that you will no longer just see this old stranger as a new friend; you will see her as part of you. This, at least, has been my experience.

Whilst gift economists ask *why not?*, you may understandably ask *why bother?* My response: if you can see the beauty in the spirit of doing things for free for the people closest to you (or the coldness of charging them), if for no other reason than to express your love and gratitude towards them, then how much more inspiring would it be to do it for people whom you don't even know yet?

THE GIFT ECONOMY IN ACTION

It was on the philosophical foundations of the gift economy that we put on a free one day festival, called The Freeconomy Feastival, to celebrate my first year of having lived completely without money in November 2009. It was to be done without a single penny changing hands, and once this novel idea got rolling, everyone wanted to get involved. It was an absolute joy to watch lots of people, from backgrounds as diverse as accountancy to anarchy, put huge efforts into co-creating something that, on the surface, had little or no benefit to them personally.

After sending out one email to my local Freeconomy[32] group in Bristol just three weeks before the proposed event on Buy Nothing Day 2009, sixty volunteers got back to me, wanting to get involved. Together we put on a one day event that saw thousands of people come along and eat and drink for free (including free ale produced using wild ingredients by brewer Andy Hamilton, see page 293) and his crew of happy brewers), attend our free cinema, go to a day long schedule of talks from inspiring voices, enjoy a three course meal made completely from waste and wild food, take (and give) whatever they wanted from our Freeshop (see page 98), and go to an extensive programme of free workshops on the day, including a make and mend area teaching people how they could make that stitch in time that, legend has it, saves nine. There was free massage and other holistic therapies too if it all got too stressful.

To watch the gift economy in full flow in this way was a moving experience. I was constantly asking volunteers to take a break, but many ended up working twelve to fourteen hours straight, telling me that they were having far too good a time to stop. The venue hosts gave the venue for free, various community groups gave us enough cutlery, cooking utensils, seats and tables to feed thousands, other groups loaned us bicycle powered sound systems and smoothie makers, brewers made the beer and showed people how to do it in the process, foragers went to the woods and showed people how to forage, as did the skip-divers and the chefs. Not only was it all done for free, and in some cases anonymously (which takes away the argument for enhanced reputation being the currency), it became a huge educational experience for everyone, meaning that inadvertently and without intention, everyone got something back.

Can you imagine any paid dish-hand, in a commercial restaurant, refusing their break? In the monetary economy, where we feel forced to do things for money, the thought is preposterous. But once you cut away the nonsense, the thing that most of us want in our lives is a sense of purpose and meaning, something beautiful to believe in and contribute towards. We want to wake up in the morning passionate about what we do, instead of being forced into doing something we resent just so that we can survive within a system that many of us feel doesn't serve us, or the rest of life, very well any more. And whilst I'm not for a moment claiming that a big one day festival run solely on the gift economy is evidence, in itself, that entire communities could work in that way on a daily basis, it does at the very least show us that there are other ways of doing things, and more uplifting ways of being.

Festivals such as Burning Man are also run on the same philosophy to a large extent, and to a much more impressive scale than the one we put on in Bristol. Why not put the word out to your local Freeconomy group and organise a similar festival in your own community?

Many forms of the gift economy existed a long time before the monetary economy, and I hope it will never completely vanish into a world where every inch of our planet has a price and where every act requires an exchange. What a horrible thought. It is my dream that we may one day move beyond these conditioned and outdated mindsets of scarcity, exchange and insecurity, and start living again in a way that is life-affirming, which inspires us instead of depresses us, and which has the feelgood factor that the monetary economy will never have.

The 100% local economy

> *The global economy is built on the principle that one place can be exploited, even destroyed, for the sake of another place.*
>
> Wendell Berry

This 100% local economy is a model where the entirety of our needs are met using local materials, produced within walking distance of where we live (or on a horse and cart, for instance, if the cart was made using local materials). This includes everything from the soles of our shoes to the cutting implements we may use to make the bow drill that starts our fire.

Even the most ardent supporters of moneyless living, such as those who call for a resource-based economy (see page 46), view this perspective as being at the more extreme end of the moneyless spectrum, despite it being the way we lived for the majority of our history, and the fact that some people still live this way. This wariness is understandable – we're currently thousands of miles away, quite literally, from this level of localisation, and living in such a manner *en masse* would require an entire redesign of society and wholesale land reform (see page 126); both of these, some would say, would require a revolution, or an almost complete collapse of the model of economy we currently participate in (which, given its dependency on infinite growth on a finite planet, is hardly out of the question). If the public and political will was there, such social redesign would still be a big task for a population the size of the UK, though by no means impossible. Without the public and political will it would take Nature and the systems' inherent flaws to conspire to create the new conditions from which a localised model could flourish. Whichever way things unfold, it is the way of living that I personally aspire to. Later in this chapter I will set out the argument for why a globalised non-monetary economy could never work.

This fully localised model only appears extreme because we compare it relative to the extremely globalised economy we have today, and because we see it through the eyes of a people who are physically and emotionally addicted to types of gadgetry and gizmotry that can never be localised.

Through the eyes of a people intimately connected to each other and their land, such as the Awá tribe of the Brazilian Amazon, extreme is how we industrialised nations live today. Extreme is a worldview that sees the majesty of life on Earth as an ingredients list of resources that by mining, clear-cutting and bottom-trawling can be efficiently turned into cold, hard cash. Extreme is not knowing our neighbours, let alone feeling comfortable enough to ask them for help. Extreme is many members of a community having spare rooms in their houses while others sleep on the street. Extreme is spending our lives doing jobs we hate, just so that we can repay the bank money that it created out of thin air in the first instance. Extreme is taking what was freely given to us and then charging another part of Nature for it, only sharing that which was gifted to us if we receive something in return. Extreme is walking towards the precipice as we smugly recycle our tetrapaks. Extreme is letting it all unfold before our eyes, as if somehow we were not powerful enough to stop it.

Authors such as Michael Shuman[33] and Peter North[34] argue in favour of less 'locally' defined definitions of local than I do, with North remarking that "localisation means producing as much as you can as locally as you can ... if you can't produce things locally, produce them as close as you can to where they will be used". Whilst I welcome such calls and would encourage people to localise as much as they can (in the next chapter I will be discussing the various degrees of localisation and moneylessness, and this is one option), I feel such a perspective is too loose and open to exactly the same globalised processes we already have. China is probably as local as I can have a pair of trainers produced for me (considering they require materials from every continent of the world). Does that still qualify as localisation? If not, where do you draw the line? Which products do we continue to manufacture and which do we stop? In a fossil-fuelled economy, where all previously natural limits have effectively been burnt into greenhouse gases, who decides what's 'appropriate'? The market? The State? Or do we resolve to take back the power to make these decisions ourselves, making conscious choices about what a truly sustainable radius to meet all our needs within is, voluntarily rejecting anything that can't be provided there? Without such voluntary simplicity, we'll have what we've already got, with just a touch more localisation that, in reality, is little more than a token gesture.

On this basis I would refine North's quote and declare that *if you can't produce things locally, begin weaning yourself off them immediately and start purposefully constructing an economy where your needs are simplified and then met with materials you can produce locally.*

Arguing for complete relocalisation may seem dismissive of well-intentioned partial localisation efforts. Of course there are degrees to localisation, and producing the things we can easily produce locally (whilst we continue to produce products such as wind turbines on a national scale, as part of a transition strategy) would undoubtedly improve our individual and collective health. Yet to argue for partial relocalisation long-term would be little more than inhabiting the fantasy realm within which the majority of us humans have conveniently placed ourselves, in blissful ignorance of the basics of economics and our globalised system's fundamental need for the large economies of scale and highly specialised division of labour (with all the social and ecological consequences of both) that are required to produce just one laptop. To produce one laptop you need to sell millions of its model to justify the investment in R&D and initial infrastructure alone. You need the global infrastructure that we know is polluting and destroying the ecological systems that support life on Earth. What's more, you need technical experts and factory line workers that only do that one task for a living, dangerously limiting, as we've seen in chapter one, their own connection with Nature, resulting in even more social and ecological consequences. These matters are complex – affecting, amongst others, an entire society's sense of self – yet are often argued in terms as simplistic as like for like calculations of carbon emissions.

The conundrum, which I appreciate authors such as Shuman and North will have considered, is that we are too many to get even close to being fully localised in the short-term, even if we did all want to, yet if we don't fully localise there are inevitable trains coming head-on to meet us as we stroll down the tracks of ecological meltdown. The good news is that it is possible for you as an individual to start preparing for a different future immediately, and through doing so inspire loved ones and friends around you to get prepared also, while more macro-scale factors ultimately force the hand of the rest of the population. My concern is that unless we choose to make a rapid transition towards fully sustainable lives soon, it may be too late to successfully adjust by the time the bubble of fantasy economics finally bursts. Start adjusting today, and use whatever parts of this book you find useful to help you on your own path.

If your main interest in moneyless living centres mainly on ecological, physical matters, and not so much on the gift economy, you could add another couple of surprise options onto the moneyless menu: local currencies and barter.

Local currencies

This is an interesting one. I am sure most of you are wondering what local currencies are doing in a book about reducing our dependency on money. A local currency is obviously just another form of money, after all. Whilst I argue that there are all sorts of unintended consequences from even using local money, I add it in here as an option for you for three reasons:

i. In the transitionary period between the globalised monetary economy and the localised gift economy of my wildest fantasies, local currencies could provide a very useful ecological function if used in combination with a local materials economy. (At the moment much of the materials and produce traded by participants in local currency schemes is imported to some extent, due to the fact that those who use it continue to also use their conventional national currency for the vast majority of their needs. The materials element of an economy will only be localised to (roughly) the inverse degree to which its members use a fluid national currency.)

ii. Local currencies undoubtedly help form relationships between local people in the short term that I believe could eventually transform into gift economy relationships in the medium term.

iii. It is a more realistic option for many people at the moment than a pure gift economy.

Thankfully, there are many local currency initiatives popping up all over the UK and the world, many as part of the Transition movement[35] – Totnes, Stroud, Brixton, Lewes and Bristol all have their own pound, amongst others. Other schemes, such as Timebanks[36] and Local Exchange Trading Schemes (LETS)[37] which I will look at in chapter five, have existed since the 1980s, and add to the menu of options available to those who want economic change. North's book, *Local Money*, is a great source of information on all of these.

Barter

This is a similar point to the one above, but more debatable, as the vast majority of people would not consider bartering to be a form of money. And technically they are correct, as it is defined as 'the trade in goods or services without the exchange of money'. Whilst bartering has even more social benefits than local currencies (though a lot less liquidity), it is in many ways little more than an awkward form of money, and is based on the same consciousness of debt and credit that we don't see many other examples of in Nature.

I include it on the buffet table of moneyless living for many of the same reasons that I've included local currencies, in that it can be a transformative experience, potentially moving people from the mindset of exchange into the mindset of unconditional giving as relationships develop. Bartering, as a social tool, is most valuable when done informally and without exact accounting (money is the ultimate form of exact accounting), like you offering me some of your glut of courgettes in exchange for sex. That has unfortunately never happened to me, I must add.

The resource-based economy (RBE)

Whilst the term *resource-based economy* could just as easily apply to the localised gift economy I advocate, it's now more commonly understood to be a high-technology, globalised version of a non-monetary economy. Proponents of such an economy include Peter Joseph of the phenomenally popular *The Zeitgeist Movement* (TZM)[38] and Jacques Fresco of *The Venus Project* (TVP),[39] two projects which up until 2011 had been strongly associated with each other.

Their central premise is that in order to enjoy what these members perceive to be a high standard of living, people don't need money, but instead resources such as food, water, minerals and other materials. In fact, they claim that monetary economics actually prevents the fair distribution of such necessities of life. Advocates of such a system argue that the world is abundant, and that all of its resources could be utilised much more wisely and shared equally amongst all of humanity, not just those with financial prowess. Fresco advocates using the high levels of technology that humans are capable of creating, but within a resource-focused, economic model in which built-in obsolescence[40] makes zero sense. It is an economic model in which machines do any job that can be automated, and are used not to replace human labour in a way that leads to unemployment and all the social implications of that, but instead to shorten the working day for all, meaning much more leisure time and complete and free access to all the resources of the Earth and the technologies that are produced. It is a design where human ingenuity is tapped to collectively create the most efficient and sustainable technologies based on best practice and highest quality, and not reduced by the pressures of the competitive market where duplication and waste are inherent and rife. The monetary economy, they argue, and again I agree, is based on scarcity, whereas a resource-based economy is based on collective abundance.

Much of this I find admirable, especially the intentions behind it. Peter Joseph,[41] in particular, is a fascinating man whose analysis of many of the major problems we face today is insightful and his courage and dedication in raising awareness of the destructive consequences of monetary economics is exemplary. Yet I feel that by aiming for a high technology, highly complex version of a non-monetary economy, both TZM and TVP are making their vision almost impossible to realise.

Why? Aside from the fact that high technology has proven to be entirely counter-productive to our sense of happiness and connection to local place and community, a point I'll explain a little further on, for it to happen would require the entire world's nations to get on board before we could even begin to think about achieving such a grand plan, as many of the minerals and materials that would be used (to make all the high technology products that RBE proponents want) come from all over the planet – oil from the Middle East, copper from China, minerals from Africa, rubber from South America. Unless all of these diverse countries and regions signed up to such an economic model and philosophical perspective, it would be unworkable. Considering the complexities of the world and its nations, politics, cultures, laws and religions that I outlined earlier, this is highly unrealistic.

With a localised economy, anyone can start living in the non-monetary economy fairly immediately without having to wait for the political and corporate leaders of the US, Iran, Namibia and Mexico to relinquish their control and unite with their entire populations under a new moneyless world order. Not that I am suggesting that TZM or TVP are advocating that we ask permission from our governments to start enacting elements of their vision – they certainly aren't, and again on that I agree.

Even if a unification of world ideologies was possible, within this version of a resource-based economy there seems to lie the assumption that 'advanced' technologies make us happy. If this were true, why is it that in easily the most technologically advanced period of human history, humankind has never been more depressed? I've no doubt proponents of a globalised non-monetary economy would point out that the reasons for our current unhappiness are much more complex than that, and they'd be right, they are. At the same time, it is widely documented that those who live in low technology societies, past and present, express stronger feelings of happiness, contentment and connection to community and place than those of us in the global West, who survive on a collective diet of quick-fix antidepressants, escapism and self-help gurus.

Research such as *The Happy Planet Index*[42] by the New Economics Foundation (NEF)[43] backs up much anecdotal evidence to that effect. I and many people I know have travelled the length and breadth of 'undeveloped' countries (the only thing developing about them is their debts to the International Monetary Fund and their cronies) and have encountered people in every village and town much happier, and more generous with their time, food and material possessions, than the vast majority of people I encounter in the 'advanced' country I live in. A twenty year study by Helena Norberg-Hodge[44] of the modernisation of the Ladakhi people, as documented by her film *Ancient Futures – Learning from Ladakh*,[45] powerfully demonstrates the effect of technology and its potent ability to destroy the very fabric of our communities. In their experience, after modernisation they had many more time-saving gadgets, yet somehow much less time. The story has been the same everywhere, and we all have experienced this to some extent.

Having lived both a high and low technology life myself, I can unequivocally state that my physical, mental, spiritual and emotional health increased as the role of high technology in my life decreased and the degree to which my life was localised increased. I don't want my table to be made by a machine, I want to make it with my own hands, or at least by the hands of my friend. Using our hands is crucial to our well-being, our sense of creativity, our relationship with the land. The only argument for a high technology non-monetary economy would be if it enabled us, and the rest of life on Earth, to live happier, more meaningful and freer lives. I have yet to see any evidence of that being the case, whilst our history is littered with examples of the opposite.

I would also argue that the separation from the rest of Nature that such high technology would inevitably cause would further diminish the lack of understanding of ecology and natural cycles, while simultaneously heightening the trauma that we endure from having no interaction with Nature in its wildest states. This disconnection would lead to the very same problems we have today and the deluded sense of self that gives rise to them. If humanity has no daily relationship and intimate connection with the Earth, how can it develop any sense of interdependence with it, or care or respect for it?

That said, there is still much we could learn from both the philosophy and practical solutions proposed by RBE advocates, and it all adds into the mixing pot of new ways of viewing economics and how we meet our needs in a more caring, sustainable and life-affirming manner. It is certainly not my intention to be unjustly critical of high technology RBEs (as I have nothing but the utmost respect for many of its intentions and efforts), but instead to help refine our collective thinking and unite us to some cause that we can actually achieve to some meaningful extent in our lifetimes.

Pay-it-forward

Pay-it-forward is a beautiful idea, popularised by a Hollywood film of the same title. It is a perspective that when you do something for somebody, and they ask you what they can do to help you in return, you tell them not to 'pay you back', but instead to look out for an opportunity to 'pay the favour forward' by doing something useful for someone else, possibly someone they've never even met before. Whilst there is still the tiniest element of conditionality about it (i.e. a request has still been made), it's the most generous, loving form of conditionality I know of.

Regardless of whether you want to start applying some of these ideas, to various degrees, in the inner city or the woods, there will be both internal and external challenges to overcome, and I'll examine these, along with proposing transition strategies to navigate them successfully, in chapter four. These challenges will take time to overcome however, even if you do want to fully live beyond the need for money. To help you make the transition, or to simply incorporate degrees of moneylessness into your life, I've co-created a tool to help you: the Progression of Principles (POP) model.

CHAPTER 3

THE PROGRESSION OF PRINCIPLES (POP) MODEL

If we don't fight hard enough for the things we stand for, at some point we have to recognise that we don't really stand for them.
Paul Wellstone

Compromise is an almost inevitable part of our lives. Many of us have some vague sense of the ideals that we, at least, aspire to. For all sorts of reasons – financial, social, legal, emotional, physiological – we're often a million miles away from actually living them out to the extent we would like to, if at all. That's OK. We're all perfectly imperfect, and our current culture and its political and economic manifestations certainly doesn't make it easy for us.

What is a more achievable prospect than going straight from wherever we're individually at now to living out our highest ideals one hundred per cent, is for us to make a transition in a series of well thought out stages that make sense to our lives. The key here is to make these steps realistic enough in the short-term as to be achievable, yet challenging enough to be considered an appropriate response to the major ecological and social issues of our time.

This book is about creating societies that move beyond the need for money for the simple reason that, as I have argued in chapters one and two, we're not going to be able live within this planet's capabilities to host us long-term unless we do. However, the world we have currently created has deified money to the point where it is now the leader of the world's largest religion, a faith that tolerates no other spiritual beliefs about the world. This tends to make living completely moneylessly a little daunting.

And so whilst some of this book is about holding the moneyless way of life up as a vision, a seed to protect until a time when external factors may leave the soil fertile enough to allow it to germinate and flourish, it also aims to deal with reality. Your reality, whatever that is.

My own ideal form of economy, as I have pointed out, is a fully localised gift economy. Yet for most of you, this may be an impossibility right now; making it to the end of the month without accruing more debt probably feels like a more pertinent challenge. Therefore through this book I want to offer you a spectrum of ways in which you can reduce your dependency on money and increase your connection with your local community and environment. Whilst the ideas themselves will be moneyless (and if not purely moneyless, I will qualify why I have chosen to include them), how many of them you can or want to integrate into your life is entirely up to you. Most will be things you can do today whatever your circumstance, whilst others will be things you may wish to strive for. No matter how much of it you incorporate into your life, whatever you do will help you diversify the way you meet your needs, reduce your dependency on money, give you more resilience, a lighter ecological impact and get you on good terms with the neighbours. The further you can go along the path the better, for the well-being of both yourself and the planet.

In my own personal journey to moneyless living, I felt I needed a framework, a route planner, to not only enable me to get from A (my circumstances in 2008) to B (what I thought was realistic within that year) and all the way to Z (where I want to be in the future), but to actually understand what A, B and Z actually look like in the first instance. How am I living now? In what manner do I want to be living in the future? Out of a long conversation with one of my close partners in this evolving moneyless experiment, Shaun Chamberlin[46] (author of *The Transition Timeline*[47]), a model emerged that would allow anyone – regardless of political, religious or philosophical persuasions – to think about what each stage looks like, and that by its nature encourages you to make your way up it, in perhaps a similar way to how you might try to ascend Maslow's Hierarchy of Needs[48] over the course of your life. It is a simple way of dealing with both the practical and philosophical issues that arise as we try to align our lives to our sense of values.

We call it the Progression of Principles (POP) model, and it is a model that could be useful to anyone who wants to live closer to their ideals, regardless of whether you want to live moneyless, as part of any religious or spiritual community, or in the Transition movement itself, just to pick a few examples.

As the focus of this book is on diversifying your personal economy and needing as little money as possible, I will apply the POP model framework in that context only, but I hope that readers will still feel able to utilise it to aid their own progress towards whatever way of life is aligned with their beliefs. The beauty about the POP model is that it is tailored by you, for you.

HOW IT WORKS

To illustrate how the POP model works let's take a couple of examples, which will be uniquely mine. It tends to naturally have between three to eight levels, depending on complexities and permutations, but it can be as long or as short as you want.

First, let's look at my POP model for 'economic systems'.

Level 1 (100% local gift economy):
Complete co-sufficiency on a gift economy basis.

Level 2:
Co-sufficiency on a local currency/barter basis within a fully localised economy.

Level 3:
Gift economies existing with minimal dependency on the dominate economic model.

Level 4:
LETS, Timebanks and local currencies existing with minimal dependency on the dominant economic model.

Level 5:
A 'greener' globalised monetary economy.

Level 6 (100% global monetary economy):
A globalised monetary economy.

Most of this particular POP model, keeping in mind my earlier comments, will be self-explanatory. For Level 1, you may ask w*hy 'co-sufficiency' and not self-sufficiency?* The answer: because self-sufficiency is an illusion. At the very least we are interdependent with bees, bacteria and earthworms, and in all reality on people from our local community, whether that be your street, village or an intentional community. So when I say community, I mean all of the community of life, and not just humans. Whilst current culture has conned us into believing that dependency on others is a sign of weakness or failure, I argue the opposite. Dependency on each other is crucial to the fabric of real community, and in the end to our sense of place, relationship and well-being. The reality now is that we're not as independent as we would like to think. We talk of 'financial independence', but this is another delusion. We have merely replaced dependence on the people around us, whom we know and love, with dependence on faceless, distant strangers who we will never get to meet or thank for what they've produced for us. Why do we choose the impersonal over the personal? Is living in a close-knit community of consciously interdependent souls really so undesirable that we will strive to earn money just to avoid it?

You may notice from the structure of this POP model that I place slightly more personal importance on 100% localised living than I do on the spirit in which the acts are done. This is partially due to the ecological imperatives of our time, but also because I believe that as personal relationships are formed through the exchange of local currency or other forms of credit exchange, that unconditional giving will come to replace the bartering/exchange element anyway. But again, depending on your own personal philosophies, your POP model could look much different to mine.

For another example, lets look at the category we'll call 'Transport'.

Level 1 (100% local gift economy):
Walking barefoot, connecting with the earth beneath my feet.

Level 2:
Walking in shoes I made myself (or were unconditionally gifted to me) from local materials.

Level 3:
Walking in shoes I bartered for, which were made from local materials.

Level 4:
Walking in trainers made in a Chinese factory.

Level 5:
Cycling on an industrial scale bicycle.

Level 6: (100% global monetary economy):
Driving a hybrid car.

I'll explain this example to aid understanding of the technique and to reveal a little more about my personal version of moneylessness. The top level, in this scenario, will be seen as quite extreme by most people and not desirable on any level. And for some good reasons: our land has been covered in cities and their asphalt, gravel and concrete; our feet have been softened by generations of wearing increasingly comfortable and warm footwear; and why put yourself to the trouble when there are already tonnes of second-hand shoes in existence?

It is OK to find it too extreme, this is my POP model for transport, not yours, and that's partially the point. But I believe that until we feel the earth beneath our feet again we will never learn to walk gently on Her. We will fail to bring a level of awareness into our lives that, unfortunately, only seems to come when necessary and unavoidable. When you walk barefoot you take notice of the flora of an area (or the amount of litter), if for no other initial reason than you don't want to get a thorn (or piece of glass) in your foot. I've often found that when I walk barefoot I forage a little more, as I become much more aware of what is around me.

Whilst bartering is most often an exercise in local economy (though this has changed a little since the advent of the World Wide Web), it's still an example of our current culture's fascination with exchange. I often wonder why we can't just share our gifts and talents with each other for no other reason than they will help somebody. Hence why bartered shoes are on the third tier, whilst shoes given to me unconditionally make it onto Level 2. Cycling, that great symbol of sustainable living, only makes it to Level 5. I don't want to be too harsh on cycling using industrial scale bicycles, as it has many benefits, and I agree it is *more* sustainable. I just don't believe that it is *absolutely* sustainable, given that it requires various materials imported from around the world using a globalised infrastructure that is inherently destructive and exploitative to the rest of Nature. If it is not sustainable in absolute terms, why do we think we can continue with it indefinitely? Cycling of any sort disconnects us from the earth more than walking, and speeds life up for us (which usually only results in us consuming more things with the spare time it affords us), which is why it falls lower down than 'walking in trainers made in a Chinese factory' in my POP model for transport. That said, it still allows you to get around without needing to spend money (especially if you can scavenge spare parts to maintain it), which may be what you are striving for – if that is the case, cycling may be top of your POP model.

Don't worry if you're still on the basement floor of your model. I currently cycle an industrial scale bicycle more than I walk, though this model has helped me clarify my commitment to doing much more barefoot walking in the future.

Bear in mind too that the 'distance' between the levels is fairly arbitrary. In a particular POP model, the 'gap' between Level 4 and 5 might be a lot bigger or smaller than the gap between Levels 1 and 2, for example. This also allows you to 'zoom in' – if your aim for the year was to move from driving a hybrid car to riding an industrial scale bicycle (Level 6 and 5 in my version), then you might want to stick those in at Levels 1 and Level 6 respectively, and add a few more stages in between.

As I describe many of the solutions available to us in the coming chapters,

I will briefly refer to this concept from time to time in order to illustrate how striving towards moneyless living doesn't have to be all-or-nothing from the word go, or ever, but as a step-by-step plan towards a somewhat more diverse personal economic model, one which I hope leads you to create a more resilient economy for yourself, one less vulnerable to a larger system founded on the absurd concept of infinite growth on a finite planet. The point of this model, however, is not to be a novel little exercise that makes us feel all warm and fuzzy about ourselves, though that can be a very nice bonus. The point of it is to help ourselves get to a place where we are living harmoniously with the Earth and each other. If it is not applied with some degree of courage and determination, we will never get to the world each one of us knows is possible.

MONEYLESS WOMEN AND MEN

Moneyless enclaves still exist amongst the retreating wilds of the world that civilisation has not yet managed to invade. Yet even within civilised, modern industrial society, there are those who have voluntarily given up using it. There are some who have been living moneylessly for over a decade, others who have travelled for tens of thousands of kilometres without money by foot or in vehicles of some sort, and those who have done it in urban and rural settings.

The reasons that all of us do it (or have done it) varies greatly, and our individual POP models would look very different. Yet there is a common thread running through them all – the simple fact that each one of us has observed a world gone horribly wrong on every level of life, and because each of us wants to create new stories to live our lives by, new ways of being that uplift instead of enslave. We want lives based on trust and relationship rather than distrust and impersonalisation.

In the interest of sharing with you as many perspectives on moneyless living as I can, and to show that you can do it in all sorts of scenarios and for all sorts of reasons, here are a few inspirational examples of people who have lived without money.

Peace Pilgrim: up until her death in 1981, Peace Pilgrim spent 28 years walking the length and breadth of the US seven times without a single dime. Her only possessions were the clothes on her back and, if you can believe it, a few small items in the pockets of her tunic. She began walking at the tender age of 44 and vowed to "remain a wanderer until mankind has learned the way of peace, walking until given shelter and fasting until given food". She has written a book, available for free both in hard copy and online, called *Steps towards Inner Peace*,[49] translated into 29 languages.

Daniel Suelo: Daniel began living without money in 2000, and is the subject of a book titled *The Man who Quit Money*. He is of no fixed abode but spends much of his time living in the caves of the Utah canyonlands, where he forages his food from the wilds (and the bins), washes in rivers, and spends his time doing whatever the hell he likes. His blog, Zero Currency,[50] is always thought-provoking.

Satish Kumar: now the editor of *Resurgence* magazine,[51] Satish first came to the UK by walking from India for over two years without money, on the advice of one of his teachers, Vinoba Bhave (one of Mahatma Gandhi's closest friends). His experiences, both internal and external, are available in one of his many books, *No Destination*.[52] He is also a founder of Schumacher College and The Small School in Devon, England.

Tomi Astikainen: this Finn gave up money "in order to see life as it is, without the veil of social conditioning". To experience this, "he became a voluntarily homeless nomad in June 2009 and has lived completely without money since July 2010". During this time, he has hitched 30,000km without money, and has written about his experiences in a free online book titled *The Sunhitcher*.[53]

Jürgen Wagner: as part of the *Schenkers (Givers)* movement, the man known as Oeffie has been living without money since 1991. As a moneyless German, most of his work is in his native tongue. If you speak German or have access to translation, you can learn more about him and his perspectives online.[54]

Heidemarie Schwermer: having founded a popular exchange circle known as the Tauschring, this psychotherapist has been money-free (with the exception of a few euros she keeps aside for train fares) since 1996. She is the subject of a documentary titled *Living without Money*, and has written a book called *Das Sterntalerexperiment – Mein Leben Ohne Geld* (*The Sterntaler Experiment – My Life Without Money*). Heidemarie's philosophy is often based on exchange, yet I believe there is still lots to be learned from her experiences, both in how it has affected her as a person and the practicalities involved.

Benjamin, Raphael, Nicola, Nieves: this band of moneyless adventurers, part of a project known as *Forward the (R)evolution*, spent fourteen months hitch- and boat-hiking their way across the 30,000km from the Netherlands to the US and Mexico, without accepting or using money, getting rides on 480 vehicles along the way. When I asked Benji why he lived without money, he said, "simply because it is the best way I have found to open myself to the world and learn how to give, share and love as if everyone was part of my family, the huge human family". An account of their experiences and inner journeys is available on their website.[55]

Sonja Kruse: On a journey that took one year, and involving 16 different cultures, nine provinces, 114 towns and 150 different families, Sonja – a South African better known as *The Ubuntu Girl* – went on a quest to find the real meaning of Ubuntu (a Bantu word that focuses on people's relationships with each other). Her thoughts and perspectives are available on her online blog.[56]

Adin Van Ryneveld:[57] Another South African who lives by the same Ubuntu spirit of '*I am because you are*', Adin gave up money in 2009 as a five year project to, some may say rather ironically, raise money for good causes. I believe that any apparent irony does not undermine his desire to help the world he has been born into, and by pursuing this path he has unique insights into an idea that could be valuable to many.

Elf Pavlik: Living in Europe without money or an identity card, and claiming no nationality, he has been responsible for bringing moneyless people from all over the world together and into some sort of cohesive movement. His website[58] contains some useful information about moneyless people and projects that can help you live in a similar way to him.

Julez Edward:[59] Despite living and travelling without money for periods of his life, Julez feels that "world wide travelling is actually completely contradictory to moneyless living, because of the plane/fuel dependency". On that basis he is now "working towards finding ways to completely live off the grid and only use what Nature provides".

CHAPTER 4

CHALLENGES AND TRANSITIONAL STRATEGIES

> *Localisation stands, at best, at the limits of practical possibility, but it has the decisive argument in its favour that there will be no alternative.*
>
> Dr. David Fleming

People who are interested in the idea of living completely freely will undoubtedly face obstacles which, for whatever reason, they can't manage to jump over at the first attempt. The most commonly cited are external: no access to land, taxes, the planning permission requirements that come with building a low impact,[60] self-sufficient dwelling, and so on.

Such examples are all major potential barriers, very much rooted in the reality of our world today, and are fairly overwhelming, especially to people who are trying to reduce their engagement with the machine economy, instead of increasing it. The issues around access to soil – such as private property, land prices, permissions and regulations – lie very near the heart of the problem. Yet many of these economic and socio-political challenges originate from the personal, internal obstacles we create within ourselves which prevent us from living a life of glorious simplicity, freedom and adventure. To perceive the land issue to be the ultimate problem is to miss the underlying cultural stories that give rise to such concepts in the first instance. Government policies and regulations are still made by people, even if it is sometimes tempting to wonder whether those who enforce them are actually of the *Homo* genus, especially when you're in the process of dealing with them.

Mahatma Gandhi, the world's greatest Luddite, once said "your beliefs become your thoughts. Your thoughts become your words. Your words become your actions. Your actions become your habits. Your habits become your values. Your values become your destiny." There is truth in this on both the individual and collective level. Yet it feels too linear, and doesn't recognise that life and culture move in spirals, not straight lines. If *The Great Soul* had bothered to consult me before making such hasty, knee-jerk comments, I'd have suggested he rephrased the ending to *your values become your culture. Your culture becomes your beliefs.* There is no destiny, no destination, just a relentless journey along a spiral.

The government policies that exist today started with a set of beliefs of one kind or another, which over time transformed themselves into many stories, which in turn married each other and created new bastardised versions. Now we have the story that someone can own a piece of the Earth, and then charge everyone else for having to be somewhere on it; there's the peculiar story of money; the anthropocentric story that some Big Man in the Sky made everything for Mankind which The Latter then has dominion over and can do with as He likes; Cartesian stories, Newtonian stories, Darwinian stories; stories by Smith and Marx and Friedman. There's the story of fractional reserve banking where our masters – the banks – magically produce money out of thin air and then lend it to us in a way that means that we have to give them not just the capital they invented, but some interest also, using money that was produced by our sweat. Let us also not forget the story that it is now only the birds, badgers and other wild animals that are allowed to make their own little nest out of local materials to live in – the same story that insists that humans must, at all times, be charged, surveilled and regulated in all that they do. This is also part of the story that Freedom is for Nature, and that we are outside it.

These are all myths, starting with beliefs that originated a long time ago, in a period when the stories they spawned may have been useful. Over the ages they have married themselves to other emerging stories, creating baby stories that on inspection are absolutely ludicrous now and make no sense whatsoever for the very real challenges we face today.

Nevertheless, the majority of our species still believe in these stories, making them valid, and we have to find ways to work with them, within them, and sometimes around them. No small feat. But it is to that effect, in this chapter, that I aim to look at some of the main internal and external roadblocks that may impede your journey to a life beyond money, or which simply obstruct the kissing gates of footpaths that lead to money-free transport, food, housing, entertainment and other such destinations. Where appropriate I will offer possible ways around these roadblocks. If I have no solution, I'll say so, and hope that one of you can in time offer up solutions as you figure them out. Part of this process is what Rob Hopkins, co-founder of the Transition Network, describes as the unleashing of the collective genius of the community.

CURRENT HUMAN CULTURE

More powerful than laws, more powerful than armies, is culture. Take an example. Whilst sharing is great for us on every level, and the health of our host, it is not so good for this creature we call The Economy, a beast that all politicians with any ambition to stay in power need to constantly feed with increasingly larger meals. To The Economy, sharing is the enemy, sharing competes for its food, and therefore sharing is the enemy of those whose bulging bank accounts depend on the growth of The Economy. Making all sharing illegal, however, would not be policeable, and it wouldn't go down well with the voter. Instead, our politicians, social architects and marketeers chose a more subtle route, co-creating a culture where sharing isn't illegal, but highly undesirable. It's a culture that asks you why you should bother to share what you've worked hard for with someone who may or may not have worked as hard. A culture of scarcity that makes you worry about the other person breaking what you've loaned them, or not giving it back, leaving you feeling like the cheated one. A culture that states that if you have to borrow something, you're not successful enough to have your own. There is no need for laws when such a culture of fear, scarcity and status makes people conform so voluntarily without them.

Culture also determines much of how we 'choose' to live our lives. As we humans are social creatures, the prospect of being socially ostracised, and the rejection and self-esteem issues that come with that, is a major influence on our behavioural patterns and the choices we make. It's hardly controversial to suggest that a person's need for conformity, a problem arising usually from a lack of self-assurance, dictates a lot of their behaviour.

Some of our social norms are pervasive and intensely oppressive. In Western civilisation, status is conferred on you by how much you own, where you live, what career you have, how much money you earn, how powerful you are, or the brands you sport. In each of these, the bigger or more expensive the better. If you choose to live moneylessly, or even a life of simplicity, you instantly forsake most culturally accepted indicators of success. Despite many who have swam against the tide reporting that making such bold moves enhanced their sense of confidence and freedom – to the point where they no longer care what people think – it can initially seem a very difficult path to take. They also realise, as Bob Dylan once penned, that "a man is a success if he gets up in the morning and goes to bed at night and in between does what he wants to do".

One of the main concerns cited to me by people pondering moneylessness – or just simple living – is what their friends, family and community will think of them because of it. After all, having no money is stigmatised with a sense of poverty and being unsuccessful in life, even if your life has never been richer in real terms. Yet the extent to how deeply embedded social acceptance is within us has still surprised me, despite our claims that we dislike the very society we feel compelled to be accepted by. As Jiddu Krishnamurti once said, "it is no measure of health to be well adjusted to a profoundly sick society", yet we often seem to prefer to make such adjustment than risk the exclusion that is perceived to come with living a healthy life.

People regularly ask me what they can do about this, how they can overcome it and live the lives they want to live. After thinking long and hard on the subject, all I could come up with was one word:

Courage.

If we want to change our culture's stories, and allow people to feel free to be whoever they want to be, we have to show courage. Billy Graham remarked that "courage is contagious. When a brave man takes a stand, the spines of others are stiffened." Nothing ever changed for the better by people just going along with the norm. This change starts with you, and in doing so will, at the minimum, affect the lives of those you touch every day. That is worth living for in itself.

All you need to do to find this courage is to ask yourself what the most important goal of your life is: is it to just do what other people expect you to do, or to live your truth as boldly as you can? If you chose the latter, all that is required is for you to begin putting it into practice.

ADDICTION TO INDUSTRIALISATION

Addiction is a powerful thing. You only have to observe an alcoholic or a heroin addict to understand how controlling and debilitating it is. An alcoholic who recognises in themselves that they have a problem knows that their life would be much better off without booze. Most understand that it is ruining all the relationships in their life that they hold dear, some even know that it will eventually kill them unless they stop. Despite the fact that it is not making them happy, they still can't help themselves from doing it.

We now know that incessant economic growth, which I've argued can only be facilitated by a tool such as money, is making planet Earth uninhabitable for between 150-200 species every day (that's up to 73,000 species a year, and that's just the species we know about).[61] It may only be a matter of time before we join that statistic, not that we should consider ourselves any more noteworthy than the others: the Dodo, the Tasmanian Tiger, the Passenger Pigeon, the Po'ouli, the West African Black Rhinoceros – the list is tear-jerkingly long. Despite this, we also know that incessant economic growth is not making us happy – the person whose thirst is unquenchable can never be satisfied.

But we're addicted. Addicted to growth, to more, to bigger, to faster, to status, to the illusion of certainty, to convenience, to mediocrity, to an unhealthy and unbalanced level of comfort, to processed food, to conformity, to non-stop round-the-clock everything. We're addicted to consuming the planet, and with it all the elemental building blocks that make up our flesh and bone. We're killing both our egocentric and holistic selves, and we can't seem to help either.

Such addiction is not the most common barrier to voluntary simplicity and moneyless living that people relay to me. Not unsurprisingly, few cite it.

Yet I regularly meet people who say they'd really like to change but who then tell me they can't. They seem so hooked on their old habits they can't let them go. Is this addiction, and if so how can we overcome it? To find out more, I interviewed Dr. Chris Johnstone, who worked as an addictions specialist in the UK's National Health Service for nearly 20 years. His books *Find Your Power*[62] and *Active Hope*[63] (co-written with Joanna Macy) apply insights from addiction recovery to tackling global issues.

MB: What is addiction?
CJ: Addiction is where we become so attached to using a substance or behaviour that we experience an overwhelming desire for it, keep repeating it even when we know it is harmful, and have difficulties controlling our use of it. This is well recognised with alcohol and drug use, but it is also seen with behaviours like gambling and over-eating. With addiction, the habit has such a strong grip on us that even when we want to change, we may find this surprisingly difficult. When we do succeed for a while, it can be hard to stick to.

MB: Can we become addicted to consumerism and spending money?
CJ: While I'd say yes, the term 'addiction' doesn't have a universally agreed definition. When looking at addiction to substances, the World Health Organisation uses the term 'dependence syndrome' and defines this by the presence of at least three of the following six features. We can use this as a checklist when looking at our relationship with money.

a) A strong desire or sense of compulsion to use the substance.

b) Difficulties in controlling substance-taking behaviour.

c) A physiological withdrawal state when substance use has ceased or been reduced, or using the substance to relieve or avoid withdrawal symptoms.

d) Evidence of tolerance, such that increased doses are required to achieve the same effects.

e) Progressive neglect of alternative pleasures or interests because of substance use, increased amount of time necessary to obtain or take the substance or to recover from its effects.

f) Persisting use despite clear evidence of harmful consequences.

When an alcoholic has a strong craving for alcohol, the desire is so overwhelming that it can be difficult to resist. It is not uncommon for people to feel something similar with shopping. A survey in the US suggests that up to 16% of the population have 'compulsive buying disorder',[64] where they experience cravings to buy things they don't need and have difficulties controlling their shopping habit.

Tolerance, where someone needs more of a substance (or behaviour) to get the same effect, is clearly visible with consumerism. The level of consumption thought of as 'normal' in the industrialised world has been steadily rising for over fifty years. We've now reached the point where our collective appetite for resources is generating an ecological catastrophe. While addiction to alcohol, nicotine and other drugs are clearly threats to health, they're unlikely to destroy our civilisation. Our collective hunger for more and more goods is another matter. That's why it is worth thinking about the role of addiction here.

MB: Why are we getting hooked on more and more stuff?
CJ: If you don't like how you feel, and you take or do something that shifts your mood towards an experience you prefer, you're more likely to do that again. People get hooked on things that seem to work – in the short term at least. The more someone goes through the sequence of a) I don't like how I feel, b) I take this stuff or do this thing, and then c) I feel better, the more deeply ingrained this pathway becomes. After a while it happens without them even thinking about it.

The paradox is that people tend to become dependent on substances or behaviours because they see them as the solution rather than the problem. What helps recovery is recognising the difference between short-term and long-term effects. A smoker may use cigarettes to calm down, but nicotine dependence makes people more anxious. Someone may turn to alcohol to cheer themselves up, yet drinking heavily makes people more depressed. Addictive behaviour often appears to be a solution to the very problems it makes worse. This creates a vicious cycle, where the more someone relies on something the more they end up feeling they need it. This is true with consumerism too. The more we rely on buying things as the way to meet our needs, the less we develop other paths to a satisfying life.

Addiction isn't just individual. It occurs at the level of organisations and society too. Our mainstream economic system reinforces our cultural pattern of looking to spending as a way of meeting needs. Tackling this isn't just about individual change, even though that's so important. We need a change in our economic system and culture too.

MB: How do we overcome these addictions? Are there a series of steps we can take?
CJ: If you've ever felt your use of resources was excessive, inappropriate or uncontrolled, the first step is just to notice the times this happens. Notice when what you're doing is out of step with your values, when it doesn't feel right. This discrepancy, even if uncomfortable, is motivating. I see it as the start of the journey of change.

The next step is to come to a decision about what you'd like to do. Is this an issue you'd like to tackle? Would you like to live a different way? Decisions are powerful, and we can make them stronger by reminding ourselves why we've made them.

Once you've made a decision, it is worth preparing yourself, selecting a specific area you'd like to tackle and identifying a first step you can take. I like the phrase 'aim for progress rather than perfection'; it focuses your attention on immediate steps you can take from where you are now. Then you take another step, and another.

Addictions recovery groups have a saying 'I can't, we can'. It emphasises that we can't do this alone, we need the support and fellowship of others tackling this too.

And lastly, *recovery needs to happen at the level of our culture and society. It isn't just an individual journey, but one we make together.*

*　　*　　*

There are a few related notes. When we talk of voluntary simplicity, whether it be in the global monetary economy or the local gift economy, we can only imagine sacrifice and loss. Most people's perception of it centres on having to give up something. But one of life's great ironies is that you gain something much more fulfilling, meaningful and rewarding when you find the courage to trust life again and to open yourself up to a more connected way of being, than the little you let go of. Yes, there is a perceived loss, initially, but it is quickly replaced by a sense of freedom and connection that you'll quite possibly have never experienced in your life before; that has certainly been my experience, at least.

When I first decided to give up money, I only intended to do so for a year. But after twelve months I had never been healthier, fitter or happier. Yes I did have to *give up* little things like going to the cinema, chocolate and delightful dealings with Her Majesty's Revenue Commissioners, but I *regained* my freedom, my autonomy to only do things my heart agreed with, not to mention a sense of real control over my life again. I found parts of me that I didn't even know existed, and I loved it. For the first time in my life I felt like I was living with awareness, with connection, with Nature. I didn't continue because it made me miserable – I continued because I'd never felt so alive. The question has got to be: what do you value most in your life – freedom or stuff?

I came across an 'extreme' example of this recently listening to Tim DeChristopher, who went to jail for successfully protecting US wilderness from drilling by simply walking into a land auction and disrupting it by bidding prices up (without actually having the money to back up his bids). In an interview after being sentenced to jail, he said, "I went into this thinking, 'It's worth sacrificing my freedom for this'. But I feel like I did the opposite. I thought I was sacrificing my freedom, but instead I was grabbing onto my freedom and refusing to let go of it for the first time, you know? Finally accepting that I wasn't this helpless victim of society, and couldn't do anything to shape my own future, you know, that I didn't have that freedom to steer the course of my life. Finally I said, 'I have the freedom to change this situation. I'm that powerful.' And that's been a wonderful feeling that I've held onto since then."

Life is the most incredible gift we'll ever be given. It is an adventure, something to explore to its fullest. We would do well not to waste it, and destroy life for everything else in the process, because we were afraid to let go of our habitual behavioural patterns. One of the tragedies of this culture is that we are so afraid to die that we never really live. We live with superficial relationships that lack dependency or depth, we live with money instead of connected relationships with all in our biosphere, and therefore we live in isolation rather than community.

As long as we are addicted, we will never be free. Let's encourage each other to face up to our individual and collective addictions, and to then help each other through them without judgement. The road certainly won't always be easy, but it's a truthful path and there are some incredibly beautiful places along the way. Grab your coat.

LAND OWNERSHIP

Growing up in modern civilisation, it would be very easy to believe that the Earth we live on has always been owned by somebody, and that to live you always had to have money. That's the culture we were born into, so it is all we know. But private ownership is a human story, and a relatively modern one at that. Once the land was free for all to roam. More recently, our land was held in common, for the commoners. Now it is owned by the few – 1% own 70% of the land.[65]

The story of the commons and the enclosures is covered in detail by authors such as Simon Fairlie,[66] but as some of it is relevant to the subject of moneyless living, I will discuss it only to the extent to which it is relevant.

Up until the Tudor period, much land was still held in common. Commoners would subsist on it and maintain it for the benefit of themselves and all. Decisions to enclose this land effectively resulted in the displacement of many villagers and the conversion of arable land into pasture land. Humans, effectively, were replaced by sheep. These displaced humans – us – were, over a period of time, forced into becoming sheep themselves, having to go off to the larger towns and cities and give their bodies and lives to the forwarding of the industrial revolution.

Whilst the reasons behind the enclosures vary depending on the agenda of whichever historian you listen to, many argue that a large part of the move towards enclosure was to force people into the cities, into the industrial factories, and therefore into the wage and monetary economies that all of us take for granted today. A smart move on behalf of the nobility and industrialists who capitalised from it, but not so good for the majority, the subsistence peasants of the time, or the 99% of today's population.

On a related aside, this move has more recently been compounded by the stealthiness of economists, politicians and journalists alike in conflating words related to *economy* with words related to *finance*. The former comes from a Greek word *οἰκονομία*, meaning *household management*, and it is little more than a logistical system for us to meet our needs and wants within the limits of what our home can sustain. This logistical system may or may not be a *financial* one, a word relating only to the management of money. This example shows the power of language, as when we hear the word 'economic' today we think of matters relating to money (finance), as opposed to methods of meeting our needs. The next time someone tells you that protecting a woodland is not *economically viable*, remind them that they really mean it's not *financially viable*. In terms of managing a 'household' that has fewer trees by the minute, protecting them is probably *economically crucial*.

Such manipulative use of language has produced profitable results for those with vested interests: few of us can even imagine a non-monetary or non-wage economy, thinking it to be a utopian fantasy dreamt up by hippies and those with no sense of reality, even though we can readily see this utopia in its most glorious action on any occasion we wander to the woods, where we bear witness to every other species living in a totally localised manner.

The trend towards enclosure, the turning of commonly held land into privately owned land, has since been rapidly unfolding across the world. This, by no small means, was helped by a biologist called Garrett Hardin, who pencilled a very influential essay titled 'The Tragedy of the Commons', which was published in journals such as *Science* magazine. Hardin claimed that when land was held in common, people acting in the rational self-interest that Adam Smith and Ayn Rand talk about would deplete it. His logic was this: for every extra agricultural unit (be it a cow or a crop) the commoner put on the land, he would gain one full extra unit, whilst it would be the entire community that would share the loss of soil fertility, vegetation and so on that the one extra unit caused.

As many commentators have noted, Hardin's perspective on the situation caught on quickly, mostly because it strengthened the case of those who already wanted to slice the Earth into privately owned segments for their own purposes. This essay gave them a credible reason to carry out what they already wanted to, the result of which was to force the rest of us into monetary slavery.

Hardin's essay was fundamentally flawed, and you only have to look at how community allotments and orchards are run to see why. As George Monbiot points out, Hardin is confusing commons with free-for-alls, citing the example of the oceans to prove this. The oceans are not collectively watched by anyone, hence they are stripped bare of fish as everyone acts in delusional self-interest towards them. Monbiot[67] argues that "in a true commons, everyone watches everyone else, for they know that anyone over-exploiting a resource is exploiting them". When people are collectively dependent on a piece of Earth for their survival, they care for it well, and make decisions around it that work for them and the land itself, and not for the nobility or the industrialists who merely want to make money from it. Small scale is critical – for good stewardship, those using the commons need to know each other in order to fairly coordinate their usage.

But Hardin's theory has another flaw. Let us suspend reality for a moment and pretend that the commoners did destroy the land they held in common by putting their own narrow self-interest above that of the collective. Even if such an eventuality was true, the necessary response would not be to put it into private ownership, which Hardin effectively advocated, but to challenge the cultural stories behind the idea of the skin-encapsulated ego. If humans fully understood the interconnectedness of all things, to destroy the land would not be in their holistic self-interest, nor even in their egocentric self-interest in the long-term.

What the enclosures did was force us all into cities and the monetary economy. You take away a human's legal access to soil and a place to build a house out of the materials which that land provides (in the same way that a bird is allowed to build a nest), and you make a *de facto* slave out of her. This movement towards enclosure rose with other stories that were being created and advanced at the time, such as the myth that humanity is separate from Nature. Such beliefs mean that, today, the countryside is for Nature – the cows, the sheep, the birds and the bees – and not humanity, as if we were less natural than a blade of grass or a gust of wind.

The end result of all of this is an inherently unsustainable civilisation. Monbiot adds that:

> *... these changes in the ownership of land lie at the heart of our environmental crisis. Traditional rural communities use their commons to supply most of their needs: food, fuel, fabrics, medicine and housing. To keep themselves alive they have to maintain a diversity of habitats: woods, grazing lands, fields, ponds, marshes and scrub. Within these habitats they need to protect a wide range of species: different types of grazing, a mixture of crops, trees for fruit, fibres, medicine or building.*
>
> *The land is all they possess, so they have to look after it well. But when the commons are privatised, they pass into the hands of people whose priority is to make money. The most efficient means of making it is to select the most profitable product and concentrate on producing that.*

History and philosophy aside, the reality is that for all of us today, there is little access to land, either for food growing or for somewhere to build a nest. This is a very real and major obstacle to moneyless living, as I personally know only too well. As I am not the Prime Minister and don't anticipate being any time soon, my ways around this are limited to some transitional strategies we can adopt for now, whilst simultaneously spreading some new cultural compost to create the fertile soil through which the seeds of moneyless societies could germinate in the not too distant future. With enough collective will and courage to stand up for our holistic selves, there is no reason I know of why this wouldn't be possible. As always, it starts with the creation of new stories.

I will outline these transitional strategies towards land in chapter six, but if we are to get back to living truly sustainable lives in the long-term, then serious land reform is undoubtedly necessary.

PLANNING PERMISSION FOR LOW / ZERO IMPACT LIVING

If you already have a house and have no intention of moving in order to partake in the moneyless economy to a wider degree, then much of the following paragraphs will be irrelevant to your situation and you may want to skip this subsection. However, if you do want to move to a piece of land that has no existing residential dwelling, in order to create a moneyless micro-economy, then read on, as the first obstacle you'll encounter is planning permission. I've seen hardy people weep at the very mention of these words, such is the scale of this particular hurdle in many countries. Those who have gone down the planning permission route and failed (usually because they take the up-front, legal approach) often lose hope of ever subsisting on the land, whilst others find it too overwhelming to even try.

Planning permission is one of those ideas whose intentions are admirable but whose current application is bordering on terrible. Before the Town and Country Planning Act 1947, which was introduced after controversial projects such as the town now known as Peacehaven (near Brighton) gained popularity, you could build what you wanted if the land was legally owned by you. *The Times*, shortly after its introduction, described this Act as the effective 'nationalisation' of the right to build your own home from materials on your land – that right now belonging to the state, "to be released only at the political judgment of local authorities".[68]

In a monetised, globalised economy where materials can be imported from all over the world and where land is viewed as a commodity to profit from, I wholeheartedly agree with author and land campaigner Simon Fairlie[69] that some sort of regulation is necessary to protect huge swaths of the countryside being turned into property development by those with the financial firepower. The downside is that, like many centralised public institutions, the Planning Inspectorate operate in reaction to the lowest common denominator, suspecting that everyone is trying to con them and profit from the system, which is usually the case in this monetary economy, to be fair. Meaning that anyone wanting to fulfil what I believe to be the closest thing to a natural human right that we have – the opportunity to make your own nest and grow crops for yourself and your community – finds it almost impossible to do so, as the planning system is designed to protect the countryside from *all* humans, even those who only want to enrich it.

If we are to do more than pay mere lip-service to 'nice ideas' such as sustainability and freedom, then a crucial first step will be to make distinctions in the planning system to separate the exploiters from the enrichers. As the need for such a system originates largely from the fact that materials can now be imported from all over the world (facilitated by money), I'd argue that the answer lies there also.

Whenever we see recently built houses in the countryside, they look like a blot on the landscape; nay, they are a blot on the landscape. This is for no simpler reason than they aren't, or never were, a part of that landscape. Houses made from local materials, by their inhabitant's own hands, compliment the countryside, give it a human touch, in the same way that a bird's nest takes nothing away from a tree and only adds natural complexity and beauty. No one who has ever seen an old stone and thatch cottage in amongst an orchard of apple, pear and plum trees has ever expressed to me that they felt that such a habitat was a blot on the landscape. Such locally made homes enliven the countryside, make it a vibrant place full of life and abundance, instead of the tourist destination it has become for depressed city dwellers who want a much needed break from the stresses of urban life and disconnected consumerism. Therefore anyone who can build their own home – one hundred percent – from materials from their land (or within a short radius of that land) should be permitted to.

Not only would these homes complement the countryside and reinvigorate it, they would encourage abundant smallholdings that improve the nation's level of self-reliance, boost local economic (ideally non-financial) activity in the countryside.[70] They would also likely lead to some reforestation, as locally produced wood would become a much sought after building material for others wanting to get back to the land but who lack adequate building materials.

As planning officers also want to protect the countryside from extra traffic, an issue I support them on, those who seek to live in the countryside under an application for a fully localised home could also be asked to sign some version of a Section 106 Agreement disallowing them from bringing a car to their site as part of such an arrangement (this lack of easy transport would also encourage those that live there to become fully self-reliant). This combination would separate the wheat from the chaff, as such homes would appeal little to developers, while appealing greatly to those who genuinely want to live subsistently and who, by their nature and values, tend to have very low incomes. Small ecologically-sound villages – places where people can grow crops for their own needs and those of their community, utilising the optimum economies of scale and division of labour that would come with such a set-up – could flourish under such circumstances. This change in planning guidance could be the basis for the beginning of a redesign of British society to a fully localised economic model.

Admittedly, such restrictions as these don't leave very many materials for a prospective home owner to choose from, and it would be more difficult to take trips into the surrounding towns, But that's the point: if you really want to live in the countryside you ought to be prepared to actually *live in the countryside*, and not in a mix of various imported materials to that countryside. If you can't make a home out of local materials and live there as part of that ecosystem, then you could argue that you no longer have that basic human right to live there. Importing stuff from the four corners of the world, and having a car, *is not* a basic human right.

Whilst I believe that we all need to support organisations such as Chapter 7[71] in campaigning for changes to the planning and building regulations systems, the reality is that things won't significantly change any time soon, and most likely not until either the financial or ecological situation deteriorates so badly that we'll have no choice but to create new, age-relevant stories. Therefore if you have some land now, or are planning on getting some, and you want to build a low impact dwelling (LID) (or better still, one with a positive impact), you will have to overcome this issue one way or another. You have two main paths open to you.

The first, and rather tempting, option is to just go ahead and build your low impact dwelling, keep a low profile, ideally hide yourself from all view (e.g. in a wood), and hope that no one ever sees you and/or makes a complaint. If you do get a visit from your local planning officer, then (in the UK, at the time of writing) you can apply for retrospective planning permission. If you are contemplating taking this route (or the second option), I would highly recommend reading Simon Fairlie's book, the *DIY Planning Handbook*. Chapter 7 also give free advice over the phone[72] to anyone who needs it, but they recommend reading the handbook first as they don't have the time or resources to explain all of its fine detail to every person who phones in with erotic fantasies of living *The Good Life* like Tom and Barbara.

This retrospective route has been taken by many intentional communities (such as the Steward Wood community in Devon and Tinkers Bubble in Somerset) and back-to-the-landers, and it has generally had a relatively high level of success, though at the cost of a great deal of energy, stress, and often money.

The second option is to apply for planning permission in advance. This has the benefits of being up-front with planners and the local community (whose needs ought to be given a lot of consideration), it is less risky (if you build without permission your house could be torn down/removed at a cost), and it has the potential to pave the way for precedents in planning guidance which can then make it easier for those who come after you. Finding good allies can be a crucial first step. One possibility is the Ecological Land Cooperative,[73] a fledgling organisation working to provide opportunities for ecologically-minded smallholdings, and to address some of the absurdities of the planning system.

The good news is that as people become increasingly aware of sustainability issues, planning officers are becoming more open to projects which rate highly in terms of their local council's sustainability objectives and have a small carbon footprint. Lammas,[74] an ecological living project in Wales, were recently successful in a landmark case which – utilising a Pembrokeshire planning policy, termed Policy 52, that takes a new approach to sustainable development in the countryside – effectively led to the Welsh Assembly Government issuing their own nationwide policy titled One Planet Development (OPD). This policy is a statement of intent from the people and government of Wales, and is part of a commitment "to reduce the ecological footprint of each Welsh citizen from 4.41 to 1.88 global hectares/person...within a generation."[75] The result of Lammas' graft and determination has meant that applying for planning permission for a LID in Wales is, at the time of writing, much more sensible, clear and appealing than in the rest of the UK. Others, such as Tony Wrench and Brithdir Mawr, have also been successful through Pembrokeshire's Policy 52, and in doing so have pioneered a path that others can benefit from.

If you do not have land yet but are determined to live moneylessly, another option is to simply leave the country you're in (presuming it is one where planning permission is required for the type of dwelling you want) to one where planning permission isn't, or is not as much, of a problem as it is where you currently reside. In Greece, for example, no planning permission is required for dwellings that are conventionally viewed as temporary, such as yurts, meaning that you can just get on with creating your own moneyless micro-economy. Given the state of the Greek macro-economy, you probably would not be alone either. One group of Greeks called *Free and Real*,[76] who have been heavily involved with *Freeconomy Greece* and with whom I stayed during the summer of 2011 in the north of Evia, are already in the process of doing just that, establishing a project very much in tune with the ideals extolled in this book. In the process they are researching and testing solutions that will be of lasting benefit to the people of their country in the not-too-distant future. Such projects will be invaluable when the time comes that localisation is an economic imperative, and not the wacky alternative that it is perceived to be today.

One way or another, we need to stop believing in the story that humans are separate from Nature, and give ourselves back the same rights that we give to the birds and the bees, as long as we accept the responsibility to live within natural limits that comes with that.

COUNCIL TAX – THE TAX ON BEING ALIVE

Income tax is only chargeable on money you earn, so this element of tax is not a problem for anyone wanting to live without money. For those of you who don't pay it for whatever reason, even those who don't claim any social welfare benefits or avail of any public services, there will be accusations of leaching and living off other's taxes, and that comes with the territory. Whilst I fully sympathise with many taxpayers' sentiments to this effect (I am one myself, as I pay tax on my book sales), I also believe that a human being must have, at least, the basic right to *not* believe in the story of money, just as much as an adult taxpayer will retain the right to not believe in the story of Santa Claus if they so wish. If other people want to use money, that's their choice. But I don't subscribe to the view that because some do, everyone therefore has to. Taxes, because they can only be paid in legal tender which most people can only obtain by trading their time in exchange for it, force people out of subsistence living and into the wage and market economy. Earthworms, trees or bees don't pay taxes, or believe in the story of money, yet it doesn't mean that they don't play an absolutely essential role in life on Earth.

However, if your heart beats and your feet tend to reside on a piece of privately owned Earth defined as the United Kingdom, you are liable to pay council tax (if you live outside of the UK this may or may not be an obstacle). Whether you have to actually pay council tax or not is an entirely different story. As it stands at the time of writing, if you are a low earner or unemployed you can claim council tax benefit to offset this, but again, it's tricky: in order to claim it, you have to prove that you're unemployed by showing a claim for jobseekers allowance or other similar forms of social welfare payment, which in turn doesn't make you very moneyless. One solution is that you could give your benefits to a homeless person who, because of various bureaucratic and personal matters, can't claim Jobseeker's Allowance, but by this point it is becoming a silly game with the system, which is hardly the intended spirit behind living in the localised gift economy along with the birds and the bees.

Another potential solution to consider is the *Freeman on the Land*[77] concept, which is a movement of people who declare themselves outside of Statute Law, using the notion of 'Lawful Rebellion' in the process. They claim that Statute Law (or Acts, as they refer to them) is contractual and therefore it only applies to their legal person as represented by their birth certificate, and not the real human being behind it to which only Common Law applies, unless they consent to otherwise. This is a huge topic in itself and one outside the scope of this book, other than my recommendation to investigate it for yourself and to then make your own conclusions in relation to council tax. Some Freemen claim that you do not need to pay it if you have not consented to their contract. I have seen some evidence of a letter from a council that would certainly back this claim up, from someone who has claimed to have won a case in relation to not paying council tax, but I cannot verify how genuine this letter was or what went on behind the scenes. If you do choose this route, you do really need to understand what you're doing and be prepared to accept all that comes with it, both legally and in terms of what it means for your life.

If you are choosing to live without the concept of debt or credit (as opposed to just being skint because the economic system you've been forced into is failing you), I feel you should strongly consider whether or not it is consistent to then avail of the benefits that the monetary economy provides, such as free industrialised healthcare, tax-funded libraries, the fire service and the like. Otherwise there is strong merit in the criticisms.

If you thought the complexities stopped there, you were wrong. Many people who argue against the monetary economy, for whatever reason, believe that we could still have our dialysis machines, fire engines and books in a non-monetary economic model (I disagree). They claim that they've been forced into this monetary model, and whilst not wanting to perpetuate it feel that they should still be entitled to use it until humanity wakes up to a more compassionate, connected economic system. This is the position many of those in movements like Zeitgeist take, and whilst I sympathise with such a stance, I have yet to see any evidence of how it could ever possibly work at such a macro-scale in reality.

Whether or not people should pay council tax is a massive philosophical question, and opinions are completely divided. It is so complex that I am even divided on the subject myself, and I'm an avid proponent of moneylessness. Philosophically speaking, I believe council tax to be outrageous, it is effectively a tax on breathing when applied in a country that no longer has any common land that one can dwell on, and it is just another tool to force people out of a subsistence, non-monetary economy and into a wage, monetary economy. For that reason alone it is worth resistance and I fully support anyone who does.

However, speaking with my realist hat on, council tax does go towards things most non-monetary economists I know like: the fire service, libraries, police protection and so on. To refuse to pay it, when you are physically able to and skilled enough to, does bring with it some responsibilities in my opinion. The responsibility of looking after your own needs in these respects, possibly with other people in your neighbourhood who don't want to believe in the story of money any longer either. Again, some will argue that it is impossible *not* to use the police, as their very existence affords you protection, unless you put up a sign on your house saying "We will not phone the police if you break in". This, in turn, could be counter-argued by the fact that, within this legal system, if someone tries to apprehend a murderer, burglar or banker themselves, they are setting themselves up to be sued.

These issues are often passionately debated on both sides, and I can see both arguments. By creating the story of money a long time ago, and by then brainwashing ourselves into believing that money is some sort of universal truism, we've got ourselves in a right pickle, and I can't hand-on-heart advise you what to do in this respect. I feel that as long as you are coming from a place of love, from the holistic self and not the egocentric self, and that you are actively trying to change the social myths that create such illusory dilemmas to begin with, then you will not go too far wrong, whatever route you take.

A fair compromise, one which respects the needs of everyone involved, may be that if you want to live without the story of money, yet still benefit from some of the services that your local council provides (whether you like it or not), that you offer some of your time and knowledge to the local community in any way that is helpful to them. I would hope that anyone living moneylessly would do this anyway, and not need it to be part of a formal arrangement, as a life without caring for those around you isn't the life without money that I advocate and I'd personally want nothing to do with it.

INSURANCE

Insurance, in all its forms, is one of the pillars of the monetary economy. Without it, the entire financial building would collapse overnight. It is vital to the way things are. But is it vital to you personally? If you decide that you do need some form of it, that simple fact forces you into the monetary economy in order to get the credits to pay for it. That's fine if all you are after is a more frugal, simple life, but how would it work if you wanted to go completely moneyless?

In the days before insurance companies existed, a family's insurance was often the connections they had with the community around them – that uncontracted, informal guarantee that if anyone's house (or teepee) burnt down, everyone in the community would look after them and help them rebuild a roof over their head. In a localised economy, this wasn't such a big deal, as houses were simpler and people still knew how to make use of locally available materials and, just as importantly, how to help each other. I'd love my insurance in life to be that: community, friendship, interdependency, as part of a people who look after each other unconditionally, no matter what. Instead we opt for official documents that do nothing to increase the bonds between ourselves and our fellow humans.

For better or worse, these are not such times, and this is where the POP model comes in handy. As my biggest advice is to live so simply that you don't have anything you mind losing, I would have 'Voluntary Simplicity' as my top level on it. Personally, I've only ever had insurance once, when I owned a houseboat, which I sold to set up the Freeconomy movement (see page 88) and start living moneyless. Since then I've never owned anything of much financial worth. However, your situation may be very different to mine, and you will likely have some possessions.

If you feel you need a car, then complete moneyless living will not be an option, as insurance is a legal requirement. If you want to insure stuff that does not legally need to be insured, that's a choice only you can make, but it obviously does mean you'll need to earn legal tender to pay for it. If you want life insurance or a pension, there are no moneyless solutions I know of, other than cultivating loving relationships and interdependent, real community. It is possible that insurance may be appropriate for you now, but less so as you work your way up your own POP model towards less money-dependent living.

Home insurance is not a legal requirement unless you have had to borrow money to buy your home – if this is the case it is almost certain the lender will legally require you to take out an adequate policy. That said, if you're paying back a mortgage then insurance premiums are the least of your concerns in terms of living moneylessly. If you want to bin the mortgage, building your own low impact home could be your solution (see chapter seven), as they cost a fraction of a conventional house (simple designs can be built without money). Simon and Jasmine Dale's 'hobbit' house[78] in Lammas (see page 77) is so beautifully designed, both aesthetically and functionally, that international media regularly feature it. Yet it only cost £3,000 to build – I know people who have spent that on a sofa or television set alone! Ardheia's dwellings in France[79] are another example of how our homes can be aesthetically exhilarating without them costing the Earth. As we have seen in the last section, there will be the issue of planning permission to overcome, but with determination you can.

If you own your home outright, which is often the case with low-cost, low impact homes, there are no legal obligations in the UK. Therefore my advice is to simply live in the present. We often negatively stigmatise people who have gambling problems, yet by taking out insurance policies we non-gamblers gamble every day. With insurance, you're betting that something unfortunate will happen to you during the course of the next insurance period. If you live accident-free for that time, you lose, but if something 'bad' happens to you, you win! I can't encourage you enough to just live in the moment, and not in the future, otherwise when you do eventually die you'll realise that you've never really lived. Jermaine Evans once quipped that "so many people tiptoe through life, so carefully, to arrive, safely, at death". Better to die fully engaged in life, I'd say.

BEING A PARENT

It's all well and fine you living without money, you're a fit young man, try doing it when you've got kids! I hear this one a lot, and I fully appreciate the truth in the latter part of it. The 'fit young man' bit I never really understood, because a) I'm not so young and b) almost anyone, except those who have severe mental/physical disabilities or debilitating illnesses, can be fit if they want to be by moving and eating well and c) my levels of fitness were mostly down to my moneyless lifestyle, as it is a life that involves you using your body instead of fossil fuels.

The part I fully agree with is that living moneylessly definitely is simpler when you don't have children who are dependent on you. In my first year living moneylessly I often thought about the extent to which it would be more difficult with a young family. But there are a number of points to note here. First, whilst it is trickier, it is by no means impossible, and throughout this book I will be recommending many tips that will be useful to parents who want to move up the POP pyramid towards their own form of moneyless living. I do this with a little apprehension – having never been a parent myself I don't feel in much position to advise an actual mother or father, so forgive me if any of my moneyless parent tips come across as arrogant or lacking understanding.

Second, bringing up a child without money is only difficult because of the myths, and the societies and institutions they have formed, that we've created and perpetuated over the course of modern history. You wouldn't be alive today if it wasn't possible to raise humans without money, as all those in the early part of your lineage brought up their children in a world where the myth of money hadn't yet even been told.

But most importantly, if you agree with my arguments in chapter one, then you will see the urgency for us all to start creating new stories, ones that are sustainable and make sense for our time, if your child is going to have any future worth having. This will require pioneers such as yourself, people who have the courage to push the boundaries closer to where they need to be. As Hillel once remarked, "if not you, then who? If not now, then when?" The next generation needs this one to develop a more expansive sense of self and to find the courage to stand up and change the culture we live in.

Make one of those people you.

CHAPTER 5

LABOUR AND MATERIALS

We – the civilised – have been inculcated to believe that belongings are more important than belonging.

Derrick Jensen, *Endgame Volume I*[80]

Anyone proclaiming that they want to give up the material world in order to live 'the spiritual life' is, I believe, deluded (in the nicest possible way) on two fronts. First, the material world is the litmus test of our spirituality, it's our opportunity to prove that our spiritual beliefs are not just abstract thoughts and words without substance. Spirituality isn't something to merely philosophise about. It's not about sitting cross-legged in the lotus position chanting OM. Reciting passages verbatim from the Qu'ran, the Bible or the Bhagavad Gītā doesn't necessarily signify a spiritual life either, no more than going to church on a Sunday morning or worshipping the Sun does. These practices in themselves have the potential to help you to lead a more connected, loving, empathic, compassionate and respectful life – which I believe is the role of whichever of these stories you choose – but they are probably less spiritual in themselves than the act of having a good old shit in a composting toilet.

I personally try to practice *applied spirituality* (despite failing miserably on a daily basis), where your spirituality is revealed through what you do everyday, and how you meet your physical needs. I believe that the depth of your spirituality is revealed by the ways in which you attain and eat your food, create fire, how gently you walk in Nature, how you interact with people that you have no personal need to get along with, your responses to tough decisions, how you treat strangers and those you claim to love, and the levels of courage you display when weakness is the easier option.

It is revealed by your respect for water, air and earth, the elements which make up your flesh and bones, and in the ways by which you share your gifts with the world.

A reporter once asked Mahatma Gandhi what his message to the world was. He replied 'my life is my message', meaning that he believed how he lived his life every day was of much more importance and relevance than telling the world how he thinks they should live or what they should believe. Words are much too easy. To paraphrase Kahlil Gibran,[81] action is love made visible.

The second part of the delusion is that it is simply impossible to give up the material world unless you accept death, which – unsurprisingly – none of the people I know want to. There are some basic needs that you have to meet if you want to survive, and they vary from one geographical region to the next. Getting close to these basic material needs has all sorts of positive benefits for you, the planet and all that you share it with, and how you decide to meet them is a deeply spiritual questioning process. Going below this minimum (which the vast majority of us are, unfortunately, in no danger of doing yet!) in the long-term can be detrimental to you and, by extension, the organism of which you are a part. The key, once again, is finding the optimal level of material requirements, the level that enriches both the egocentric and holistic self.

I believe that exploring the spiritual aspects of ourselves is crucial to our wellbeing and will be central to how gracefully we face the converging ecological and social crises that are upon us, so I don't mean to offend anyone's spiritual practices in the slightest. But I feel we would do well to stop seeing the material and the spiritual as separate realms, and instead to see the spirit that is invisibly running through every mosquito, every act, every rock, through each and every plant and animal, through ourselves. Seeing the mundane imbued with the glorious enables us to treat the Earth, and the community of life it supports, as if the quality of our lives depended on it – and oh how it does. Meeting our needs in the most sustainable, community-enhancing and connection-creating way we can is one of the most potent spiritual practices we have available to us; that has, at least, been my experience in life.

If you do decide you want to live moneylessly or much more simply, there are certain physical needs you are going to have to meet, regardless of whether you decide to do it in the city or the woods. Whether you meet those needs by using palaeolithic methods or by logging on to the expanding array of gift economy websites, or a mix of both, is up to you, and will depend largely on your unique situation, what you have access to, the reasons why you want to live with little or no money and your proficiency at surviving in both the urban and wild landscapes. To meet your needs you need labour (whether it be your own or someone else's) and materials to some degree.

LABOUR

Given the political and economic systems we've grown up in, along with the myths that such societies have spoon-fed us since birth, it would be easy to believe that the only way in which we could manage labour in our economies is with money.

As with everything, it really doesn't have to be this way. It is just a story, one of many, and one which we can change if it no longer serves us. Our current way of living may be theoretically convenient, but if convenience turns out to be soul-destroying, is it still convenient? Modern economics does little for the human spirit; it has left many of us miserable and hating what we do every day. Contrary to what money's most enthusiastic proponents would have you believe, it actually inhibits our sense of freedom, and through its mechanisms stops us from pursuing the things we really want to do in life. The US, the self-proclaimed and flagship land of the free, does not legally require its employers to provide any paid leave, and almost one out of four workers has no paid leave at all.[82]

There are other ways of living and working, ways that uplift us, that build resilient communities of people who trust and depend on each other, systems that create unity instead of division. Some of these that I will list in the menu below are still based on the concept of exchange (a couple are even forms of local currency), yet I include them because they may help you move along your own POP model in this respect, and act as stepping stones towards living fully in the gift economy. They are divisible into two general categories: the modern, which is what will be useful to most of you in the immediate term, and the palaeolithic, also known as the art of survival.

Modern skills and labour systems

Since I gave up money in 2008, I have noticed a huge surge in the gift economy, most of which is organised online. This presents a problem. There is no truly moneyless solution to the internet due to the complexity of the technologies involved. You can access the internet without money by making use of your local library. Yet whilst this is free at the point of delivery, libraries in the monetary economy are funded by council taxpayers. Therefore, projects such as these in this section should be regarded as transitional strategies, as opposed to something to strive for long-term.

Freeconomy

I created the Freeconomy in 2007, partially in response to the fact that all of the other alternatives to the monetary economy that I knew of were still based on the old mindset of exchange that lay at the heart of the dominant monetary economy they existed within. I felt an alternative to the alternatives was desperately needed.

Freeconomy involves sharing your time, skills, tools and knowledge to whatever degree you are comfortable with – completely for free – safe in the knowledge that whenever you need help with something else, or the loan of a screwdriver, another member of your local group (whom you may have never even met before) will then help you in the same spirit. There are no credits, IOUs, ratings systems to be filled in or boring administration to be done; unconditionality is much more efficient, and less bureaucratic, than conditionality. This philosophy sounds radical when considered within the mindsets we hold today, but the old adage 'what goes around comes around' just about sums it up.

Using it is even simpler than the idea itself. Once you sign up, you instantaneously gain access to the entire skill pool of all other members in your local area, whose radius you can define as anything between 1 and 25 miles, depending on whether you live in London or the Forest of Dean. From that point onwards, think of the Freeconomy as your online Yellow Pages, but where everyone does everything, and shares everything, for free.

Let's take an example to show how simply it works. Your bike is punctured. Instead of trudging your bike off to the bike shop, you log on and search for the word 'mechanic'. The software will then inform you of every single member within your chosen radius who has signed up with 'bicycle mechanic' as one of their skills, listing those closest to your doorstep first and those further away in descending order. You can contact them through the site, and if both parties are happy you can arrange to meet up on whatever terms suits you both (all we ask is that no money changes hands). You, or they, get the job done for free, learn how to fix a puncture in the process, and you both may even become good friends. Feedback I've received indicates that people often cook dinner or lunch for the person who has helped them to say thank you, but this is by no means expected.

If you're worried that only Reiki and Hopi ear candle practitioners take part, think again. Freeconomy members have offered up over 500,000 skills at the time of writing, with over 2,000 pre-listed types of skills to choose from on the website. Skills range from hairdressing to plumbing. I've – rather ironically – helped a local children's charity with its accounts and cash flow forecasts, and have had free legal advice from another member who I'd never even met before.

Against all the expectations of friends who originally told me that it was too idealistic to succeed in a dog-eat-dog world, the Freeconomy is flourishing. I'm not too surprised. Whatever conventional economists may believe, a glance at the one truly functional economy we know about – Nature – taught me that dogs actually show a strong preference for helping their fellow dogs rather than eating them.

There are now Freeconomy groups in over 160 countries around the world, and its success reflects people's desire and need for a decent level of the gift economy in their lives, especially as the cracks in the monetary economy continue to widen and become visible to all. Members seem to be positively enthusiastic about doing things for no other reason than the simple fact that another human being needs help, and that they have been gifted the ability to be able to help them. What reason, other than the understanding that we can help another living soul, do we need to help someone? Do we always have to get something in return nowadays? Freeconomy has thankfully been teaching me that we don't, and that people really enjoy giving unconditionally. Don't believe those who will try to convince you otherwise.

Gift circles

The gift circle is an idea originally developed by a group of people, including Alpha Lo,[83] in California, but which is now spreading worldwide. It's the equivalent of a small-scale, off-line Freeconomy group. Creating one, and then running it, is easy. Everyone (the optimum number is somewhere between twelve and twenty people, give or take a few) sits around in a circle and begins by stating a handful of their needs. This may be anything from a tennis partner, a desk, help with tax returns or learning how to make a bow drill, the loan of a sleeping bag or a lift somewhere.

Once everyone has said what they need, the group then go around again and say what they're happy to share. Again, this can be anything from skills and stuff to knowledge and time. Once this is complete, there is an optional round, where everyone can say thank you to others in the group who have helped them in some way, or to the group in general. Although this can seem to be superfluous if time is limited, it is crucial to the long-term sustainability of the group. Hearing the ways in which others have given freely inspires the rest of the group to do so too, it uplifts everyone involved, and showing gratitude for that which we receive is an important part of life.

A few tips: it is wise to have a facilitator who has a fair understanding of gift economies (this can be a different person each week, and you can have multiple facilitators at each gathering), and for someone to take notes of all attendee's contact details, what they want to receive and what they can offer, so that everyone can follow up on things afterwards if they need to. Groups can meet up as often as they find useful – some meet every week, some once a month. Organisations can also create their own gift circles as a way of getting things done without the need for money or funding, in a way that brings people of that organisation together under a common purpose.

The benefits of this over a web-based model such as Freeconomy is that it gets a group of people together face-to-face in a way that builds and nurtures real interdependency. It also doesn't require the internet and its global infrastructure in order to exist, meaning that anyone can utilise it. Its only downside is that it doesn't work as well when the numbers go over twenty, whereas a model such as Freeconomy (which is in effect a large online gift circle) can handle any number of people. In my POP model, I'd describe gift circles as the ideal and Freeconomy as a tool we can utilise as we transition to a point where each street has their own real-life gift circle.

Help Exchange[84]

HelpX works in an almost identical way to the more renowned WWOOF scheme (see page 112), with the main difference being that it's not limited to organic farms and smallholdings. Through this scheme participants spend a few hours of their day doing work for their hosts, often in places such as B&Bs, sailing boats, hostels or on farms, for which they get food and accommodation (along with the chance to experience a new culture or learn a language and skills) in return. It opens up the possibility of having the moneyless experience of WWOOFing in the city as well as the countryside. Usually people work for their hosts for about four hours per day, and then have the rest of the day off to do whatever they please. Again, combine this with hitching or cycling and anyone could live for a year or longer without needing money, bureaucracy or banks accounts if they wanted to give it a trial run. While the ecological benefits of this scheme are only utilised if done through an organic farm, it does allow anyone an easy opportunity to get a sense of how it feels to live without a penny to your name. Such experiences can have a huge impact on your own personal growth and provide you with a stepping stone to a more localised and gift based form of moneyless living.

Local Exchange Trading Schemes (LETS) and Timebanks

Adding these schemes to a book on moneyless living is questionable but, as I mentioned in chapter two, they can be a stepping stone for anyone who is currently embroiled in the monetary economy, enabling them to eventually make their way into the gift economy if they so wish.

LETS is a network of people who agree to use a local currency (LETS pounds for example) to share their skills. Its members create and exchange credits which, as Peter North points out,[85] "they back with their commitment to do enough work to pay this 'commitment' (not 'debt') off in a reasonable time in the future ... you don't need any local money before you start – you just make a commitment to work for someone else who asks you in the future." It's a bit like Freeconomy, but without the uplifting feeling of unconditionality that only the gift economy really creates, and without the bonds of interdependency that only money and immediate-and-exact crediting can so efficiently destroy.

Timebanks are much the same as LETS in that credits of one form or another are exchanged. When you help Mary with her car for an hour, you bank one hour of time. When Jake calls around to your noisy neighbour with a baseball bat and sorts him out, as agreed, he banks one of your hours. The critical difference with Timebanks is that everyone's time (and therefore life, as what is life but time?) is valued equally, with the person who helps you get your garden into shape earning as much for their time as you do when you provide them with your plumbing or web development skills.

So how are these any different to 'normal' money? They're not different enough to be seen as a long-term solution, and whilst they still perpetuate the old story, albeit in a healthier way, they do provide communities with extra resilience against shocks to the national currency, though this is marginal unless they have fully localised their material economy along with the currency. They also allow their members to get things done while reducing their dependency on banks, loans and the fundamentally corrupt money creation process that goes along with both – that can only be a good thing. Their role as a stepping stone to a new way of living, a new type of economy, is crucial. But local currencies ought not to be our holy grail.

Other skillsharing schemes

Swapaskill(.com)[86] and LocalSkillSwap(.com)[87] are straightforward barter schemes, with no credits or pounds being registered or accounted for. On their websites you simply post what skills you are willing to share with others and what skills you would like in return. In terms of my POP model for labour and skills in a moneyless economy, this is somewhere between Freeconomy and local currencies – they're not unconditional, but they feel much more informal and value everyone's time and skills equally.

Ancient skills

The reason I described the menu of moneyless options early in chapter two is because the moment you mention the concept of moneyless living, different things spring to mind for different people. Some, like resource-based economists such as Peter Joseph and Jacques Fresco, envisage a technotopia where machines do almost all the work within the context of a world that has consciously evolved beyond the concepts of debt and credit, concepts which money represents in physical form. Others, like Derrick Jensen,[88] believe that the only sustainable way of living is one where the level of technology used is close to that of the palaeolithic era. The case Jensen presents in both volumes of *Endgame* is refreshingly rooted in reality and a place of deep ecological understanding, and it stands in stark contrast to the fantasies held by a people who want it all: an abundant, alive, healthy planet, and at the same time all the gadgetry that can only come at its expense.

Regardless of which side of the moneyless fence you fall down on, there is absolutely no reason not to learn the basics of survival – eating, drinking and staying warm. All of these can often rely on you understanding the art of making fire: food will often need to be cooked to make it edible, water may need to be boiled to purify it in a polluted environment, and in cold wet climes fire may be essential to avoid freezing and to stay dry.

Depending on your personal reasons for wanting to live moneylessly and your unique situation, the ways in which you could go about making fire can vary widely. In my POP model for personal economy that I outlined in chapter three (see page 53), I declared that my own reasons for living moneylessly stems from my desire to reconnect with Nature and Her people and places. Holding such a philosophy means that, on my POP model for fire-starting, the simple bow drill comes out on top.

Others amongst you will want to live moneylessly so that you don't ever have to burden yourselves with the wage economy, and all that goes with that, ever again. If this is the case, using discarded lighters may be top of your POP model. I find them regularly on pavements outside pubs on a Sunday morning.

However, there are many good reasons for you to resist the use of lighters, even ones that are destined for landfill before their time, and other mass produced forms of fire-lighting equipment. And there are many good reasons to use a bow drill.

First, it's not reliant on an industrialised system that is killing the planet, and that is something that is important to me. I find cognitive dissonance difficult to deal with, and speaking out about the personal, social and ecological consequences of industrialisation (and the concepts on which it relies) whilst simultaneously benefiting from it causes me quite a lot of cognitive dissonance. Convenience is uncomfortable.

Second, it ensures that I have to stay alert about where I am, what the meteorological conditions are, what plants are around me and what time of day it is. The emotional, physical, mental and spiritual benefits of this are substantial and grossly underestimated. If it's a wet day, I need to collect some tinder and kindling early in the morning, keep it close to my body as I move around all day, so that by the evening I have enough dry material to get a fire started. Such low levels of technology keep me present in the moment, and deeply aware of my surroundings. In comparison, the lighter is much less beneficial for the overall wellbeing of both the egocentric and holistic self. Convenience makes us feel less alive.

Third, the industrialised system that creates such useful little gadgets may not exist at some point in the future. Therefore learning how to create fire without them could save your life in an apocalyptic style scenario that we would all like to avoid. Likewise, if for some reason you find yourself in the middle of nowhere (like a forest) without a functioning lighter, then knowing how to utilise the natural materials at hand could be the difference between life and death. Convenience can leave us dangerously unskilled.

Fourth, it's just a lot of fun. Convenience is boring.

Once you master the art of fire-making you've taken your first step on the road to knowing how to live amongst the land on which you find yourself. But it is only the first very basic step. All the skills you need are a book in themselves. Ray Mears' *Outdoor Survival Handbook*[89] and *Essential Bushcraft*,[90] along with John 'Lofty' Wiseman's *SAS Survival Handbook*,[91] are both very useful guides, for widely different reasons. Mears speaks eloquently about our need to walk very gently in Nature, to leave as little trace as possible (which is also a good survival skill in countries with animals who want to eat you), whilst still providing you with all the skills you will need. Lofty is much more of a survivalist, which is understandable given his military background, and his focus is on the basic survival of the egocentric self alone. I'm much more in the Mears camp, but there is so much practical knowledge packed into Wiseman's book that makes it worth having a copy on you if you are ever lucky enough to adventure out of civilisation.

Reading about such almost forgotten skills is one thing, the practice is another. I strongly recommend doing a course close to wherever you live, with a teacher that has a good reputation and a deep regard for Nature. The longer the course you can do the better, as it will give you the experience of practising and honing these skills in all sorts of scenarios and weather conditions. Alternatively, why not organise a local group of bushcraft enthusiasts, where you meet regularly and teach each other whatever skills you know, or run a series of Freeskilling (see page 236) evenings or weekends on aspects of bushcraft? It really could be an essential and valuable skill in the future.

Another crucial element to moneyless living for the purist is flint knapping, as it solves the question of how we produce cutting implements (which are central to much of bushcraft) in a way that doesn't require a level of technology that is higher than what is necessary for us to be sustainable in absolute terms.

THE ART OF FLINT KNAPPING

Will Lord, flint knapper, teacher
and founder of Beyond 2000BC[92]

Flint knapping is the art of creating tools (such as knives) and projectiles by chipping away at silica based stones such as flint. This skill, tragically almost unheard of now in the global West, was a very important part of the lives of some peoples for over ten thousand years.

Flint, when found, is often encased in a skin called cortex. Once the flint is broken open, either accidentally or intentionally, it will have smooth surfaces and razor sharp edges. It was these edges that were of interest to our ancestors. The colour of the inner surface can range greatly, but black is often deemed best due to its high silicon content.

Keeping this in mind, you will be looking to create a shape in the flint that is suitable for whatever its purpose will be, whilst being safe for the user.

The two 'tools' used to knapp flint are the:

- *Hard Hammer*: these are stones such as quartzite or basalt.
- *Soft Hammer*: these are made from deer antlers, using the heavy section (that connects to the deer's head) as the hammer surface. This is called the coronet.

The process begins by using the hard hammer to remove large sections of the flint that aren't required. This is only achieved with great thought given to the detail of the surface you are going to strike, such as the angle of the flint and the volume you are attempting to detach. Once you can describe the process as controlled, and you have a basic shape, then you will gently abrade the edges to tilt them and produce what we call a platform. This is then struck with the soft hammer, which produces longer and thinner flakes, leaving the edge of the item you are making sharp, as intended.

So why bother with the ancient art of flint knapping in a world full of bustling technology (and knives)? There are many reasons for this, archaeology being one. But many of us are now realising that we need to revert to a more gentle way of living on the Earth, and that we need to look at some of the examples given to us by our ancestors who lived here for such a long time in harmony with the Earth. What better place to start than with an every day skill that is required to make one of our most basic tools and weapons.

As you go through the process of flint knapping the past seems to open up to you, and you gain a sense of personal empowerment similar to the feeling you get when you light a fire through the friction process – that feeling of freedom, that you can survive without the modern world's products and all the destruction and exploitation that comes with it.

MATERIALS

Aside from labour, the second major component of any economy – monetary or otherwise – is materials. How much you need depends on a number of factors: your unique situation, whether you have children or not, and how simple or complex a life you want to live. In our world of mass consumerism, living moneylessly doesn't have to mean a life of austerity, as there are so many waste materials to mine before producing anything else. Despite this, a life of voluntary simplicity can have far more rewards than drawbacks. I found that once I overcame my addiction to stuff I realised how much it had been stunting my happiness and adding very little meaning.

Therefore, whilst I am about to list an overall menu of ways in which you can meet your wildest desires without the need for money, I am in no way encouraging you to fill your life with pointless clutter just because you can. The things we own only end up owning us, eroding our sense of freedom and over time conning us into thinking that we could never live without them.

General stuff

Considering the amount of 'things' in the world, and that this book is limited in size, it is impossible for me to list how to get every single material in the world without money. The best I can advise is to first decide what you need – and really question if you actually need it – and then find a book or internet resource that specialises on that material. There are many free resources out there that will be of significant use in helping you get whatever materials it is you need, all with their own merits; I'll briefly outline them here. There are also some common items, such as nappies, paper and books, which I will describe my solutions for. If you can come up with your own innovative creations, even better.

Freecycle and Freegle

Both of these projects do exactly the same thing. In fact, Freegle[93] was set up by a bunch of ex-Freecycle[94] moderators out of a long-term frustration with the US-based administration of Freecycle.

So what do they do and how do they work? Both are very intelligent logistical systems which match people who have things they don't need with people who don't have things they do need, and vice versa.

Take an example. Your child has grown too big for her bike and no longer needs it. If you don't have a friend who wants it, you can sign up to your local Freegle or Freecycle email list. You post an offer to everyone on the list by sending one normal email, simply stating the offer and postcode in the subject line (OFFER: Child's Bike BS2), which everyone else on the list has an opportunity to see. Anyone interested will be able to email you in private, and you then choose who you want to give it to. First come, first served is my preferred policy, unless someone badly in need gets in touch. From there you can both arrange a time for collection, which is normally, but not necessarily, down to the recipient to do. If there is something you need, you can also make a simple request (WANTED: Kettle SW19). And that's it. Much more simple than making a trip to the tip. It's a system in which everyone wins, not least our over-burdened planet.

The first UK Freecycle group was set up in 2003; the country now has 540 groups holding 2.5 million members (there are over 8 million members worldwide), at the time of writing. Freegle, only formed in 2009, has already over 1.2 million members across 320 groups. Meaning that, no matter where you are, there will be a group near you with enough critical mass to meet your needs. The rise in the popularity of such projects also shows just how far the gift economy has come in the last decade, and how much potential it has at a time when the deep flaws of the dominant economic model are becoming increasingly exposed. Between Freegle and Freecycle alone, millions of tonnes of usable stuff are kept out of landfill every year.

One problem is that both of these projects are based online. Luckily, there are now many offline versions of Freecycle – *the Freeshop* and *street freecycling* are two well established examples of this.

The Freeshop

Bristol, and a growing number of other areas of the UK, has now got its own Freeshop. This concept varies from a regular stall organised by a local group, to the standard format of a High Street shop. The latter works in much the same way as a normal shop, except that there are no cash registers, CCTV or security guards watching your every move. You are both supplier and customer, bringing in the things you no longer need and taking the things you do. Think of it as an offline Freecycle, one not reliant on the internet, and one with a greater sense of real community about it. Freeshops also have the benefit of allowing you to be able to look at something, and test it if need be, before you take it.

Healthy Planet,[95] a UK charity, runs a national network of free book (and DVD) shops from empty premises on High Streets across the country. Cara Sandys, who is behind the Southampton branch, says it is a win-win situation for everyone: landlords get reduced rates for having a charity in premises they can't let; the council have one less unoccupied shop to think about; the volunteers get a community space for free; and the customers get books for free. She adds that she sees no reason why the same free shop model couldn't be used 'for furniture or children's clothes'.[96]

Another recent version of the Freeshop has been The Really Really Free Market[97] (RRFM) that grew out of the anti-globalisation protests of the last decade. Whilst no two RRFMs are the same – thankfully – they often involve the sharing of both materials and labour.

Contradicting what our culture would have us believe, nobody comes along and cleans out everything from a Freeshop. Empirical evidence has shown that when people know that they can take whatever they need, when they need it, they have little or no tendency to take more than they need at any given time. Thomas More's fictional island *Utopia* was based upon such a philosophy; maybe Utopia isn't as utopian as monetary economists would like us to believe.

If there isn't a Freeshop already in your local area, then why not organise a core group of people to set one up (contacting existing Freeshops or Healthy Planet for advice)? This could be anything from a weekly or monthly stall to begin with, to premises that are open seven days a week.[98]

Street freecycling

This idea is widespread in a number of suburbs of Bristol. It is very similar to the ideas above, except you put whatever it is you don't want outside your house with a sign saying something like 'Please take everything outside the front wall for free'. Be careful to clarify what exactly you are giving away, otherwise you may come out to see your garden gnome or recycling bin gone by mistake!

I could almost give a guarantee to anyone looking to furnish a house that they could do so by spending a day or two travelling around three suburbs of Bristol alone. If such a culture doesn't exist in your area yet, then be a pioneer and start it yourself. You'll be surprised how quickly the idea takes off. Putting out a sign advertising free stuff causes people to take notice – before you know it, all the neighbours will be doing it. Ideas can spread fast with just one simple action.

Skips

If someone has a skip outside their house, full of stuff they are evidently wanting to get rid of, have a look to see if there is anything in it you need that is salvageable. If there is, it is polite to knock on its user's door and ask first, but you will almost always get permission, due in part to the fact that few people like to dump stuff and partially because it will free up space in the skip for them, potentially saving them money into the bargain. Ask nicely – if you're friendly, you tend to find that other people will be too.

Sharing – not giving away – your stuff

If you have stuff you would still like to make use of, but only use irregularly, you may be up for sharing it with others instead of giving it away completely. To this end, there are a host of sharing websites willing to fill the breach, and all in slightly different ways. Out of the lot, my favourite is a project called Streetbank(.com),[99] which they describe as "a giant attic, garden shed, toolkit, fancy dress chest, library and DVD collection for you and anyone living within one mile of your home". If for some reason that doesn't fit the bill, you could also try FavorTree(.com),[100] LetsAllShare(.com),[101] or Ecomodo(.com).[102] The latter two websites do include functionality that allows you to rent and hire stuff too, but I'd highly recommend taking a leap of faith and just sharing your stuff for free – you'll be much more likely to create a new friendship that way, something that many of us have realised is impossible to put a financial value on.

I should add that I see all these online schemes as transitional strategies. In my ideal world, we'd all know our neighbours well enough to not be dependent on such high technology. But in reality, we don't. People today have become apprehensive about asking to borrow things from the people they live beside, which perfectly summarises the bizarre culture we live in today. Projects that utilise high technology software such as these can help us bridge the gap between reality and the ideal, until external issues transform the former into the latter.

That said, there is nothing to stop you organising your street, town or village to do something very similar to these websites but in a way that isn't online (which can often exclude older people). Why not knock on your neighbours door and organise a meeting (maybe at the pub) to see what system would work best for your community, enabling you to address any concerns people have about lending and borrowing each others stuff? It may be as simple as creating a photocopied list of stuff that each interested member in the area is willing to share with others in the scheme.

Nappies

One thing you probably don't want to share, or get off Freegle, are your child's nappies. Most parents are aware that you can make reusable, washable cloth nappies. If these were used by everyone it would save 8 million nappies from being dumped in landfill every day (3 billion annually) in the UK alone,[103] saving parents an average of £500 a year into the bargain.

Yet there is an option that saves you both the bother and expense of making and using washable nappies. It is called Elimination Communication (EC), also known as Nappy Free Baby.[104] This is a toilet training technique where a parent uses methods such as signals, cues and intuition to cope with a child's toileting needs. This method's ideal is to use no nappies whatsoever, but you may combine it with washable nappies when the situation requires it. Not only would the widespread use of EC take a big chunk out of our landfill sites, save all the energy and materials involved in producing nappies in the first place, and reduce the workload of parents who use washable ones, it also empowers parents to be more attuned to their kids. EC was initially inspired by the traditional methods of preindustrial times, so it is nothing new.

Having no children myself I do not speak from personal experience on this. Close friends of mine have used this method, however, and do speak very highly of it, in terms of their relationship with their children, the money it saves them, and their ecological impact.

Books and paper

Booksharing websites

ReaditSwapit(.co.uk)[105] is a website that utilises some very smart software and functionality to enable you to, first, find people who already have the books you want and, subsequently, swap them for any of your books that they want. You simply sign up, enter the ISBN numbers of the books you're willing to pass on (the website finds all other information on the book, including author, edition and an image of the cover), before beginning to search for the books you want. If no member currently has a copy, you can add it to your wishlist and the website will automatically let you know once it is added. Once you request a book that is available, your book list will be sent to the current owner, from which he or she can pick one of your titles. If they find one they like, they accept the swap and the website forwards you each other's postal addresses so that you can post your books to one another (or hand deliver it if you are in the same area, meaning no money on postage). And unlike the library, you don't have to give it back, which is great for books that take longer to read and for people who are too busy to read them in the allotted time.

Bookmooch(.com)[106] is another very similar website that uses a slightly different system based on points. It also allows you to easily donate books to charities, and, unlike ReaditSwapit, its functionality permits international sharing. If you can't immediately find the book that you want on either of these, then why not give others, such as Bookhopper(.com),[107] a try?

Booksharing clubs

One step better than a booksharing website is a real-life booksharing club, as it doesn't require a money dependent internet to exist. It could work exactly as above (or, better still, by people just giving their books away with no condition on getting one in return), except it has the benefits of real life interaction – local residents getting to meet their neighbours, the opportunity to talk about the books which you may consider sharing, and an exposure to titles and subjects that you wouldn't even have thought of searching for if you were using a website. Because it is fully local, no postage expenses apply. If you love books and you would like to meet new people locally, why not organise your own book club and promote it on Freeconomy and other local networks.

Bookcrossing

A really fun alternative to the websites above is Bookcrossing,[108] a project more aligned to the ideals of the gift economy which incorporates the pay-it-forward philosophy. It works like this – you register a book on their website, which then allows you to print off a label for it containing a unique identification number (if you are completely moneyless and printerless you can write this number on the inside of the cover using a mushroom ink feather pen, see page 104). All that you then need to do is leave it somewhere random, such as a park bench, bus, or on a coffee shop table. The lucky recipient can then go online, see where it has been in the past and mark its new destination. At any point in the future you can use your unique online identification number to see where in the world your book has got to – members often find it has made its way around the planet to all sorts of unimagined places, inspiring and informing many people along the way and uplifting them through the spirit of the unconditional gift.

If you don't use the internet then why not just leave a book lying around anyway, with a nice little note on it saying why you wanted to pass it on and that you hope the lucky finder enjoys it. Some pubs, cafés and community centres have little book corners that allow for this also – you bring in a pre-loved book you're happy to pass on, and if you happen to see one you like then you can take it with you.

Libraries

This is one of the few moneyless tools that is obvious to everyone, despite the fact that it is only free in its delivery and not in its operation. Yet libraries are under-utilised, when you consider the size of the market for new books. This is in part due to the fact that none of our political leaders encourage us to share resources. As we have seen in chapter one, sharing is the enemy of a high technology, globalised economy. We're told that more economic growth, and not the efficient use of all the resources we already have, is the answer to economic austerity.

As much as I love the idea of libraries, they are a classic example of why the moneyless economy has to be one that is based on simple technologies. If everyone stopped buying books today, and got them instead from the library, the book industry would collapse overnight. Why? Because sharing is the enemy of a high technology, globalised economy. I can't say it enough. And today's mass produced books are a form of high technology, like it or not.

Newspapers

If you need a source of paper for lighting your woodburner (as tinder or for making paper logs), then approach your local newsagents and ask them if you can utilise the waste newspapers they normally have to recycle. The bins of newsagents are often full of papers, as they only have to send the newspaper's title back to the wholesaler in order to get a credit for it. You can help them reduce their waste and make use of it yourself for free by simply going and asking them, a gift economy relationship they are often more than happy to enter into.

This is also a good resource to mine if you want to make papier-mâché. Or, as we'll see in chapter nine, for cleaning your bum in combination with a compost toilet.

Paper and pens

High up on my own POP model for paper and pens would be to make your own, which you can do using a combination of inkcap mushrooms for the ink and a molted wing feather from a large bird to make a quill pen, and some birch polypores (*Piptoporus betulinus*) or Dryad's Saddle fungus (*Polyporus squamosus*) along with a mesh and deckle to make the paper.[109] I find that when you have to find the materials for doing so, and then actually make it yourself, you're less likely to waste it than you are some cheap A4 slabs that you can pick up for a couple of quid from the stationary shop.

Unless you want to connect with Nature to that extent, there are easier ways to acquire paper without it costing. Using the backs of envelopes is good, and especially satisfying if it is letterbox spam. If you have friends who work in an office, ask them to save you some of the printed paper that has only been used on one side and that they don't shred. Like with everything regarding moneyless living, looking at all waste as a potential resource will usually help you come up with your own creative solutions, which is the way it ought to be. Homogenisation and uniformity have no place in the moneyless economy I envisage.

Tools, gadgets and equipment

I want to let you into a little secret – I hate lawnmowers. It is not just the fact that they ruin the peace and tranquillity of an otherwise glorious summer afternoon; they're also tamers of potentially wild gardens everywhere. Letting your garden go the way it wants to has become a social faux pas, and a neatly trimmed patch has somehow become some bizarre ideal to strive for. The perfectly tended lawn has become the most illuminating symbol of how deeply the story of our separation from Nature has affected us.

I have something to thank lawnmowers for though: they stimulated me into embedding a world-wide (but localised) toolsharing scheme (this includes over 2,000 pre-listed 'tools' such as digital cameras, scythes, drills of all sorts and printers) into the Freeconomy movement. In the summer of 2007 I was living on a street of 45 houses. In all of my three years there, not once did I ever hear more than one lawnmower going at the same time. Despite this observation, one out of every two people on the street had one. It was blatantly obvious to even a fool such as myself that this was not a good use of local residents' hard-earned cash (or time), nor the planet's dwindling resources. The solution wasn't very complex – a piece of software that we had already developed for the skill-sharing side of Freeconomy. All it would involve was applying the same principles and methods for the tool-sharing scheme.

Despite its origins as a skill-sharing project, Freeconomy is also the world's largest toolsharing website. It works in the same way as its skill-sharing department (see page 88). You simply sign up, choose whatever tools you are willing to share with other members in your local area, and search for whatever ones you need whenever you need them. The terms on which members share is up to the individuals involved; again, the only requirement is that no money changes hands.

As I argued in chapter one, it is important to remember that even sharing our high technology tools is not a long-term sustainable solution.

The lawnmower can only be produced (especially at anything near the prices they are today) if every second person on a street has one. If there really only was one lanwmower for every forty five houses, the industry would collapse from not being able to benefit from the required economies of scale. So I wouldn't go feeling too smug about sharing your lawnmower – the only long term solution is to simplify our technologies so that they can be made on a local scale. That said, schemes like Toolshare remain potent transitional strategies, which we should fully utilise as an interim step to reducing our ecological footprint until external forces conspire to help us construct the economies of the future.

Freeconomy's Toolshare system is just a poor man's alternative to actually knowing your neighbour well enough to know that they have a lawnmower, and being on good enough terms to ask to borrow it (or to show them how to use a scythe!). I would love Freeconomy to become obsolete in ten years time, on the basis that such a technological solution is no longer necessary.

FIVE THINGS TO DO WITH A PALLET

Dave Hamilton, author of *Grow your food for free ... well almost* and co-author (he wrote the best bits apparently) of *The Self-Sufficient-ish Bible*

Famously, prisoners in the notorious Guantanamo Bay made their own veg patch with nothing more than the seeds from their lunches and the plastic spoons they were given to eat them with.

This goes to show that growing your own food does not have to be expensive and that it doesn't even have to cost anything at all. If they can do it with as little resources as that, then anyone can.

Pallets

Pallets have become a universal part of modern life. Necessary for shipping and flying around all the crap that many seem to find essential for existence, they can turn up in the most unlikely of places. I think they have become so ubiquitous that if we ever colonised the stars the pallet would go with us.

Unlike a lot of the debris of life in the 21st century the pallet does at least have some uses and many of those are of a horticultural nature.

Compost bay – Compost bays are one of the easiest and most practical things you can make with discarded pallets. Simply screw or nail three together into a 'U' shape before submerging it to a planks depth to keep it from falling over. Then use another pallet lashed to the front as the door. It is best to have three: one to brew, one to add to and one to use. However, if you don't have room you can get away with one.

Planter – Prize some planks off a pallet with a crow bar. Using four as uprights/corner posts, screw three planks lengthways and three widthways to the uprights before cutting the uprights down to size. Fill with a mix of compost and soil and feed any sick looking or fruiting plants with homemade comfrey feed.

Seat – Have a look online for a template to make a seat. Failing that, if you have a futon look at how it is put together and use it as an outline.

Shed – Sheds are a little more complicated but very possible. I found it best to make a framework from discarded posts used for old internal stud walls, then use pallets which did not have holes between the planks as the outer façade. Other methods involve screwing two pallets together for the back of the shed and four (two high) for the sides. The walls won't be rainproof unless you cover them but it should make for a sturdy frame. The roof in both cases can be made from discarded plywood.

Fence – Use the pallets intact as fencing panels, or just leave one side intact, removing the blocks and lower supports and screw to fence posts, shaping the top to a point.

Things only become rubbish or trash when we can no longer find a use for them. Pallets are just the tip of the trash filled iceberg. There is a world of discarded items waiting for a use – horticultural or otherwise.

CHAPTER 6

LAND

'How can one own stars?' [asked the little prince]
'Whose are they?' the businessman asked peevishly.
'I don't know. They don't belong to anyone.'
'In which case they are mine, because I was the first person to think of it.'
'Is that sufficient?'
'Of course it is. When you find a diamond that belongs to nobody, it is yours. When you discover an island that belongs to no one, it is yours. When you are the first to have an idea, you take out a patent on it: it is yours. And I own the stars because nobody else before me thought of owning them.'

Antoine de Saint-Exupéry, *The Little Prince*

Since the Enclosure Acts, access to land has been the biggest obstacle for anyone who has wanted to live subsistently, and it remains so for anyone who dreams of creating a localised gift economy. Every inch of the land we were born out of is now owned by someone or something, and the combination of that cultural creation with the subsequent land prices and planning permission constraints has led us to a scenario where the human has been forced out of her natural habitat. Are we less worthy than a woodpecker or an otter to live freely upon the land?

One of the most significant impacts of this is the fact that the overwhelming majority of people now need to take out large mortgages in inherently unsustainable cities where they have little opportunity to have control over their own lives, instead being forced to work in the wage economy so that they may pay back their mortgage lenders the money that the latter created out of thin air to begin with. In effect, making the rich financially richer and the poor more enslaved. The consequences of the privatisation of our land on our freedoms and our ability to live in a truly sustainable manner are grossly underestimated.

Land reform, as we've seen in chapter four, is crucial to the movement towards a moneyless economy. The corporatocracy, that merging of corporate and political powers (I was once told that politicians and corporations are not actually in bed together – they are, in fact, the same people!), will not relinquish control over the land easily. The land was taken off us in order to force us into the industrial and wage economies, after all. Until such reforms happen one way or another, there are plenty of transitional strategies we can employ to enable those of us who do want to live off the land in a subsistence, non-monetary, economy to do so, or at the very least give ourselves access to soil so that we can be as self-reliant for food and our other needs as possible. The good news is that many people and organisations have already pioneered these transitional strategies, meaning you just have to decide what path best suits you and then pursue it with determination.

In the course of this chapter, I aim to provide you with a range of strategies that could offer you the potential to access the land in a way that will help you live outside of the monetary economy to some degree, regardless of whether you live in the city or eventually aspire to get back to the land.

THE LAND OF THE FREE

Getting access to soil allows you to be self-reliant for food and other needs (and, as we'll see in this chapter and the next, potentially gives you the chance to create a home that is designed to enable you to be self-reliant, with no bills and needing no external inputs). If you are living in the city, you may think this is impossible for you. The good news: it is much easier than you think. There are possibilities to access land everywhere, surprisingly so in cities, and you do not need to own land to do so. Even if you can only grow a little, it will help you build resilience into your own economy by introducing more diversity, and that can only be a good thing for you and the planet. In this chapter I explore all the options available to you in this respect.

Windowsills and small spaces

Even if you live in an apartment block or a flat that has no back garden, you can still grow many useful plants in small spaces such as windowsills and balconies. From these alone you could become moneyless for your herbs (grown in pots or troughs or old tin cans) at the very least, which you can then pick fresh as you are cooking. Salad leaves will also work well here. Sunny south-facing windowsills are best, or any that get more than five hours of sunshine a day. These are also ideal for germinating seeds, which – if you are lucky enough to have access to an allotment or garden – you can then plant out as the temperature outside increases, remembering to harden them off first by putting them outside during the day and bringing them in at night for about a week or two first. Do make sure that your plants have enough room to grow, make sure they have enough water, and don't let them get scorched by direct sunlight during the hottest part of the day – this you can easily do by creating a little shade for them.

Landshare

How we have shared the Earth with each other has changed dramatically over the years, from our time as hunter gatherers when no formal structures existed, to modern society where the concept of private property is ubiquitous. Due to a range of economic mechanisms and social factors, we have ended up in a situation where many people who own land don't have the time or energy to grow food whilst others, who do have that time and energy and dream of being able to grow their own food, don't have the financial capability to buy land, especially if they are not allowed to construct a simple, cheap (or free) dwelling on it.

It was to solve this problem that Hugh Fearnley Whittingstall,[110] through *River Cottage*, set up a UK wide initiative called *Landshare*[111] in 2009 shortly after he paid a visited to Transition Town Totnes' Garden Share project the year before. Given the fact that there are at least 86,000 people already on allotment waiting lists in the UK (though the real figure is likely to be somewhere between 100,000 and 150,000), that the grow-your-own movement is becoming increasingly popular, coupled with the obvious reality that there is so much land all over the UK (both in cities and the countryside) going unused or drastically under-utilised, it was a niche waiting to be filled.

Landshare, through *River Cottage*'s public profile and some great online functionality, has a huge potential to suit people who want to grow their own produce but don't have anywhere but their windowsill to do it; who have some spare land that they're prepared to share with others in their local community; or who can help with local food production in some way, from sharing knowledge and skills to lending tools to a particular plot.

The strength of this organisation is that it allows anyone to get involved. According to their website, "Landshare arrangements can range from an individual sharing a patch of their garden to a national body such as the National Trust creating allotments for many people at grand sites across the country. Land is also shared by schools, companies and communities."

So if you need land in order to be self-reliant and moneyless in terms of food and a range of other needs, or if instead you have land that could be used to help your community localise its economy to some degree (and all the personal and social benefits that can stem from that), then avail of the mutually beneficial relationships that projects such as Landshare facilitate. It also allows for people who can be Landshare food doctors, who can offer advice (both online and in real life) to those who are learning as they go.

WWOOFing (World Wide Opportunities on Organic Farms)

WWOOFing has a very similar approach to Landshare, in that its main focus is to match up people with different but complementary needs in a mutually beneficial, win-win way. With national organisations in over fifty countries around the world, WWOOF[112] lists all the organic farms, smallholdings and such that have signed up to the scheme in each country (most organic farms are now involved, such is the success of this approach). If you're looking to spend time on an organic farm (for any of the reasons listed below), you simply join up to the scheme, contact the farms that most appeal to your needs and ideologies, before hopefully coming to an arrangement with them regarding how long you stay for, how many hours you will work whilst there, and any food and dietary needs you have. It is generally accepted that 25 hours of work a week, in return for comfortable accommodation, adequate food for your time there (including your days off) and the opportunity to learn a wide variety of skills (including the language of your host), is a deal that often works for everyone concerned, but it really is up to both parties to come to any agreement they like beforehand.

Most people seem to use this scheme when they are on their travels, and therefore it tends to often be a short term endeavour. There is also no reason why it can't be used as a long-term, ongoing option that benefits all involved. I spent three years working on an organic farm, and whilst it was not a normal WWOOFing relationship, it worked on the same principle of being mutually beneficial to all.

I'd highly recommend WWOOFing to anyone who wants to dip their toes into moneyless living for a period of time, short or long, as it is possible to hitch or cycle from farm to farm, and no money is needed once you are there. Living on an organic farm has an amazing ability to cease any previous cravings you had to go out and buy needless stuff. Some of the skills – both practical and non-practical – that I subsequently needed in order to live moneylessly were learnt during my time WWOOFing. But most importantly, it enabled me to get a sense of how it feels to not use money for long periods of time, along with the understanding that there is little in life you need to be happy and fulfilled.

Turning urban wastelands into growing spaces

Due to a variety of personal and external factors, there is a huge movement of people who want to reduce their dependency on money and fossil fuels in relation to their food. To put it into context, in 1986 there were 13,000 people on waiting lists for allotments in the UK. Compare that with the figures I mentioned earlier, and add all those people who want an allotment but don't put their name on the waiting list because they believe it to be a waste of time (and with good reason – waiting lists vary from three years to a decade), and you get a sense of the scale of the public plea for more growing space.

But there is hope, and as long as this hope is acted on, there are solutions. Everywhere you look in cities there are brownfield sites and wastelands waiting to be transformed. According to a report published in 2009 by a think tank called the New Local Government Network (NLGN),[113] Britain has an estimated 12,710 hectares of vacant brownfield land, 85% of which is within five hundred metres of an urban area.[114] That's 31,407 acres of land that could be used to help British people become more localised for food. For those of you who want to grow your own, it would be a damn fine place to start.

In order to get your local council to investigate a particular piece of wasteland, with a view to it being turned into allotments or other growing spaces, you don't need to do much. Section 23 of the Small Holdings and Allotments Act 1908 states that "on a representation in writing to the council of any borough, urban district, or parish, by any six registered parliamentary electors or ... resident in the borough, urban district or parish, that the circumstances of the borough, urban district or parish are such that it is the duty of the council to take proceedings under this Part of this Act therein, the council shall take such representation into consideration" (the law is slightly more complex than this so please read the full briefing[115]). In plain English, you need six people, as long as one of them isn't a Irishman who refuses to go on the electoral register (so don't ask me). If you have trouble finding six people, contact a nearby allotment group and you should find that some of those waiting on their lists would be more than happy to join you.

Note that after you make the request, the council are only obliged to investigate it, and they don't necessarily have to provide you with these allotments. However, councils are now tending to be very supportive in this respect, partially in response to The Localism Act, and you may be surprised by how much time and assistance they give you in transforming such wastelands into areas that would benefit residents in the surrounding areas in a plethora of ways.

If the unlocked potential highlighted here isn't enough to jolt you into getting a community run allotment group together, then take some inspiration from four pensioners in Preston who, with a combined age of over 300, "transformed a run-down patch of wasteland into a tranquil [wildlife] haven for the community".[116] If they can achieve that, then what's stopping the rest of us doing something similar for food production, in a way that hopefully builds community resilience, interdependence and bonds of friendship, along with creating habitat for wildlife?

You don't need an allotment to grow food in the city, however. There is space everywhere. So much so that the Capital Growth project[117] was set up with the aim of creating 2,012 new community growing spaces across London in 2012. In Bristol, Eastside Roots[118] set up a community food growing project in a piece of unused land by the side of a railway station, and has become a hub of social activity for the surrounding suburb of Easton in the process. You can grow crops in the communal area of a block of flats. If it is covered in concrete, use whatever containers you can get your hands on to plant in. Or why not do like the folk of Hollingdean and grow food on the roof of your community centre? These are just examples – you and your friends and neighbours can come up with your own inspiring ways. The key is to look at your local area differently, and see the potential for growing food and other useful crops in every unused space.

CREATE AN INSPIRING VISION AND PURSUE IT PASSIONATELY

I believe that there is a certain magic to life (though this may just be one of my own personal stories – nevertheless, it is one I find useful), an element that is beyond reason and which packs our experience here on Earth full of mystery and enquiry. Things happen all the time that we cannot intellectually explain, yet we all too readily dismiss them because we can't scientifically prove them, as if we humans had reached ultimate knowledge and understanding. The fact that we don't know how certain aspects of life work doesn't mean for a moment that they haven't got as much validity as those aspects we do fully understand. When a cat watches a car drive past, the basicreality that the cat has no idea what the car is, or the mechanisms that make it work the way it does, doesn't mean the car isn't real or is less valid; it just means the cat hasn't the capability to understand it. The same applies to us – there are levels of understanding that we have either lost or have never developed, and may never develop. I have found that happiness often comes in the acceptance that there are things that we will never understand in life; instead of relentlessly trying to explain them, we could just sit back and wonder at their majesty.

Passionately and relentlessly following your own beliefs in life, without worrying exactly how it will all come together, is often enough to bring whatever you envisage into existence. That has certainly been my experience, and ever since I have integrated that level of trust and surrender into my life I've had the most incredible experiences and adventures.

It was the magic of life that, in the end, led to the creation of an inspiring project in Devon called Embercombe, founded by Tim Macartney. Whilst Embercombe is not a moneyless community, there are very valuable lessons to be gained from its creation that I believe would be of great use to anyone considering setting up a fully localised gift economy.

EMBERCOMBE – THE STORY OF ITS CREATION

Tim 'Mac' Macartney, founder of Embercombe,[119] storyteller, public speaker and author of *Finding Earth, Finding Soul*[120]

There is a piece of land out there, perhaps closer than you might imagine, that is calling to you. In your heart you know this to be true, because you have heard the song of that land on the breath of the wind, or in the longing of a child dear to you. Of all the deeper needs that our people have, the desire to truly inhabit our land, find community, and develop meaningful work, matches any. Many of the aspirations we burden ourselves with do not belong to us. They were sold to us and the price bore no relation to the value, but rediscovering kinship with each other and the shared experience of growing food is an authentic longing that belongs to you and me and our children.

It is forty years since I stood in that field of wheat. Transfixed, I experienced a profound sense of knowing. I think I was experiencing a moment of grace. We might call it a vision. In those few hours I saw and felt what I most loved. At some cellular level, I knew that I was being called. It was beautiful but it was also frightening and I had not yet accumulated the knowledge, the courage, the discipline, or the commitment to bring it into reality. I was, like many other young men or women, eager to explore but not yet to focus. Looking back I realise that on some level I agreed to undertake a curriculum of experiences that, providing I kept the vision alive in my heart, would eventually equip me with the means to bring it to life.

I am stubborn and many times over have been my own worst enemy, but early on I also realised that life has no meaning for me unless I know that I am walking a trail towards the things I call sacred. To do otherwise would be to betray myself, and I am too proud to consider that an option.

It took me 28 years to travel the distance between that warm summer day in the field of golden wheat to the moment of true joy when I awoke to my first morning at Embercombe on May 1st 1999. Fifty acres of meadows, woods, gardens, and hills purred and pulsed as the spring sun warmed the moist earth. During those 28 years I lived and loved as passionately as I could. I was lost and found time and time again. I remembered and forgot, went to sleep, had numinous dreams that left me weeping with joy, and nightmares that nearly killed me. Nevertheless, I did not forget. I still walk the invisible path. I still journey.

I was a drama teacher, managed a restaurant, worked as a medic in a mine, picked apples in Washington State, ran a landscaping company, and then trained as a gardener. At the same time I scouted the underworld, and explored trails marked, 'Danger. Do not enter', trails that could have left me hurt or in prison. I followed other kinds of trails as well, searching for people who still held the keys to ancient spiritual traditions honouring our Earth. With great effort, a battered pride, and scraped knees I found these people and began what turned out to be a 20-year apprenticeship. My first job as a gardener was at an outdoor leadership development centre to which many of the large corporate businesses sent their aspiring leaders. Interested and intrigued I asked my boss for a day off to watch how our firm went about developing Sainsbury's deputy store managers. The privilege was granted on the condition I promised to remain silent and refrain from adding in a gardener's perspective on the trials and tribulations of Sainsbury's best. Things didn't go as planned that day and I had to break my promise when tempers boiled and the fragile boundary separating peace and war was breached. While discomforting and embarrassing for some, I emerged with a new career and entered the world of corporate leadership development and entrepreneurship. The field of wheat vision never disappeared but for the first time ever I finally accepted that if I truly wanted land upon which to gather and explore new ways of living, I would have to earn the money and not just hang-out waiting for someone to give it to me. I was right and also wrong. For ten years I applied myself to building a successful international business developing people in organisations, and our team came close to realising this success on several occasions when we nearly sold the business. Then, one day, sat in front of a client, I received a project briefing that eventually placed the field of wheat in my hand.

"We have a very small business and even though the markets we serve are in turmoil and many similar firms are going under, we believe that we have the strategy, expertise, energy and will to create a phenomenal success. We have a set of core values that mean everything to us. We do not wish our success to be at the expense of our values. We'd like you and your firm to work with us, so that we can make this journey and achieve our commercial ambitions with our values intact."

This is what we did and five years later my client sold the company for a pot of gold. Meanwhile, and at the same time, my training with the First Nation people of North America continued. Two parallel paths. My client and his co-founder came to me shortly after the sale.

"We have achieved our goal and it feels good, yet there is also an emptiness. Chasing this goal has occupied all our creativity and energy. Now what? Do we do it all again but even bigger?"

For the first time I revealed my other life to them. I suggested that their questions were spiritual and deserved their full attention. I offered to take them on a vision quest journey and they accepted. Life spoke to my client as she always had, but in the deep contemplative quiet of the quest I guess he had more time to listen. Later when we returned he asked me what my dream was and I told him of my time, almost thirty years ago, when I stood transfixed and allowed what is most profoundly beautiful to enter my heart and fill me with gratitude. He asked me what I needed and I told him, and he wrote me a cheque.

On the last day of April, just a couple of days after my fiftieth birthday I drove to Devon and began a new life. I fancifully imagined that the hard work had already been done, but it was not so. I have been tested, and along with others many times I have knelt on the earth of Embercombe seeking guidance, drawing deep on reserves, shedding tears of frustration, and doubting my ability to sustain. With each test I have grown stronger, my commitment, deeper. A deep relief that I am walking the path of my calling and in company of many friends, some whom I know and many I have never met, nor will I ever meet. We are a people and we are returning to ourselves and to our land.

Join an established community

There are many landbased ecological and spiritual communities already established all over the UK and across the world. I've yet to come across one that has a policy on using zero money, but that is not to say one doesn't exist. Either way, there is nothing to suggest that a number of these groups wouldn't be willing to accept you as a long-term resident in the knowledge that you don't use money. Some would potentially view it in a similar way to WWOOFing, but with the benefits of having you live there long-term. From your perspective it would give you access to all the basic infrastructure you need to live a life beyond money.

If this option interests you, I'd recommend getting your hands on a book called *Eurotopia*,[121] which lists three hundred intentional communities and ecovillages from around Europe, providing detailed information and descriptions written by the communities themselves in a prescribed and easy to compare format, along with maps and contact details for each one. Before you contact anyone, I would advise you to be clear in your own mind what your needs are, the types of personalities you generally feel drawn towards, what your philosophies are on general living, and what you are and aren't willing to compromise on. Once you know this and have read the book through, you are then in a great position to contact the groups most likely to be a good match, and take it from there. You may have to try quite a few before you settle on a particular community, as in reality the human dynamics of intentional communities are often different to how they seem on paper.

Ghost towns

These formerly inhabited villages and towns exist throughout many countries of the world. In some instances they are maintained and managed by the state as tourist attractions, but often they are just abandoned habitats waiting to be reoccupied. Of course many have been abandoned for a reason – either they were the scenes of massacres, suffered epidemics, lost economic activity, had political problems, became depleted of natural 'resources' or befell a disaster of some sort. It goes without saying that some of these are no longer adequate to support micro-economies of self-sufficient moneyless people – that is partially why some of them were abandoned in the first place.

However, often there are reasons for their abandonment that are not relevant considerations for people who want to live in a localised gift economy, and many will be packed full of potential as places where people could, with no small amount of graft, transform them from run down old buildings into areas abundant in life and activity that could act as the initial examples of how the economy of the future could work.

There are dozens of known examples of established 'ecoaldeas' of this sort in Spain, mostly built from the ruins of Medieval towns. One of these, an abandoned hamlet in northern Navarra called Lakabe, was found in 1980.[122] Fourteen people initially moved in, slowly rebuilding the homes and gardens with barely any money. They now generate all their own energy with a windmill they erected by hand, having carried the iron structure and materials up the hill themselves. They also grow lots of food and, despite the fact they were all urbanites originally, they are now almost self-reliant with very minimal money. Mauge, one of the original people who discovered this ghost town, says there is now a "wait[ing] list of people who'd like to move in," but that "the answer is not for people to join what they have created, but to try to emulate them somewhere else."

If you're feeling like you've missed out, keep in mind that there are an approximated three thousand other abandoned villages such as this in Spain alone. As long as you are prepared for a life of voluntary simplicity, and the beauties, joys and occasional hardships that can come with that, there is little reason why anyone could not start a moneyless community within a handful of years.

Depending on your country of residence, this path could require you to cross borders into another part of the world where such abandoned towns exist. This would mean that you'd be setting up in a part of the world, far from family and friends, where you may not have fluency in the language and where support networks are likely to be non-existent in the difficult initial stages. This problematic aspect could be offset by organising a group of interested individuals who are looking to do the same thing, as opposed to trying to start it up by yourself.

If you do form a group to explore this as an option, make sure that everyone getting involved shares a similar philosophy, that they know how to work together in ways that are beneficial to the whole group, and that they are looking to create something positive as opposed to simply running away from some difficulties in their own life. Ideally you'll have spent some time living or working with them in the past, so that you all know how compatible you are.

Other than that, I would highly recommend spending as much time finding out as much information as possible about the ghost town you plan on reoccupying, and what that country has in relation to laws around squatting and the like, in order to minimise the risk involved and to make sure that your energies are being put to the most productive and positive use.

Buy land

This is, of course, an absurdly odd option in a book that is primarily about moneyless living and the inevitable negative consequences of private ownership of land. Let me be clear: buying land is a million miles away from my ideals, and it is an extremely awkward and sensitive subject to broach within this context. However, the reality of the legal, political and economic society we've all been born into means that every square metre of land is now owned by somebody. An associated reality is the fact that, for whatever reason, people often find themselves with a chunk of money. I've found that it is often people who have worked all their lives in well-paid jobs in the City who are looking for a new way of living on the Earth, having witnessed first-hand the intrinsic horrors of the current economic model. Others inherit money (or less liquid forms of it) and want to use it as an escape from the madness of consumerism. Therefore there is an argument for using what we have already got in order to more rapidly put in place the infrastructure and culture of self-sufficient micro-economies, in a similar way that the flotsam of industrialised society may play its part in what David Holmgren, who along with Bill Mollison coined the term *Permaculture*, refers to as a 'creative descent',[123] in this context towards fully localised, gift economy living.

PERMACULTURE AND RELOCALISATION

David Holmgren, co-originator of the Permaculture concept and author of many books including *Permaculture One* and *Permaculture: Principles and Pathways Beyond Sustainability*[124]

The peaking of global oil supply suggests a permanent decline in the energy available to support humanity. This energy descent future will demand ways of thinking and organisation that are fundamentally different from those that guided the continuous energy ascent era since European cultures conquered the Americas and began to tap fossil fuels. Peak oil promises to make 'living with less' a non-negotiable reality faster than the alarming evidence of emerging climatic catastrophe.

Most people who have seriously considered the energy descent future recognise that it will lead to, amongst other fundamental changes, the faltering and reversal of globalisation. A revitalisation, in some form, of local economy, community and politics should follow. This structural change reflects a deeper level of thinking and action than imagining which fuel source or sources we will use in the future.

Permaculture is a design system for living and land use in the energy descent era. It emerged during the first oil shock era (1970s)[125] and has steadily grown into a worldwide movement of practitioners, designers and activists. Permaculture strategies range from using local organic wastes to create fertile food gardens, or making use of microclimate to grow a greater diversity of crops, to natural building heated by the sun, or collecting rainwater and reusing grey water, as well as local currencies and community supported agriculture. All of these examples can all be thought of as localisation strategies.[126]

Permaculture design starts with getting our own house (and especially garden) in order, then making the connections across the back fence, around the neighbourhood and throughout our networks. Instead of a focus on what is wrong with the world and what 'they' should do, Permaculture design and activism focuses on what we can do to live more self reliant lives with less dependence on distant and centralised sources of water, food and fuel. Rather than a survivalist strategy for holding onto essential resources, Permaculture harvests wastes and generates renewable abundance that will support the modest needs of self, kin and community.

Systems theory suggests that these micro-scale solutions that grow to modest economies of scale, but spread like weeds, are more likely pathways to successful relocalisation than the contraction and breakup of mega systems, although that may also make a contribution.

While Permaculture solutions vary greatly depending on the conditions and culture, they are all informed by universal design principles that collectively generate localised solutions to ecological, economic and social needs. For example, the design principle *Use Small and Slow Solutions* demands we look to resources and opportunities which tend to be localised and distributed rather than global and centralised. The principle *Use and Value Diversity* encourages a variety of solutions from place to place. The principle *Apply Self Regulation and Accept Feedback* demands a move to more self-reliant ways of living that take account of natural limitations. The principle *Obtain A Yield* requires us to extend financial literacy to energy literacy so we know which parts of a system are providing the goods. Permaculture design principles combine the common sense of our grandparents with the latest understandings from systems ecology.[127]

Oil has been the quintessential global energy solution and the design thinking developed in the energy ascent era leads us to believe in the next singular and global energy solution and to dismiss solutions that, by their nature, cannot be applied on such a scale. This apparently self-evident truth from the passing era is now a dangerous mindset that blinds us to the myriad of small local solutions and how they fit together to make for a prosperous way down from the peak of fossil energy. Permaculture helps us find and create those local solutions. At the same time it provides the thinking tools to detect the red herrings, false paths, dead ends and 'Trojan horses' we will face while charting our descent off the energy mountain over the next few decades.

If, through whatever means, you find yourself with a wad of cash that doesn't require paying back, then this is an option that, one could argue, would be silly to refuse without at least some thought. There are a number of potential ways you could use this money to take a piece of land out of the monetary economy to put back into the gift economy.

One option is to buy a sufficient number of acres and design an infrastructure and logistics system that allows you (and others) to grow and produce all your goods without the need for money from that point onwards, enabling you to then give away any surplus the land produces to local people in the same way it was given to you – unconditionally. Ideally, the people you give it to would, over time, want to get involved in collectively producing it.

If owning land is something you ideologically disagree with or are uncomfortable about, this admittedly isn't a brilliant option. Our dilemma lies in the predicament that all land is now owned, meaning that unless you play the same game as everyone else you have usually no legal right to grow any substantial amount of food, with the exception of limited options such as allotments. To ease your discomfort, there are various options open to you.

First, you could do as the Tolstoyans of Whiteway Colony in the Cotswolds did over a hundred years ago and burn the deeds of the land over a pitchfork as soon as you purchase it, effectively leaving it as owned as the day it was born into cosmic creation. This is certainly more difficult today with institutions such as The Land Registry involved, but as long as you don't register with them I see no good reason why it isn't at least possible. The anarchists of Whiteway even went to court to ensure that no one could lay claim to the land, and it was a case which the court upheld. Either way, there's no doubt it would be a powerfully vivid message to send out to the zealots of the Capitalist religion and a world obsessed with the concept of private ownership.

Another option could involve you buying the land without setting torch to the deeds (thus making a minor reduction to your carbon footprint), with a view to putting as much land as you can into the hands of a community allotment organisation, under a legal structure (such as a land trust) that you and your local community could set up specifically to protect this piece of land from those who would see it merely in terms of its financial value to them. In this way the land would be collectively managed and looked after, again giving local people the opportunity to be moneyless in terms of their food and any of the other basics of life they wish to grow.

The benefits of some of these methods of returning land back to the community are many: getting neighbours together; optimising the economies of scale; the pooling of the community's skills, knowledge, tools and other resources, therefore reducing duplication of equipment whilst optimising their effectiveness and the potential for learning; the creation of non-financial employment; a sense of genuine community and interdependence with each other; having others to look after the produce and animals if you are on holiday, and vice versa; free, locally produced organic food; and not least making the community more resilient (in terms of meeting its needs) from external shocks such as oil price hikes, hyper-inflation and the potential of national or international economic collapse. This latter point will become increasingly important in an age where we may not be able to depend on the current economic model to supply us with our food.

These are just some of the paths available to anyone who wants to use money to create less money dependent (or moneyless) micro-economies, as ridiculous and ironic as it sounds. The irony does fade though when you accept the logic of using what we have available to us now to hasten the transition from this globalised, conditional economy to the one we would like in the future.

CAMPAIGNING FOR REALISTIC LAND REFORM

Though it is undoubtedly a more long-term strategy, I do feel that it is imperative that the people of Britain address the fact that so much land is owned by so few. The Royal Family is a perfect example – they own 677,000 acres of land in Britain. The Ministry of Defence own 750,000 acres. Insurance companies, 500,000 acres. Whilst a small percentage of this (figures vary) is already used for food growing, the New Local Government Network argue that our government should create innovative ways to free up the land they leave unused, so that it can be made use of by people who simply want an opportunity to grow their own food, a very basic need for many people, perhaps even a necessity for some in the current economic climate. The NLGN have suggested three routes to doing this (in sequence):

- To appeal to land owners' altruistic side. NLGN's director and former MP Chris Shipley believes that Prince Charles, as "a vocal advocate for farming and the countryside ... will be supportive of the idea" of giving over his unused land to communities and allotment organisations for the production of local organic food. Given historical evidence, I must admit I do not share his optimism but I would be very happy to be wrong. If Prince Charles isn't, I feel he should ease off on the rhetoric regarding his commitment to sustainable farming (I'm not suggesting for a moment that the Duchy is supportive of non-monetary economy, but the ideas are interlinked in many respects) and admit that he isn't prepared to put his assets where his mouth is.

- For the Government to offer tax incentives for landowners to allow allotments to be built on unused sections of their property.

- Should a "voluntary system not work, the Government should consider a Large Private Estates Commission which could have the power to temporarily transfer unused plots of private land to the local community for agricultural use"[128] if "the landowner refuses to countenance the redevelopment of vacant land."[129] This is obviously a controversial point, but I believe that within an economic system where we import the majority of our food when much of our own land simultaneously lies well below the optimum level for sustainability and wildlife, something drastic needs to be done if those who own and control the land haven't got the decency or motivation to do it themselves.

Given how essential land reform is to our future sustainability aims and to those of us who desire nothing more than to not be forced into the monetary and wage economy, we should all get behind proposed reforms such as this. I'd go much further to say that we must stop merely asking for such reforms from those we elect into government, and instead demand them.

If ecological collapse isn't enough of a motivating factor to make these demands, what will be?

CHAPTER 7

HOME

Most of you reading this book will already have a place you call home, regardless of whether you own it outright, rent or have a mortgage. Unless you own it outright, then complete moneyless living will be an impossibility to you, for obvious reasons. Fear not, there is still much you can do to reduce your dependency on money.

For starters, I'd get rid of the TV set. I packed in television long before I even heard of the words *climate chaos* or *peak oil*. It wasn't that I particularly cared about the Earth back in 2002, I can't remember even considering it. I just found television a waste of my precious life. I was watching other people living instead of experiencing life for myself. Once the TV has been taken care of, there are some basics you can do to get yourself moving towards moneylessness.

Instead of letting the bath water out, use it to water the plants or give it some other use. To conserve even more water, remember the phrase "if it is yellow, let it mellow, if it is brown, flush it down"; that is if you don't have a compost toilet, which most of you won't (yet!). There is no need to flush the toilet after every pee (we use on average 70 litres per day flushing,[130] multiply that by millions, and you see the impact). Turn off the lights when you leave the room. Better still, have a 'Power-off weekend'[131] or a 'Slow Sunday',[132] invite your friends around for a game of cards or chess (only for matchsticks, remember) and get some musicians playing acoustic tunes. Winter was once a time of the year when we slowed down, partially because we had to as we hadn't enough light to work. Now we can effectively have light all year round, so we never get to hibernate with larders full of preserves. Powering down connects us with the seasons.

Instead of using the grinder, use a pestle and mortar. Instead of the electric blender, make yourself a bicycle powered smoothie maker.[133] The list of ways in which you can save energy in the house is almost endless, and there is a plethora of books that concentrate on that subject. The key to this is simply questioning everything you currently do around the house that uses energy, as it is this that has the biggest cost, both financially and ecologically. Everything has a moneyless solution – the fun is in coming up with your own, and these will be tailored to your unique needs.

In terms of your house's internal infrastructure, I'll be looking at elements of that in other areas of the book – furniture earlier in this chapter, showers and baths in chapter nine, heating in chapter eleven, and toilets at the end of this chapter.

If you are looking to redesign your life and eventually go completely moneyless, you may want to explore possibilities for finding or building a house than can allow you to do so. In the previous chapter, I looked at some of the ways of getting access to land. In a number of these cases, there will only be an option to utilise the land for growing plants, as planning permission may be a non-starter. Yet with some of the other transitional land strategies I've described, there will be potential for building a low impact dwelling or renovating an existing dwelling, ideally in a way that needs both a minimum of external inputs and zero or little money. If you're lucky enough to find yourself in this position, you may decide to go for either of the bureaucratic approaches I described in chapter four – applying for permission before building, or looking for retrospective permission after you've been caught being a naughty little boy or girl.

In terms of moneyless living, the ideal is obviously to build a house that is free in its construction, maintenance, and energy usage. Despite popular misunderstanding, it is still possible to build a house without money (it was standard once upon a time, when we were guided by different stories). All you need is materials and voluntary labour. As Irish artist Frank Buckley proved, one of these materials could be money. As part of an artwork he was creating called 'Expressions of Recession', he built a house made out of 50,000 bricks he made from $1.82 billion worth of decommissioned and shredded Euros that the Irish mint gave him. Frank remarked that "he wanted to make something out of nothing," and that "whatever you say about the Euro, it's a great insulator." This, to the best of my knowledge, has been the only time money has actually been useful for its own physical qualities and not the stories and beliefs we attach to it.

Even if your house does cost you a little, it will still be a fraction of the initial cost of a normal house, and it will allow you to remain bill-free and off-grid for life. As I mentioned earlier, it'll also mean that you probably won't need the mortgage that would have otherwise forced you into the wage economy, and all the personal consequences of that. This will be a big step up in your own POP model towards moneyless living. I got the dwelling I lived in when I lived moneylessly from Freecycle (see page 97). Admittedly, it was a caravan, not a semi-detached four bedroom house in the suburbs.

How much money you will need to construct your house will depend on how simple or complex it is, and how long you want the house to survive before you have to build another one. On one end of the spectrum you have what I call the bird's nest – simple, fully localised and not requiring a single penny, but not matching current human expectations of comfort and certainly not meeting all building regulations (I'm sure bird's nests don't either). In practice, these are the types of homes we built when we had to build them from local materials – in the UK that meant stone, wood, cob, thatch and so on – a time when no one would threaten to flatten your house on the basis that the airflow was a bit less than the regulations stated.

On the other end of the spectrum you have ex-Manchester United and England footballer Gary Neville's £6 million, 8,000ft^2 future eco-home, which claims will be Bolton's first zero carbon house. Despite the obvious extravagance, there is still lots of merit in aspects of Neville's approach, and some lessons to learn from it like there is from everything. Not to mention how encouraging it is to see professional footballers start to take our imminent ecological crisis so seriously (unless, that is, you are a Liverpool fan). Use a POP model to see where in the spectrum you currently lie, and what you would eventually, and ideally, like to move up to within a realistic timeframe. The most important point is to then take proactive steps towards making it happen.

The simplicity to complexity ratio of your house will determine how moneylessly you can maintain it, as the more complex materials you use in its initial construction, the less likely you are to be able to find the repair materials locally or be able to make them yourself. By using waste materials, however, you could build and maintain a house with little or no money and still maintain a level of comfort that we soft, civilised Westerners have grown accustomed to.

There is an almost endless list of potential dwelling designs to choose from, using a range of different local and waste materials. I will only aim to outline the main genres of moneyless housing, briefly touching on the essence of each. The techniques involved in each one of these designs are entire books in themselves. If one of them piques your interest then I recommend reading more on them yourself (I have referenced some useful reading material on each of the designs below), before adding your own touch and your own style. No two homes should be the same, just as no two residents are.

FREE HOUSE

If you don't want to build a house, or can't because of any of the obstacles we looked at in chapter four, there are a number of choices available to you, depending on whether you want to live in an urban or rural setting.

Squatting

Depending on your political and social viewpoints, this is a mildly controversial subject. Squatting usually involves occupying a particular space which the squatter doesn't rent, own or generally have permission to use. Reoccupying the ghost towns I mentioned in the previous chapter would technically be one rather unusual and positive method of squatting. The most common version occurs when people take over residential or commercial buildings in cities that have been left unused for a long period of time, turning them into social centres or homes for people who aim to live outside the political and economic systems that they've been born into.

What Transition Heathrow,[134] through its *Grow Heathrow* project, have managed to do on an old and abandoned market garden site in Sipson – one of the villages that had been earmarked to be concreted over to pave the runway for ever more flights at Heathrow airport – is widely regarded as one of the many really positive examples of squatting. First, they have they set themselves up to be self-reliant, by growing their own food (chapter eight), using a rocket stove (see page 216) to heat their water, utilising greenhouse roofs to collect water for the plants (see page 179), producing their energy using both solar and wind and creating four compost toilets (see page 142) – they are completely off-grid. Yet, just as importantly, they've become an integral part of the already established community there, as both locals and the 'blow-in' environmental activists have worked hard together to "return the Berkeley Nurseries site back to its intended purpose – a thriving market garden that will provide [their] community with locally produced, organic fruit and veg as well as a venue for new and interesting projects and workshops."[135]

During their first two years they have hosted many skill-sharing sessions, some big events, and cleared up 30 tonnes of rubbish from the site. Also, according to a statement from the Metropolitan Police, "there is evidence to show that crime has reduced since the Grow Heathrow Group has occupied the neglected Berkeley Nurseries. Possibly the presence of the group acts as a deterrent for crime in the surrounding area. Positive feedback has been received from local residents regarding the group, and the local residents feel safer knowing that there are people staying there. The evidence shows a reduction in motor vehicle crime in the area by 50 per cent, and a general reduction in crime of 25 per cent." Grow Heathrow is a perfect example of one of the many ways with which we can take back control of our land for the benefit of the people who live there.

The subject of squatting, and its history and legalities, is a book in itself, and for anyone who is considering this as an option, whether temporarily or long-term, I would recommend contacting the *Advisory Service for Squatters*,[136] and reading their book, *The Squatters Handbook*. At the time of writing, laws around squatting are looking likely to change, and this advisory service is best placed to give you the most up to date information on how to go about it at any point in time.

Squatting, in combination with other activities such as volunteering for your local community allotment, guerrilla gardening, foraging, skipping (see page 171) and other methods of utilising urban soil and waste, can easily provide you with an opportunity to live completely without money in the city, especially if you incorporate enough of the other ideas on how to demonetise your life described in this book. This is not a model that could work *en masse* without the complete collapse of society as we know it.

Yet it has definite value as a transition strategy as it presents those who are ready for moneyless living, and who want to test how it feels on every level, with an immediate route through which they can begin. Macro factors, along with our own efforts, will eventually merge to create the moneyless solutions of the future.

This urban approach also allows those involved to then devote their time to the causes – whether they be rape crisis centres, soup kitchens or campaign groups – they really want to support and help, projects that in many cases have no means to pay people by their very nature. While we work to proactively change the stories of the future, and the economic models we live within, it is important that we fully utilise what we have now in order to bring it about with optimum speed and efficiency.

House- and boat-sitting

House sitting is always a mutually beneficial arrangement. What usually happens is this: somebody who owns or rents their home needs to go away for a few days, weeks or months, leaving a cat or a dog or some plants behind that require looking after. The period they want to go away for generally isn't long enough to justify getting a tenant in, yet they still need something in the house looked after. Some like to have people in their house because they're afraid they'll have a higher risk of being burgled if not.

Because of these commonplace occurrences, there is a high demand for trustworthy house-sitters. I've spent the majority of my time writing this book house-sitting for various people around Bristol, including a stint on a houseboat along a beautiful stretch of canal near Bath. I spent two months looking after one large house where all I had to do was feed a gorgeous cat called Treacle twice a day. Daniel Suelo, who lives moneylessly in the US, spends half of his year doing this also.

There are plenty of projects out there designed to match house-sitters with house-owners. Many of these projects charge a small membership fee to join their list and access their databases, so I've always used the Freeconomy network to find my sits. After a few jobs you'll often find that word-of-mouth spreads and friends of those you have house-sat for ask you to come and do the same for them. Some people even offer to pay a house-sitter, but I would strongly recommend declining such offers and just doing it for free, as introducing money into the equation changes the entire feeling around the relationship, in the exact same way it does in other realms of life.

Like squatting, this isn't possible for more than a fraction of the population to do at any one time, and so it's obviously not a long-term housing strategy for society. However, if you're spending all your time volunteering for organisations who do work that you really believe in and want to support, this can be a very useful transitional strategy in the same way that squatting can be. Moneyless living doesn't have to be puritanical. Like a pigeon living in a church steeple eating food from the ground below, we could do worse than to live freely using what is at hand until a time when we're so surrounded by the abundance of Nature that we no longer have to.

Caves

This most original of human homes is both land and dwelling all-in-one. If you do decide to go and live in a cave, the caveman name-calling of anti-Luddites will refreshingly have some literal truth in it for once. Empty caves exist in all countries – I even know one on the outskirts of Bristol, a medium sized UK city – but not all countries have climates that are conducive to living in a cave, unless you're what is commonly referred to as a double hard bastard.

The good news on this front is that there seem to be more of them in countries where it is hot enough to live. The even better news is that due to the stigma Fred Flintstone and his family and friends have helped attach to cave dwelling, they're not much in demand either. If you fancy it, all I can say is go off on an adventure and find one. A good place to start, for beginners, would be Cappadocia in Turkey, where caves are rather unique and plentiful. Hitching or cycling there, before finding one once you arrive, is the challenge I put up to you.

There are a couple of things to consider if you do go living in caves:

a) Wild animals who see you as a nice tasty piece of meat, and an even scarier prospect,

b) Local authorities.

In order to avoid run ins with either, do plenty of local research before you set up camp. Preparation is also crucial, so don't just go in as some arrogant Westerner thinking you're Crocodile Dundee because you went camping one night in Dartmoor with a bag full of supermarket food.

Cave dwelling can be a long- or short-term moneyless living option, depending on what path your life is taking and what you want most out of it. Daniel Suelo (see page 58) spends the other half of his year in a cave amongst the canyonlands of Utah, and he speaks very highly of it. Others I've known have done it for a couple of years here and there, but I have yet to meet anyone who has done it all year round over a long period of time. Except for our ancestors, for whom it was the norm.

The blackhouse

This was a house traditional to many of the Celtic nations, most commonly in Ireland and the Highlands of Scotland and its surrounding islands. The reason for this was simple: they were made from materials the locals could source from their land, they required no money and, with the right skills, they were reasonably simple to construct and maintain. Blackhouses usually consisted of an earth or flagstone floor, drystone walls rammed with earth, wooden rafters covered in thatch (reed or straw) and a fire place.

Without adaptation (they generally didn't have chimneys, instead leaving the smoke to escape through the roof, for example) there is no way they'd pass modern building regulations and most people would see it as a definite step backwards in terms of comfort. My personal opinion is that, because of fossils fuels and the subsequent economic model that they have helped mould, our expectations around levels of comfort have risen to a point that is highly unsustainable in the long-term. As unpopular as it is to actually say this out loud, I believe that an adapted blackhouse could offer us a fine balance between comfort and true sustainability and the non-exploitation of the rest of Nature. That said, I'm not sure I'm up for sharing my house with a couple of sheep and pigs, which is what many people did in the days when the blackhouse was a commonplace structure.

This dwelling is one which I believe complements a landscape. I could never look at a blackhouse and consider it a blot. There is something about them that is just very aesthetically attractive. It is partially the skill, the art, the craft involved, but I feel it is in no small part due to the fact that the house has emerged from that particular landscape, and therefore is naturally a part of it, as opposed to being imported from a hundred other far-flung countries and their quarries and factories. The understanding of what it represents – simplicity, a care and respect for the land – also adds to its appeal, as the beauty of a thing lies as much in what it represents as it does in its physical qualities.

CHEAP (OR POTENTIALLY FREE) TO BUILD, FREE TO RUN HOUSES

Theoretically, you could build any house for free, especially in a model such as the resource-based economy that participants in the Zeitgeist movement propose. Realistically, a dwelling could only be built for free to the degree that it was made from local materials. Therefore any design that involves imported materials will very likely have some level of financial (and ecological) cost attached to it in most instances, though as we will see throughout this chapter this is not necessarily so, as we can often use the detritus of industrialised society to produce the sustainable homes of the future.

In the rest of this chapter I will look at houses that could be built for free but are likely to cost something, even if it is a fraction of what you would spend on a modern bricks and mortar house. To keep costs to the absolute minimum, use your imagination and try to use what you have at hand, as much as you possibly can, in the construction process. In all cases, once they are up they can easily be free to run on an ongoing basis. For inspiration, Lloyd Kahn's books *Shelter*,[137] *Home Work*[138] and *Tiny Homes*[139] are excellent sources.

Passive solar designs

If you want to eliminate heating bills, and your corresponding ecological footprint into the bargain, then one of the best things you can do is build using a passive solar design, ideally using a locally sourced material such as cob, which has high thermal mass, as a means of storing the energy created.

Designing in a greenhouse, where you propagate and grow whatever plants you want to eat or use, onto the south facing side of your house is one of the best methods of doing so. The sun shines in through these windows throughout the day, heating up the dwelling behind the greenhouse. If you want a house that heats up quickly in the morning, but are happy for it to cool down in the late evening, then fitting your interiors with wood may be a good option within such a design. However, if you would prefer to have a house that takes a little longer to warm up in the morning (for example, if you are out of the house until evening) but which then stays warm throughout the evening until the following morning, then cob may be a much better alternative, as it slowly radiates the sun's warmth that it stored throughout the day.

Earthships

This is one version of a passive solar house, developed in the US by pioneering architect Michael Reynolds, for parts of the country that can get as cold as -20ºC. Passive solar homes can be made using a variety of materials, and usually are. Earthships[140] are a specific variety that are made out of recycled and natural local materials. Rainwater harvesting methods, used car tyres rammed with earth, glass panes (which you can pick up for free from your local double glazer, who often are burdened with glass that they've cut wrong or that a customer no longer wants), wind turbines, solar water heating systems, photovoltaic panels, even beer cans and glass bottles (used to create wonderful lighting effects inside), all constructed using methods that very much chime with permaculture principles. The result is that you have a model of home that will enable you to be self-sufficient for energy and water, and with a little bit of elbow grease, food also.

Given that 40 million tyres are disposed of every year in the UK, the Earthship is a solution that simultaneously solves two problems: what to do with all these tyres, and the ecological impact of importing all the building materials that we currently use to build our homes, materials these otherwise useless tyres could come to replace. The fact that this untapped resource would provide high levels of thermal mass just adds to the notion that the Earthship design, adapted to use less complex equipment than they currently are designed with, really could be the model of a sustainable, moneyless future.

Earth bag construction

As an alternative to the rammed earth tyres of the Earthship model above, which pay great long-term dividends but which require a massive amount of time and human energy to begin with (each tyre can take approximately 40 minutes to an hour to fill, though numerous friends and acquaintances have told me that the weeks they spent ramming the tyres had a powerful bonding effect on their group), there is the option of using earth bags[141] instead, which only take a few minutes to tamp depending on how strong and energetic you are feeling. For this purpose you could reuse the rice and grain sacks that your local wholefoods and organic retailers and/or wholesalers may have.

Depending on how simply you want to build these, they could be done without money, but it is more likely that they will be low cost in their construction. In the wake of the earthquake, the Haiti Christian Development Project built around a dozen such dwellings at the cost of £1,400 each, which included wage costs. To bring that figure as close as you can to zero, and as a transitional strategy, you could instead employ a bunch of volunteers to help, whom you'll find are often enthusiastic about getting involved, whether to learn some new building technique or apply those skills they already have to help others build the sustainable homes of the future. With such a model of working, the volunteers get to learn all the skills which they can then pass onto others or use to build their own dwelling, whilst you get some much needed labour and morale boosting support, without any financial cost.

Straw bale homes and guest houses

These are exactly what they seem – houses made in large from straw bales. For a localised (and hopefully moneyless) straw bale house, the type of straw you would use is country specific. In the UK that would be rye, oats or wheat. For more information on how to do this, I recommend Barbara Jones' book *Building with Straw Bales: A Practical Guide for the UK and Ireland.*[142]

A very useful take on the straw bale house is a mini-model which I stayed in whilst visiting a well-known self-sufficiency project in the UK. The owners built a little straw bale guest house for visitors and volunteers, which was effectively a pimped up tent, but much warmer and cosier. It consisted of old wooden pallets on a base which they levelled out, covered in sheep's fleece (though any insulating material you can get your hands on for free could be used), with a recycled mattress on top, surrounded on three sides by load-bearing (and small) straw bales, with a south-facing wall of windows (constructed using waste glass and free reclaimed wood), with a green roof to help it blend into its landscape. Alternatively you could use the roof for water collection, depending on other factors in your unique situation. The one I stayed in was sited at the top of a large hill and the views waking up at dawn were quite stunning. It was also a very cosy place from which to watch the sunset on an autumn's evening, especially if you have a lover's arms tucked around you.

These mini straw bale guest houses take less than a day to build, they can be done using locally sourced and waste materials, and can be completely free of any financial cost. If you were happy with very basic housing and just wanted to hide away in the woods, this could be easily adapted to allow you to stand and walk around in; the only problem with this adaptation is that you are then more likely to attract attention.

Subterranean houses

This underground model was popularised by Mike Oehler in his book *The $50 and Up Underground House Book,*[143] which shows you the basics you need to know in order to build one. The benefits of these are many, and include that:

- Due to their subterranean nature, they do not impose on the landscape they exist within, a point that is especially advantageous if you do not have planning permission.

- They require no foundations and only half the building materials.

- They are energy efficient due to the fact t hey benefit from geothermal mass and heat exchange by their very nature; with good design they can stay warm in winter and cool in summer.

- Subterranean homes can also make best use of space if you are trying to be completely moneyless and your land is under an acre.

- The materials you gain from the excavation can be used in the building process.

- They are resistant to everything from earthquakes to the much more common threat of wind.

The folk down at the building regulations department may have a few thoughts on it; that is, if you tell them about it!

Circular houses

Whenever a child draws a picture of a house, it always involves straight lines, such is the ubiquity of the rectangular or square house. Such dwellings haven't always dominated, however, and some circular models are still used as low impact and moneyless homes today. If such a round structure appeals to you, and there are many good reasons why it would, I'd recommend looking at *Circle Houses: Yurts, Tipis and Benders*[144] by David Pearson or *Simple Shelters: Tents, Tipis, Yurts, Domes and Other Ancient Homes*[145] by Jonathan Horning for more information and inspiration.

Four main types of round dwellings spring to mind:

1. *Benders*:[146] These are easy to make and can be made moneylessly out of local and recycled materials. All you really need to make one is enough coppiced poles (hazel is best but ash or willow would do), a canvas (which you may be able to find for free) or some other waterproof covering, and some string, which you could make yourself out of fibres from locally growing plants.

2. *Roundhouses*: These are regularly made from a number of locally sourced materials, including cob and cordwood, wooden posts, wattle and daub panels, all finished with either a thatched or reciprocal frame green roof. A great example of one of these exists

in Tinkers Bubble, an ecological community based in Somerset. Tony Wrench, who has built quite a well-known roundhouse, has written a very good book on the subject also.[147]

3. *Yurts*: A standard yurt is usually made up of a circular, wooden lattice frame covered in canvas. The roof is composed of a transparent crown, which allows light and heat in, held up by poles. You can add to their ability to retain heat by stuffing old rugs and duvets, or other insulating materials, in between the frame and the canvas. If this design appeals to you, I would recommend investigating geodesic domes first as a similar option, but one which you are more likely to be able to construct using zero money.

4. *Tipis*: These dwellings, traditionally used by Native American Indians (the name itself was given by the Lakota) and adopted by hippies worldwide, consist of wooden poles covered by some waterproofing material. Originally animals skins were used, though these days many people use canvas. The main difference between a tipi and other circular dwellings is its conical shape and opening at the top end, enabling the dweller to cook and heat themselves with an open fire. If you decide to use animal skins then tipis can be made 100% out of locally sourced materials and can easily be done without money. If you use canvas, they can still be made for free but you will need to mine the vast amounts of waste at our disposal (see chapter five).

If you live in the UK, all of these round structures will require planning permission; again that is if you inform the authorities. Due to their fairly mobile nature, many people just erect them and hope for the best, safe in the knowledge that they are easily moved if they get caught. In other countries such as Greece, which I spoke about earlier, many of these temporary structures do not require any permission, and given their climate and land prices, it can be a tempting place to go for anyone who wants to live outside of the absurd story of money and credit and debt without having to attempt to navigate the minefield of bureaucracy that exists in the UK.

The ideal home is one which makes the most of the best elements of all the above designs, tailored to the ecological context within which it is built, which is an important point in itself. As long as you have a sound understanding of the materials you are working with, and the landscape and climatic conditions you are working within, you can do a pick-and-mix with all the materials and designs above. A large part of your decision may simply come down to what materials grow locally to you and what you already have at hand.

COMPOST TOILETS

You may have noticed that in the centre of the Indian flag there is a spinning wheel. This came about because, at the time of India's independence from Britain, when the flag was designed, Mahatma Gandhi believed that true national independence would only be achieved through *Swadeshi*, which roughly translates as self-sufficiency. He believed that India would only truly earn political independence when it achieved economic independence. In order to do this, he encouraged the millions of Indians to start spinning their own cloth again and to stop buying it from industrial fabric centres such as those in Lancashire in England. This culminated in bonfires of Lancashire cloth lighting up the land as a powerful symbolic act. Therefore, the spinning wheel became the symbol of true political independence.

If I were to create a flag for the planet, it would have a compost toilet on it. The flush toilet represents everything that is psychopathic about our current culture and mindset – we shit and piss into a life-giving liquid, spoiling it in the process, instead of using both of these potential resources (in different ways) to fertilise the soil which, in turn, makes the food that we eat more nutritious. Instead, we import polluting fertilisers from distant laboratories once we've finished polluting our waterways. Somehow we've managed to take a really beneficial resource for the soil and turn it into a major ecological problem.

I urge you to ditch your flush toilet and install a compost loo as a symbolic and, dare I say it, spiritual act. It's a no-brainer for anyone who wants to simultaneously stop polluting their source of life, drastically reduce their water consumption, and obtain a high quality organic fertiliser for their soil free of charge. Every single one of us could do it immediately, no matter what our circumstances. There are many models to choose from, but as human shit guru Joseph Jenkins points out, and Nicky Scott describes below, the simplest version is actually the best, looks much the same as a 'normal' toilet, and can be incorporated into any home.

If you want to collect some of your urine separately to this, but can't pee in your back garden for various reasons, I'd recommend making a simple urinal (possibly in your garden shed if you have one) that channels your liquid gold (aka pee) into a bucket of some sort, which ideally you would dilute using greywater you've harvested from your sink, bath tub or from rainwater harvesting (a water:urine ratio of 5:1 is accepted as good). If we all captured our urine, either by compost toilet or urinal, it would save us flushing 18 million gallons of useful fertiliser into our waterbodies each and every day in Britain alone[148] (not to mention the hundreds of millions of litres of water used to flush it 'away'). Instead of being a major pollutant, it would provide us with an easy and organic way of supplying our plants with a large percentage of their needs for nitrogen and potassium, meaning no more costly (ecologically and economically) imported and industrialised fertiliser into the bargain. If you can't build a urinal, just pee in a bucket and transport it to wherever it is most useful.

Taking responsibility for our own excreta can seem like dirty work to modern humans, below us even. Yet doing so is an act of humility,[149] a spiritual act, one of respect and honour and gratitude, and all it takes is a change in our perspective. If we can't even be bothered to, quite literally, sort our own shit out, then let us stop paying lip-service to caring for the planet, for our actions are much more revealing than our words. This is the very least we can do.

COMPOST: ONE MAN'S SHIT IS ANOTHER MAN'S FERTILISER

Nicky Scott, author of *How to Make and Use Compost: The Ultimate Guide*[150]

Being a 'no-dig' gardener (see page 167), I can never seem to get enough compost. When I was young – a few months ago now – I had a Saturday job with a remarkable man called Dick Kitto,[151] a composting pioneer and author who collected all kinds of organic matter from around Totnes and mixed it with spent mushroom compost to make huge, steaming heaps of nutritious, free and organic fertiliser. It was he who convinced me of the importance of composting, and suggested that I go to the Henry Doubleday Research Association, HDRA (now Garden Organic), where I was once a 'student' in the early 80s. Lawrence Hills, its founder, was passionate about not breaking the cycles of fertility, and he showed me how crucial it was to follow the simple principle of returning organic matter back to the soil. So many farmers and growers today 'mine' the nutrients of the soil, taking away from the bank balance of fertility without thinking to replenish it with compostable materials; instead choosing to import synthetic nutrients for the quick, short-term fix. He exhorted us to collect materials from wherever we could – autumn leaves, wasteland weeds, the trimmings from the fruit and vegetable market, belly button fluff, skipped food from bins, hair from the barbers; basically, whatever we could find. It is only when you start looking for it that you realise how many free sources of compostable material there are out there to gather in. Doing so is absolutely crucial for anyone who aspires to live in a fully localised, non-monetary economy.

Humanure

We had compost toilets on one of our sites, in Braintree, and it felt really good not using up precious drinking water to flush and transport my bodily wastes away. Flush toilets are, upon thinking about it, a bizarre concept. But it wasn't until I read Joseph Jenkins' excellent book *The Humanure Handbook: A Guide to Composting Human Manure*[152] that I fully understood how ridiculously simple it is to set up a composting system that could incorporate what we normally flush out of sight and mind. Indoor composting toilets can potentially be expensive and take up lots of space (the other option involves constructing a special structure outside). So instead, we had the downstairs toilet removed and in its place a simple box was made with a hinged lid and a wooden toilet seat. It now consists of one large bucket (you can obtain five gallon containers from almost any food business, and they will be more than happy to off-load as many as you want onto you) under the toilet seat and another beside the box, full of 'soak' materials (such as sawdust, soil, compost, paper, cardboard, autumn leaves) that we use to cover the deposits. When the bucket needs emptying it is taken to the compost heap and covered, layered with other compostable materials. Admittedly, there is more to the art than that, depending on your situation, and I would strongly recommend reading Jenkins' book if you are at all interested (*The Humanure Handbook* is also free online[153]).

Composting is easy: it's just water and air

After years of learning, experimentation and experience, I have finally distilled the essence of the composting system down to 2 things that you need to balance: water and air. You also need warmth, but unless you get a mixture of materials which contain enough water and allow airflow, then your composting will not be a satisfying experience.

I couldn't possibly tell you how many people get hung up with dealing with grass cuttings (which, in my view, should simply be left on the lawn in order to maintain its fertility). Many people tend to dump all the grass cuttings from the lawn in a pile, which inevitably heats up quickly and goes smelly and sludgy, generating methane in the process. This isn't any good for anyone. Instead, if these fresh and moist grass cuttings (along with fruit and vegetable peel, tops and tails and any soft sappy weeds) were layered or mixed

(50/50 is good) with materials which allow airflow and others which absorb moisture (like shreddings, twigs, sawdust, prunings, cardboard and paper), a very useful compost heap would be created. The bigger you make your heap the more likely you are to generate and maintain high temperatures.

The best time to start a hot composting system is in midsummer, when there is no shortage of compostable materials around. My approach is to scoop the top layer off a current bin, dig out the bottom finished layers for use in the garden, before relaying the bin. I start this new bin with a coarse layer of dry, structural materials. On top of that I layer some soft greens, before adding the top of the old heap I just dug out, plus any weeds I've managed to gather. Always remember that you want to mix wet with dry, soft with hard, and if possible old with new. Balance is key.

Following these simple guidelines, you will see temperatures shoot up day by day. I tried an experiment with the ubiquitous 'dalek' bin your local council probably promotes, and recorded an initial ambient temperature of 20ºC. The temperature went up 10º every day until it peaked at just over 50ºC. In an insulated or larger bin it would have probably gone up even more. The level of compost in the bin, not coincidentally, dropped pretty dramatically over the same few days. This is the first really active stage of composting, and is driven primarily by bacteria and other micro-organisms. The more heat that is generated, the quicker the pile turns to useful compost. As it eventually cools, it goes into a longer maturation stage which can last months or a year. This is when the worms move in to finish off the job and transform it into the most amazing, life-giving substance.

Wormeries

Worms always come into compost discussions, and I found there to be a bit of a mythology surrounding them. It's true that they are amazing creatures, but they really only work as I've described above, moving in as the heap cools and the materials are partially broken down; only then can they eat the soft parts.

If you want more worms for your compost (which you ought to), I'd recommend building yourself a wormery.[154] Wormeries are worm farms, a sealed container of some sort where you breed worms for your compost and, ultimately, your garden. Wormeries are perfect for dealing with small amounts of cooked food which, due to its ability to attract rats, can otherwise be tricky in small domestic composting systems. Word of caution: because worms hang around waiting for the materials inside to fester long enough for them to eat, it is important to add only a little food waste at a time to a wormery, otherwise they tend to be rather airless and smelly, and become too hot for the worms. Therefore, try not to think of a wormery as a bin, and instead a farm for little things. Get it right, and your compost and land will thank you for it, especially if you plan on using a no-dig system where the worms do the work (willingly, I should add), instead of you.

CHAPTER 8

FOOD AND WATER

Milton Friedman, through a book of that title, foolishly popularised the phrase 'There's no such thing as a free lunch'. It is instantly obvious to anyone with half their wits about them that Milton spent much too much time reading economics textbooks and no time at all taking strolls through the woods foraging food. To be fair, this phrase is used by economists to convey the concept of 'opportunity cost', an idea that author and economist Campbell R. McConnell[155] states is "at the core of economics" and which stems from the belief that in order to have or do one thing, we must sacrifice another. The idea is that even if we do something apparently free, like sit and contemplate the beauty of a quiet evening by a lake, it 'costs us' the opportunity to do all the other things we could have done with that time. Like making money.

On this I would note a number of points. First, I would alter McConnell's statement to say that it is at the core of *modern monetary economics*, and that it is more symbolic of humanity's current mindset and culture than it is any universal truth. It reveals how modern economics and culture views everything as a win-lose situation, as opposed to the win-win-win scenario that is possible with non-monetary, gift economics. Take this for example. I'm feeling the need to get some fresh air and stretch my legs, knowing that I'll also be hungry when I come back. So I head off to the hedgerows with the willow basket that I thoroughly enjoyed making earlier, searching for fun adventures and food. And oh how I get both in abundance! I return home feeling great, having no need for the gym and all its high technology machines, my lungs brimming full of country air, with a basket full of the most alive food I will ever have the pleasure of putting into my body.

My question to McConnell and Friedman is: *in what way was that lunch not free?* The opportunity cost of lounging around the house feeling physically and mentally unhealthy is hardly a cost, nor is having to go to a busy supermarket to pick up bags of food that are nutritionally equivalent to cardboard, and possibly less flavoursome. In fact, if the exercise and good food helps me towards health, fitness and a longer life, I might actually have more time remaining in my life after my walk than I did before – not so much an opportunity cost, more an 'opportunity dividend'.

The mindset that believes that *there is no such thing as a free lunch* is symptomatic of, and a perpetuator of, an economy that compartmentalises life into distinct activities, one where the ways in which you meet your needs must be dour and boring. In the mindset of the gift economy, you meet your needs everyday by doing the things you love to do, integrating your private life, work life and social life into one inextricable whole. My favourite times are when I am out in Nature planting seeds. That it just so happens to supply me with all my own dietary needs months later is a bonus. Give me the choice between growing food or going to the cinema, or going on a holiday to some ghastly tourist resort, and I'd be out playing in my natural habitat every time.

Life doesn't have to be separate and compartmentalised. We could just as easily design lives that are fluid, lives where we always mix business with pleasure.

On that basis, I hereby refute Friedman's claims and state that there is such a thing as a free lunch. How you go about getting such lunches is a bigger question, and will depend largely on whether you live in an urban or rural setting; what your philosophies around food are; and how much soil, hedgerow or woodland you have access to.

In this next section I will introduce various methods for eating for free, suggesting further reading for each technique (as some are books in themselves) so that if one chimes with your practical needs and ideological stance you can explore it in a lot more depth in your own good time. Some options will be suitable for urban life, others for rural. The ideal is to incorporate a number of methods into your food economy, as diversity builds resilience. In the monetary economy, you're dependent on the local supermarket having shelves full of food stocked – if that system failed, would you have a Plan B?

I'll also look at ways of drinking for free (water that is, see page 293 for a free pint of the fermented stuff), again exploring various options so that we find a solution for everyone's situation.

FOOD

There are three general ways in which you can eat food for free – wild food foraging, the various forms of growing (ideally some Permaculture approaches I will look at in this chapter), and skipping. If you live in the city and this is all new to you, once you start looking you'll be surprised to realise how much food there is going unused (nettles, for example are highly nutritious and great for a soup), you'll see growing spaces everywhere and, if you're prepared to do it, the bins of supermarkets would keep you and your friends feasting every night for as long as you wanted.

From the produce you get from some mix of these three methods, you can also include bartering to the list. This is particularly useful at harvest time if your allotment or back garden has a glut, or if you've had a bounty from the bins, though in such circumstances I prefer to just give it away for free to neighbours.

WILD FOOD FORAGING

Foraging is defined as the act of looking or searching for food or provisions. The term is usually used these days in relation to going out harvesting food from the wilds, which in England usually (and sadly) means hedgerows, woods and other areas that have seen minimal human cultivation, interference and management.

Anyone can go out and forage. There is wild food everywhere, much more than you would imagine in cities, as long as you know where to go and what to look for. Rocket and Jack-by-the-hedge, growing through the cracks between the wall and the footpath, both disappointed about not being picked; sumac in your local park waiting to be made into 'lemonade'; and dandelions crying out to be put into salads. However, I would strongly recommend learning it by adventuring out with someone very experienced for a period first, unless you are planning to harvest only commonly recognised species such as the stinging nettle, ramsons (wild garlic) and blackberries. Richard Mabey's book *Food for Free* is a now a classic text, but hands-on experience (and lots of it) is required before you will gain enough proficiency at it to go eating some of the more obscure plants. Plants that are toxic to humans often look very similar to ones that aren't, and only going out with a very experienced forager will give you the confidence you need to eat well from the wilds. Until you become fairly competent at foraging, start making full use of those plants you do recognise but have never got around to utilising.

WILD PROTEIN: LEAF CURD AND ROADKILL

Fergus Drennan, broadcaster, professional forager
and wild food foraging teacher[156]

On 1st January 2013 I'll be beginning my third attempt to live on entirely wild/foraged food for a year. When I tell people that the diet will be predominantly plant based this usually elicits one of two questions: 'How will you get enough carbs?' and, 'What about protein?' Carbohydrate is relatively easy to come by; obtaining sufficient protein on the other hand can be more of a challenge. One answer to the challenge lies in the wild food adventure that is leaf curd production – the extraction of protein direct from multiple leaf varieties. Actually, in 15-20 years time I wouldn't be surprised to see leaf curd complimenting meat as a common and nutritious source of protein. Before then, forward thinking mechanical engineers, enthusiastic experimenters, determined vegans, and those committed to alternative and more sustainable food production must devise equipment that can extract the protein more efficiently than that which is currently available. Still, in the meantime, and on a small scale, leaf curd can significantly contribute to a healthy and more sustainable diet with very minimal investment in equipment.

Leaf curd – what exactly is it?

Leaf curd or leaf concentrate isn't just protein, although a well made curd will consist of up to 70% protein; it also includes vitamins and minerals such as vitamin A (as beta-carotene), iron, calcium and essential micronutrients. Not only that, the resulting dry fibrous residue need not be construed as waste but rather can be composted or, better still, made into card or paper – edible paper in fact.

Given that the curd is so nutritious, it has been produced on a small scale in countries where malnutrition is endemic. Given, also, that over half the population in this country is seriously overweight; I reckon that counts as bad or malnutrition. So let's get to work!

At present I have successfully utilised wild garlic (*Allium ursinum*), alexanders (*Smyrnium olusatrum*), charlock (*Sinapis arvensis*), ground elder (*Aegopodium podagraria*), lime (*Tilia* species) and stinging nettle (*Urtica dioica*). The flavour of the first three is intense. Consequently the finished curd from these combines well with the milder tasting nettle, charlock or lime curd in a ratio of 1:6.

The leaves of many plants can be used, and although fresh grass cuttings are a good source of bulk leaf material and can be used, generally speaking it is safest to use plants with a well established use as human food. Note: fungi and seaweeds are unavailable for home protein extraction due to their small cell size.

Selecting your leaf maceration and juice extraction method. Possible techniques:

- Home liquidiser with added water (ideally using a bicycle to run the liquidizer) and manual straining and squeezing through a fine cloth or bag.

- Manual meat grinder (no added water) and manual straining and squeezing through a fine cloth or bag.

- Very good quality general juicer or wheat grass juicer.

- Giant pestle and mortar. Pounding leaves in a large water butt or other suitable container with a big wooden stake, followed by manual straining and squeezing through a fine cloth or bag.

- Impact macerator.[157]
- The Super Efficient Ingenious Device (invented by you, my dear reader)!

How to make leaf curd

First, collect young and tender leaves. This is best done in the spring from March-May before leaves have laid down too much cellulose. 12kg of stinging nettles will give about 1 kg of damp crumbly curd; for wild garlic it is slightly less at 12kg to 800g, but the flavour is super intense and a little goes a long way. The aim is to break open as many of the leaf cells as possible to release the protein. This is best achieved if the leaves are washed and used as soon as possible after collecting. The three most convenient small scale methods involve either liquidising the leaves in a blender, passing them through a meat mincer or pounding and grinding using a giant version of a pestle and mortar. The latter two methods will give you a little juice and much wet pulp that then needs to be squeezed in a cloth to extract the juice. I prefer to use the liquidising method, although the pounding method is excellent if you fancy a workout. Place about 250g of washed and roughly chopped leaves into the liquidizer and top up with water – spring water preferably. Blend for a minute or so to produce a fine pulp. Repeat this process until all the leaves have been processed. If using wild garlic, after 2-3 times using fresh water, strain out the solids and use the same liquid to blend the next batch of leaves. Once all the leaves have been pulped, tip the leafy pulp into a pillowcase resting inside a large bowl. Strain out the liquid and squeeze the residue to get out as much liquid as possible. Place this green liquid in a stainless steel pan and bring to the boil for 1 minute. The protein will coagulate into solids. Once it has cooled a little, strain through a fine cloth – I use silk, squeezing until no more water will come out. For large quantities one could use a hydraulic press or apple press perhaps. If using wild garlic leaves the strained liquid can be used as a stock base for soup. It can be bottled for subsequent use (note: with many if not most leaves the liquid is not safe to consume regularly).

How to store and use the curd

Fresh curd should be used as soon as possible although it will keep in a sealed airtight container in the fridge for a few days. Dividing into cubes and freezing or mixing in 200g of salt per kg and then refrigerating also works well. Drying is possible in a low oven; above (but not in contact with) a radiator; or in a food dehydrator. Nevertheless, it should be manually crumbled up half way through the drying process; this avoids the formation of apparently dry lumps that remain moist inside. I tend to mix it with salt and use small pieces as stock cubes or freeze and thaw to use as fresh.

So, after all this effort how can it be used!? Well, it's surprisingly versatile. I have used it in all of the following ways: in spicy Indian sauces, risotto, vegan burgers, vegetable smoothies, salsa, savoury seaweed mousse, pesto, bread, pasta and noodles, pastry, pancake mix, soup, stews, as a salty spread, pâté, stock cubes, in seitan (i.e. combined with wheat gluten flour and cooked) and even to make green fried eggs! Perhaps the most intriguing experiments have been my attempts, partly successful, to make green cheese. This has involved adding salt, coconut oil and acidic whey (extracted from milk, yoghurt or, as a purely vegan alternative, separating the liquid from sour dough starters), then wrapping in cloth and increasingly compressing over the course of several weeks (in cool conditions).

Wild food and roadkill

Of course, let us not forget that there are many other fun and efficient ways to obtain high protein foods from the wild. Perhaps the best and most easily obtained plant based source is the delectable walnut. Particularly in the south of England, feral, abandoned trees, or simply those in public places, can be readily found. There are over 40 such trees within a short cycling distance of my home. Last year I gathered 50kg nuts. These can be used whole or have the oil extracted, the resulting meal being a wonderful and protein rich food source. Then of course there is the whole coastal larder of fish and shell fish, the inland larder of snails and insects and, dare I say it, yes I do, accidental meat, a.k.a. roadkill. Given the tragic fact that every year in the UK,[158] 3 million pheasants, 800,000 rabbits, 50,000 deer, squirrel and badgers, as well as 25,000 foxes are killed on our roads, (and extrapolating from these appalling statistics, whilst taking into account the differing size of the various animals and, for arguments sake, assuming that 50% of such animals are serviceable as food – i.e. avoiding the tabloid cliché that anyone who eats road kill 'scrapes it off the tarmac') then (when accounting for the differing number of servings from each animal) we're looking at least 8,900,000 potential meals for the practical, discriminating and opportunist forager. *Bon appétit*!

For an extensive and detailed account of leaf curd production techniques, preservation and storage methods and recipe suggestions, see the excellent free online document: *Leaf Concentrate: A Field Guide for Small Scale Programmes* by David Kennedy.

The classification of wild food, as separate from food cultivated by humans, raises some interesting questions here; questions which highlight the extent to which we have perceived ourselves to be separate from the rest of Nature.

First, what exactly is 'the Wild'? Second, why are humans commonly not considered to be wild, or a part of the Wild? If a human plants a seed, and it germinates and spreads itself across a landscape over a short period of time, are these new plants wild or cultivated? Most people would suggest the latter, though with little confidence or clarity. Yet if a so-called wild animal eats some fruit before, very kindly, dropping the seed bomb composed mainly of its own – ahem – potting mix, and that seed then germinates into another fruit producing plant, most people would consider that to be the work of 'the wild'. Is the planting of a seed only a domestication issue if it is done consciously by humans? Gary Snyder, author of *The Practice of the Wild*, suggests that a plant is wild if it is "self-propagating, self-maintaining, flourishing in accord with innate qualities".[159] But who is to say that plants haven't evolved in the ways they have to manipulate us into planting them everywhere – they've evolved with the wind to do this, so why not with the human also?

We believe that we are in control, that we are the manipulators, but maybe it is the plants that are manipulating us. If you think that is completely barmy, consider the fact that unless we continue to spread seed (on their behalf) every single year now, we will die. Who is really in control here – us or the plants?

Humanity is no less or greater a part of Nature than a fox or a deer. We may currently be a more destructive force that anything else that exists, but we are still Nature. And within us still resides a piece of The Wild.

GROWING

As the ecological crisis that we now find ourselves in is exacerbated, so too does the collective desire to understand where it actually began. Jared Diamond,[160] and an increasing number of anthropologists, scientists and ecologists like him, argues that it was the emergence of agriculture that triggered many of our converging ecological, social and personal crises, and that agriculture is "in many ways a catastrophe from which we have never recovered,"[161] the "worst mistake in human history". Diamond adds that "hunter-gatherers practised the most successful and longest-lasting life style in human history. In contrast, we're still struggling with the mess into which agriculture has tumbled us, and it's unclear whether we can solve it." Historically, agriculture was heavily dependent on slavery and serfdom; now it is heavily dependent on fossil fuels. It is no coincidence that we finally abolished the slavery of humans (though the monetary, wage economy is just a more subtle form of slavery) during the advent of the Industrial Revolution, which effectively enslaved the rest of life on Earth instead. A litre of oil, remember, is less hassle than keeping a slave. As fossil fuels are a finite resource, it is self-evident that we cannot continue with this. Meaning we either need to go back to slavery, or kick our fossil fuel habit by redesigning our economies and drastically changing the way we think about our place in the world. We need to abolish the slavery of the rest of life on Earth too, otherwise it is just narrow minded, anthropocentric speciesism.

If human history thus far was a 24 hour clock, and each hour represented 100,000 years, then we have lived for the first 23 hours 54 minutes as hunter-gatherers, and only the last six minutes as agriculturalists. In the time it takes to make a cup of cosmic tea, we've somehow managed to create for ourselves a conundrum of epic proportions.

I agree with Diamond to a large extent. The concept of agriculture has paved the way for the mess we see today, despite this view contradicting the views of many environmentalists over the last fifty years who have believed that simply getting *back-to-the-land* is the solution. However, I argue that our present problems began a few stages earlier than the advent of agriculture. They began when we slowly started seeing ourselves as separate from the rest of Nature, and started believing that our fates are not interdependent on everything that makes Her up.

Regardless of when we diverged down the ill-fated track we now find ourselves on, it's clear that sixty one million people in the UK (a population size that agriculture has facilitated) cannot feed themselves from a hunter-gatherer diet, given that we've destroyed the Wilds that such a food supply would have once come from. Therefore, new solutions are required that mix the reality of our dependence on what is an inherently unsustainable agricultural model, with the reality that we simply cannot keep on going like we are, and the reality that we need to eat. Luckily, many such solutions already exist.

In terms of eating without money, I want to present a menu of methods and techniques for you that, though not as sustainable as our hunter gatherer ways, provide a manageable target for us to work towards. For a food system to be moneyless, it needs to be based on a circular model and not the linear type that most modern farming is based on – cradle-to-cradle as opposed to cradle-to-grave. The linear model only functions through the importation of resources that attempt to replace the fertility that their methods have stolen from the Earth, and the fossil fuels that allow one farmer, and a few farmhands, to control hundreds of hectares of land. The importation of such resources would not be possible without a tool such as money.

These options and methods I describe below will provide you with all the practical tools you'll need in order to grow your food without money, and offer a middle ground between the ultimate model of sustainable food – hunting and gathering – and the reality of feeding 61 million people from the 54 million acres of potentially productive land the UK has 'at its disposal' (and at the minute, disposing of it is exactly what we are doing).

Seed saving and swapping

In order for you to achieve the type of closed loop food production system that would give moneyless living its least complex and most realistic form, saving seed is crucial. Seed is usually very cheap to buy, which is why most gardeners don't bother to collect it (another example of money's marriage to the maximum economies of scale proving extremely wasteful), as it can be a bit fiddly depending on the plant. However, whilst it only costs a pittance, it is obviously not free to buy, meaning that unless you save seed you must enter the monetary economy and accept all that goes with that. This highlights the difference between living frugally and living completely without money. With frugal living, innumerable seeds go unsaved up and down the country every day. Without money, saving them is a matter of survival. Therefore moneylessness doesn't just avoid waste, it forces us to be highly attuned to Nature's rhythms.

Saving seed is easy once you know what you're doing, and as long as you store and label each batch correctly, including all the relevant information, it can be a very rewarding practice. Each plant will obviously require methods that are marginally specific to them, but you will quickly learn these through a mixture of reading and experience. If you want to be completely moneyless for food, I'd recommend Sue Strickland's book, *Back Garden Seed Saving.*[162]

As Dave Hamilton, in *Grow your Food for Free*[163] points out, "in terms of food security and biodiversity, [seed-saving] is the most important thing you can ever do". It also presents us with our best opportunity to allow plants to evolve and adapt for the future climatic (including micro-climate) and soil conditions of our geographical region. Just as importantly, it really connects you to what is going on during each season and the effect of meteorological factors on plants, encouraging you to stay awake to everything that is going on in your garden.

If there isn't one already in your community, why not set up a local seed and plant swapping group – you'll get to meet other local growers, get access to a wide range of seeds, and create a supportive network of people who can advise each other on all aspects of growing.

Perennial Plants

Even better than seed saving is growing perennial plants. The definition of a perennial vegetable is a source of constant debate amongst the green-fingered, but it is generally accepted as plants that live for two or more years. As Charles Dowding[164] notes, "perennial vegetables grow again, every year, from roots that survive over winter. There is no need to start again in the spring, and early crops are assured, growing vigorously while newly sown seedlings of annual vegetables are only just underway." If grown using methods such as forest gardening (see page 165) or no-dig (see page 167), there are even more time, fertility and energy saving benefits. Commonly recognised varieties include plants such as rhubarb, asparagus, and artichoke, but there is a huge list to choose from.

Any gardener who has grown both perennials and annuals knows how much less work there is with the former. Considering that the moneyless world I envisage is one with less drudgery, not more, this is an important advantage. But there are many other advantages just as important. As Patrick Whitefield points out,[165] they can be used instead of terracing to protect the soil on steep slopes, generally have a higher nutritional content (sometimes at the cost of a little of the flavour our modern palates have become accustomed to), are generally more resistant to diseases (meaning you don't need to buy in pesticides), and most importantly for moneyless living, they will help you to get you through what is known as 'the hungry gap',[166] that time of year when there aren't many annual crops ready to be eaten, a period when we import a lot of our food from warmer climes. Whitefield also adds that "the fact that almost all the plants in natural ecosystems are perennials suggests intuitively that a garden of perennials may be more sustainable than one of annuals".

I would recommend Martin Crawford's book *How to Grow Perennial Vegetables*[167] for anyone who wants to eat for free without breaking their back in the process.

Closed loop systems

Closed loop food models are essential to creating simple moneyless micro-economies. Therefore maintaining the fertility of the soil, so that it can support you and the rest of life without any need for imported and industrially produced fertilisers, is very important. Modern agriculture intensively grows annual crops which rapidly depletes the soil of nutrients, then replaces this lost fertility using raw materials imported from outside of that region, often from the other side of the world. These fertilisers include ingredients such as zinc, phosphorous, potassium, sulphur (all finite), and they are mostly synthesised in a laboratory. In other words, they would not be possible without the high economies of scale and specialised division of labour that money allows us.

Similarly, there is no place for industrialised pesticides in a moneyless system. Beside the well documented ill effects of pesticides (insecticides, fungicides, herbicides etc.) on both the egocentric and holistic self, they again have to be imported into a system from the outside, which means that not only are they inherently unsustainable, they're also an impossibility without money.

Yet moneyless people still need food that hasn't been decimated or destroyed by pests. To deal with these two needs, there are a number of farming methods based on circular thinking that we can utilise.

Organics

A moneyless food system needs to be, at the very least, organic. This is obviously a large subject in itself, but in terms of moneylessness it replaces industrialised fertilisers with soil improvers such composts and mulches, and pesticides with methods such as companion planting, crop rotation, slug traps, the utilisation of heirloom seeds, encouraging beneficial micro-organisms and insects through increasing biodiversity, along with a host of other methods.

There are countless books on organic growing, so if you are a beginner to gardening then pick one up from the library that best matches your abilities and needs. For making compost – a crucial skill for the moneyless human – I'd recommend Nicky Scott's *How to Make and Use Compost* for a very comprehensive guide.

Understanding organics is at the very heart of moneyless food growing. It's Moneyless Living 101. If you're seriously considering fully localised living, or just meeting your own needs in as respectful a way as possible, you'd be wise to get versed and experienced in approaches such as the no-dig method, agroforestry (including forest gardening), and biodynamics. My advice would be to do so either by taking an initial course (which may cost money) or, ideally, by finding a farm that has already adopted the approach you're interested in and volunteering with them for a period of time. The WWOOFing directory is perfect to help you find something suitable.

HOMEMADE NATURAL, ORGANIC PESTICIDES, FERTILISERS AND PLANT AND SOIL ENHANCERS

Steph Hafferty, organic no-dig grower, teacher and speaker[168]

Herbs and wild plants have many uses in the garden, as companion plants to enhance growth, attracting beneficial predators and pollinators, as organic liquid fertilisers, compost activators and insect repellents.

Spray the garden early in the morning or late in the evening to minimise disturbing bees and other pollinators.

Rich in nitrogen, potassium, calcium and other important minerals, comfrey has a chemical composition which is similar to manure. Although it is extremely beneficial, it is highly invasive and so it is best to grow it in a part of the garden where it's enthusiastic nature will not take over your vegetables! The best comfrey is Bocking 14 which is sterile and propagated from root cuttings, so ask a friend if you can have some of theirs. Alternatively, wild comfrey (leaves only) can be gathered whilst foraging.

Comfrey is a superb compost ingredient, adding essential nutrients and helping the heap to heat up. Research has shown that it can reduce composting times by up to a half. I layer comfrey leaves whilst building the heap up. Never add roots or flowers or you may end up with baby comfrey plants inconveniently popping up everywhere – it is extremely difficult to eradicate, the deep tap root which brings up so many minerals from the subsoil ensures that even when 'dug out' there is always a piece lurking which will regrow.

Chopped and used as a green manure or mulch, comfrey is especially beneficial for fruit bushes and trees. In the vegetable garden the layer of damp leaves provides a habitat for pests so is best avoided in sluggy UK. Gather large bunches of leaves during the growing season and dry in a warm airy place (I hang mine in the shed). Crushed and stored in sealed bags or containers, these dried leaves can be added to the compost heap, potting compost, used to make a feed in winter or sprinkled on top of the soil as a beneficial enhancer.

A potent and valuable liquid feed is made simply by filling a container with leaves and topping up with water (if you are using dried leaves, half fill the container). I make mine at the New Moon. Stirred occasionally, it is ready just after Full Moon, and the waning moon is the best time to use liquid feeds. Strain into another container (put the sludge onto the compost heap) and dilute 1 part feed to 10 parts water. It is very good for tomatoes, melons and cucumbers and any plants you are growing in pots.

Warning! Comfrey liquid smells terrible! Wear your worst clothes when straining and using.

Familiar everywhere, the stinging nettle (*Urtica dioica*) is a wonderful help to the gardener, rich in iron, copper and calcium. Ladybirds, whose larvae eat hundreds of aphids, lay their eggs on nettle leaves which also provide a home for the caterpillars of comma, tortoiseshell and peacock butterflies. Nettles grow too abundantly in the wild to necessitate cultivating in the garden: they are very invasive and this is best avoided.

Nettle leaves are an excellent compost activator. Either remove the leaves with a gloved hand before adding to the heap or chop into 4 inch pieces with a sharp spade or secateurs, after checking that there are no flowers or roots which may invade your garden. Nettles can be dried like comfrey for winter use.

Nettle liquid feed is an excellent fertiliser, helps to build plant resistance to pests and disease and also can act as an insect repellent. Fill a container with nettles at New Moon and top up with water, before covering. Stir occasionally. Just after Full Moon, strain (adding the sludge to the compost heap) and store in sealed containers. To use, mix 1 part liquid with 10 parts water. For a foliar spray, mix 1 part liquid with 20 parts water.

The leaves and flowers (not seeds or roots!) of the dandelion can also be made into a beneficial fertiliser in this manner, or add a handful to the nettles or comfrey before soaking.

Horsetail (*Equisetum*) is highly invasive and almost impossible to eradicate so do not introduce into the garden, but the foraged plant makes a wonderful magnesium rich spray which can be sprayed on the soil or directly onto plants. Boil one handful of fresh horsetail with 3 cups of water (½ cup dried plant) for 5 minutes. Remove from heat and cool, still covered, for 6 hours. Strain and dilute 1 part horsetail liquid to 4 parts water.

In late May, when the larger plants die back, shoots resembling baby Christmas trees appear. Harvest these to make Little Shoot Spray – a beneficial fungicide. Simmer 2 cups of fresh shoots (1 cup dried) in 2 gallons of water for 20 minutes. Remove from heat and leave, still covered, for 24 hours. Strain and dilute 1 part liquid to 2 parts water.

Yarrow (*Achillea millefoliuim*) is a renowned compost catalyst. Tests revealed the perfect 'dose' to be two finely chopped leaves mixed through 1 cubic metre of compost (about the size of a domestic compost bin). A larger quantity of yarrow actually reduces its potency. Grown in proximity with other herbs, it increases their fragrance and yield, although be wary of its invasive nature. Yarrow can be easily found whilst foraging and grown either from seed or a piece of root. Yarrow further benefits the gardener by attracting hoverflies.

A tea made from chamomile (*Anthemis nobillis* and *Matricaria chamomilla*) helps to prevent damping off in seedlings (as does careful watering and good ventilation). Add a handful of flowers to 3 cups of hot water and steep for two hours. Strain and use. Chamomile has an ancient reputation for benefiting nearby plants and is a valuable addition to the compost heap.

Pests

Dried crushed tansy leaves (*Tanacetum vulgare*) repel ants, flies, fleas and other insects. Sprinkle on the ground to deter these pests. Rich in potassium, the herb is an excellent compost plant and the flowers attract many beneficial insects.

All types of chillies make a potent deterrent for mice, rats and other rodents including squirrels. Sprinkle fresh or dried chopped chillies to discourage them from eating pea, squash and other seeds either in the greenhouse or garden. Always be very careful when chopping and sprinkling chillies. Wash your hands thoroughly and especially avoid touching the eyes or other sensitive areas.

Mice – and slugs too! – also dislike a spray made from southernwood or wormwood. Simmer 1 cup of fresh herb with 3 cups of water and cool, still covered, for 6 hours. Strain and spray onto the soil. Alternatively, use pieces of the fresh or dried herb, crushing the leaves first, to repel rodents.

Biodynamics

Originating out of the work of Rudolf Steiner, biodynamic agriculture shares many of the same principles and methods as other organic production approaches. Yet it differs in two major additional ways: the compost preparations it advocates (which includes no less than the urinary bladders of red deer being stuffed with yarrow blossoms and buried in the earth between summer and the following spring), and the fact that it takes into consideration the celestial and terrestrial influences on the plants. It specifies what time of the month (i.e. phase of the moon) is best for all stages of growing – planting, cultivating and harvesting – for each variety of plant that we grow.

This all sounds wacky at first glance, and biodynamics does receive a lot of criticism – the fact that it has been proven to be very successful seemingly being secondary to the fact that science can't seem to work out exactly why.

Because it views a piece of land holistically, within which all the parts – soil, people, plants, animals, water – are interdependent and considered in their relationships to one another, it makes it a particularly useful tool for anyone wanting to grow their food without any need for external inputs. If this is a method you'd like to understand in more depth, I'd recommend Hilary Wright's *Biodynamic Gardening: For Health and Taste*, or any other book on the subject (especially Steiner's writings) depending on your previous knowledge and experience of it. Better still, I'd spend some time volunteering on a biodynamic farm to understand it in practice.

Forest Gardening

One wrung down, below wild food, on my POP model for food is forest gardening. Forest gardens have the potential to optimise both vertical and horizontal space through their layered design of trees, shrubs and ground covering vegetation, making them ideal for small growing spaces in cities.

Martin Crawford[169] describes them as gardens "modelled on the structure of young natural woodland, utilising plants of direct and indirect benefit to people". This often means edible crops (fruits and mostly perennial vegetables), but the useful plants which they have the potential to abundantly produce can be used for cordage, dyes, firewood, medicinal purposes, furniture, basketry materials, poles and canes (useful for normal gardening), spices, soaps, honey, building materials, salads and herbs, mushrooms, nuts and seeds and sap products. You can see why I'm a fan.

A well designed forest garden ought to be at the core of moneyless living for anyone, regardless of whether they live in a rural or urban setting. It represents the best closed loop model, outside of the Wilderness, that I have seen in practice. A very well designed forest garden requires little or no composting or manuring, simply by using multi-purpose plants such as the autumn olive, a crop I have fallen in love with. Not only do these produce great fruit for jams, they also just happen to be an excellent nitrogen fixer for plants living in the layers below them, due to their ability to "convert free air nitrogen into fixed nitrogen for eventual plant protein assimilation and storage".[170]

Supplemented with some annual and wild food crops, forest gardens will play a central role in the moneyless micro-economies of the future, and they are at the core of how I intend to meet my needs over the coming years. The only downside is that they require a long-term perspective towards life (insofar as that can ever be a bad thing) – depending on their size and the crops planted, they can take many years to reach maturity, so harvests will be low to begin with (which largely explains their otherwise inexplicable absence from the hundreds of thousands of under-utilised gardens of rented accommodation in cities).

AGROFORESTRY: ESSENTIAL FOR A SUSTAINABLE FUTURE

Martin Crawford is Director of the Agroforestry Research Trust.[171] His books include *Creating a Forest Garden*[172] and *How to Grow Perennial Vegetables*

Agroforestry is the growing of trees or shrubs with other agricultural crops. It can range from lines of trees intercropped with a cereal like wheat, to fully integrated forest garden systems incorporating trees, shrubs and perennial crops in a self-sustaining system.

Over the last few hundred years almost all the research and agricultural effort has been focussed on annual plants, to the extent that most of the world's population depends on them. This wasn't always the case, though, and many people have forgotten that the mass growing of annuals on a field scale is never going to be sustainable because they take a huge amount of energy to grow. As long as energy is cheap and available they can continue their dominance – but it is clear now that energy is not going to remain cheap for much longer.

We need to move much more towards perennial crops – whether it be tree-based crops (for example, nuts to take the place of some of the cereals) or smaller plants such as perennial onions. In other words, we need a move towards agroforestry.

Perennial plants, once established, take much less work to maintain than annuals – you only have to plant once (in a long while anyway), and most plants look after themselves with far less susceptibility to pests, diseases or the vagaries of the weather than annuals.

Perennial plant products are often more nutritious than their annual counterparts too, because their roots systems are larger and can get more nutrients out of the soil.

Sustainable growing requires a change in attitudes too. Agriculture has been misled into thinking that every bit of ground needs to be productive – in other words needs to have a crop coming from it. This is never going to be sustainable. Truly sustainable growing systems must devote a proportion of the land to plants with 'system' functions – in other words, plants which increase the health and resilience of the total growing system (whether or not they produce a crop). Such plants would usually include nitrogen-fixing species (to make the use of nitrogen fertilisers unnecessary), and also plants to deter pests and diseases by, for example, attracting predators of likely pests or by confusing pests with aromatic emissions.

The most sustainable systems will be closed-loop systems, where no extra nutrients are brought in and the growing system sustains itself. Forest gardens are an example of this.

Agroforestry systems are less suited to very large scale production than monocultures, so by their nature they will be smaller scale – which also means that they are much more likely to be integrated far better with their local economy: crops are likely to be sold and used locally, so the mass transportation of food should decrease significantly as these systems become more popular.

They have many other benefits – wildlife value is very high, they can provide shelter and thus reduce energy usage for heating or cooling, and so on. Once understood we'll wonder how we ever did without them!

No-dig gardening

Conventional modern agriculturalists, and their books, almost always advocate digging the soil as if it was some sort of universal truth that needs no qualifying. In fairness, it is well intentioned advice and it is recommended by them for a number of reasons: to incorporate manures and composts into the soil, to open it up from compaction (often caused by heavy machinery), to loosen the soil and produce a crumbly tilth, and to bury weeds. Most of these reasons are flawed and come from a lack of understanding of what the soil actually needs, resulting in lots of unnecessary graft and damage to the very ecosystem on which our lives depends. Needless to say, such results as these are not exactly the goals of moneyless living.

Showing a new (or rather, old) way of growing food without disrupting these delicate, finely tuned systems, and saving you from a life of drudgery into the bargain, are pioneers of the no-dig method such as Charles Dowding.

THE NO DIG (NO-TILL) METHOD

Charles Dowding, author of *Organic Gardening: The Natural No-dig Way* and *How to Grow Winter Vegetables*[173]

My advice for growing your own food is to garden little and often, to treasure your soil and to be realistic in what you attempt. Supermarkets have created an attractive impression of year-round abundance and it is false. Every soil and climate is different so you must adapt to local conditions and seasons, ensuring that whatever you sow and plant comes to fruition. Growing the right food for your climate and locality, although bringing you less food range, will result in tastier meals and extra vitality every day.

Some homework before starting is a great investment and helps avoid sowing the wrong seeds, or growing plants in the wrong way. For example, cauliflowers need a lot of space and tend to mature all together, aubergines are a hot climate vegetable which are unproductive in Britain, and tomatoes as well as potatoes will succumb to fungal blight if it rains regularly when their fruit and tubers are developing. So for example, in my damp climate I grow just a few caulis, one or two aubergine plants in a polytunnel, tomatoes only where their leaves can be kept dry, and varieties of second early potato which mature before the blight arrives.

Our most precious resource for growing healthy food is soil and it needs careful attention, but does not need to be dug or cultivated, except by its inhabitants. Worms and other soil life do the job better than we ever can, leaving soil aerated and firm at the same time, with a stable structure which can bear the weight of a gardener and wheelbarrow. There is a common misunderstanding that soil needs to be loose and fluffy for growing food, and this is absolutely wrong: I garden on dense clay and roots travel happily through my soil, which has been undisturbed for fourteen years.

Soil improves when fed with organic matter and this serves to increase the amount of both air and nutrients. In moist climates I recommend a thin mulch of compost to feed soil life, and hence all plants growing in that soil. In dry climates a moisture retaining mulch has a similarly beneficial effect, but is not a good idea for growing annual vegetables where rainfall is common, because damp mulches of half rotted organic matter encourage slug damage.

We should all be able to nourish our own soil with humanure (and litter from any animals we keep) but attitudes need to change in order to allow this if food is being sold. Stacking manure for at least six months allows it to compost and retain nutrients when spread. Once a soil is fertile it is possible to 'close the loop' and keep it productive with your own waste materials, including all weeds and garden residues, preferably composted. But infertile soils will improve no end if you can import an initial, one-off dressing of compost or manure on the surface.

Should you have more land than is needed to grow food, green manures can be sown to build up soil humus, but this is slower than using compost and before growing vegetables again, you need to allow time after they mature for decomposition in the soil, even if you dig them in, which reduces their value compared to using a mulch. I often feel that the space devoted to green manures could be sown or planted with a second vegetable instead, and that time spent on growing and killing green manures would be more profitably spent on scrounging extra additions for the compost heap from verges and edges. Remember also that weeds will grow and set seed amongst green manures, unless you weed them as if they are a crop.

Fruit can be cropped at the same time as vegetables and herbs, but be careful to choose the right kind of tree. In Britain I find that apples complement many vegetables, with a spacing of about four metres square, for trees that are grafted on medium size rootstocks. I have trained them in espalier style, to increase light available to vegetables underneath. On the other hand I have not succeeded in growing annual plants under plum and apricot trees. Before planting trees, do as much research as you can to be sure of their suitability and productivity, because it will be years rather than months before you know any results, and that is a long wait if it is an unproductive or greedy tree!

Perennial vegetables are an option and are generally considered quite easy, but bear in mind a few things: the range of food is less extensive than from annual vegetables, some flavours need getting used to, such as small leaved lime instead of lettuce, harvesting may take longer (small wild raspberries compared with garden varieties such as Autumn Bliss), there are no native perennial root vegetables in Britain for a substantial meal, an issue in winter when leaves and fruits are scarce, and perennials are not zero maintenance, still needing some clearing and tidying.

For fast and abundant results, salad leaves are wonderful and offer a great range of flavours. Keep soil around salads clear of weeds at all times and also clear any overgrowing, surrounding vegetation to reduce slugs. Sow seasonally and pick with fingers rather than a knife, so that plants live for longer. Seasonal salads means sowing lettuce, spinach and pea shoots in spring, then endives, chicories, more lettuce and kale in high summer, oriental leaves and herbs such as coriander and chervil in late summer, followed by a wonderful range of winter cropping plants in early September. If you can afford them some shelter, it is possible to have tasty leaves every day of the year, from a small area.

Guerrilla gardening

This most recent of gardening methods usually involves gardening some other person's land without their express permission. This land is usually neglected or abandoned by its legal owner, and in effect the guerrilla gardener is often a productive squatter who doesn't even bother to move in – guerrilla gardeners should be in demand! It is obvious that, for some, this is a political statement about land ownership, but it is also a way for some people to access soil and grow their own food – not just for themselves, but often for others in their community.

Depending on the motivations and locations of guerrilla gardening squads, this can involve working in the middle of the night. Other groups make a point of being seen, in order to provoke thought about the neglect of potentially productive land in a world that needs to rapidly localise – this means that many teams also go out in waking hours, you'll be relieved to hear.

If you want to set up your own guerrilla gardening cell, or join an existing one, go to GuerrillaGardening(.org)[174] and get involved. Not only will you get to meet a network of like-minded people, it's also another way to meet your food needs for free and turn wasteland into something productive.

SKIPPING

Known as dumpster diving in the US, skipping food is the term given to the act of salvaging food that has, for one reason or another, ended up in somebody's bin – usually that of a supermarket. If you live in an urban environment and want to live moneylessly, utilising waste food will play an important part, due to the general lack of sufficient growing space in built up areas to produce all of your nutritional and calorific requirements. The fact that an average UK household wastes 25% of its food (and "an estimated 20 million tonnes of food is wasted in Britain from the plough to the plate"[175]) is depressing on many levels; the good news for you is that there will be no end of choice for dinner.

Technically, taking food out of someone else's bin is illegal, as it – rather bizarrely – is still regarded as their property, despite it being blatantly obvious that they no longer want it. Our council's waste collectors seem pretty confident that its legal owners no longer want it when they come to pick it up every week. That said, it is highly unlikely that you would ever be convicted, or even prosecuted, for the offence of 'stealing' waste. The only case I'm aware of is that of Sacha Hall, who got a twelve month conditional discharge for lessening the levels of waste within Tesco's bins, but that case was lambasted enough in the media to deter other cases being brought against freegans.[176] A much more likely scenario, if you are caught, is that you'll receive a reasonably friendly ticking off from a police officer, have your name taken and told to move on. If you'd prefer to avoid that, I recommend going on a reconnaissance mission to the skip's site before entering. When you feel that you know a time when the chances of anyone being around is unlikely (night time is good, as it is also dark), go there as often as you feel it is worth it. Sometimes you'll go and find everything you need, other times you'll find nothing, whilst on another occasion you may find a hundred chocolate bars and a years supply of baked beans. Bring along an 8mm triangular key, the type you use for a gas meter box, to gain you access to the bin; if you don't have one, ask for one from the Freeconomy network.

I personally feel we've an obligation to use every ounce of food we can, given the amount of energy, destruction and exploitation that is embodied in our diet today, coupled with the fact that half the world is undernourished. Word of warning: I wouldn't recommend living off a purely skipped diet, unless it contains a lot of fruit and vegetables that are sufficiently alive to still be nutritious. If the weather is warm and you suspect that meat or dairy has been in the bin for a while, then there are obvious risks attached which you should strongly consider. As a general rule, if in doubt don't eat it and put it back. If you have a compost heap yourself (or your community allotment has one), the fruit and vegetables you find in supermarket bins will be suitable for it, even if they are not fit for you belly, so it may still be worth taking if you can motivate yourself to do so.

OTHER IDEAS

Eggs

One win-win way of getting a portion of your protein needs met without money is to rehome ex-battery chickens through organisations such as the British Hen Welfare Trust.[177] The hens – whom will have led heartbreaking lives up to that point but whom, surprisingly, can make a very quick recovery once they are introduced to healthy conditions – get a chance to start over again and live a life in which all their needs are met and where they can do all the things that hens like to do, like scratch and forage around. As well as knowing you've given an abused animal its freedom, you also get to eat eggs that, contrary to popular belief, the vast majority of ex-bats will continue to lay (initially the eggs may get bigger in size and eventually get laid less frequently).

If you have some hens, you may also want to get a cockerel.[178] The ladies will happily lay eggs without the man around, but as chickens need a pecking order keeping a cockerel will stop the girls from fighting amongst themselves and from wandering off too far. If you decide you do want to keep a cockerel and you have housemates or neighbours close by, you may want to talk to them first about it as he will cockadoodledoo at the crack of dawn, and don't just assume everyone (including yourself) will be OK with that. Usually neighbours can be persuaded with a regular supply of excess eggs, but as always your unique circumstances will dictate what is best for everyone involved.

How you feed them depends on your situation. If you have a big garden, and it is designed with the chickens dietary needs in mind, you should be able to feed them without any commercial feed – manufacturers' websites would have you believe otherwise, but surprisingly chickens did actually eat and survive prior to industrial civilisation and pet shops. If you live with a small garden you probably won't have enough room to provide for all their needs, and in such circumstances you should seriously consider whether or not your living situation is suitable. If you decide it is sufficient, it will be appropriate to import some of their dietary needs into the system, which could potentially be done by means other than money, such as bartering, foraging or skipping.

You can easily build a safe and comfortable coop for your chickens out of salvaged materials at no cost, and the World Wide Web is replete with designs on how to do so. For a simple beginners guide to keeping chickens, the late Katie Thear's books, such as *Starting with Chickens*,[179] are very useful, but there are many books and free online resources that can help you get started.

Honey

The bee is under attack from industrial civilisation. All sorts of reasons are cited for their demise, from neonicotinoid pesticides, electromagnetic radiation by mobile phones and their accompanying towers to a lack of biodiversity, global warming and the Varroa destructer. A mixture of all of the above and other factors, some of which we may not even be aware of yet, is in all likelihood responsible for some frightening statistics. According to the *Centre for Ecology and Hydrology*, three of the 25 native British species of bumblebee have recently gone extinct, over 50% of the remaining species have suffered declines of up to 70% since the 1970s[180] and 25% of native bees are on the Red Data Book list of endangered or threatened species. This would be disturbing news even if bees weren't a crucial part of the world's ecosystems and life on Earth; the fact they are should demand immediate action from us all on the matter.

If that isn't enough reason to provide habitat for all species of bees, there is an added incentive to keep one subset in particular, the honeybee: yes you've guessed it, honey. Honey is a very healthy replacement for bought-in sweeteners such as white refined sugar, and has many medicinal properties. Not only that, honeybees are important pollinators for your other food crops and, as we'll see in chapter eleven, can provide you with other materials that will help you localise and demonetise your life.

If looking after bees is something you feel inspired to do, it is best to educate yourself fully first. Spend time with a local beekeeper learning the art, join your nearest beekeeping association and borrow a good book on the subject. When you feel competent, you can build yourself a simple horizontal beehive without bee frames, a model which is ideal for a beginner and someone who wants to create a closed-loop economy.[181] Such a design means your bees produce both honey and – because they have to build the entire comb themselves – lots of beeswax. Bees are great for people with little space as a hive takes up little room in your backyard.

Strangely enough, honeybees do not exist solely to sweeten flapjacks and herbal teas for humans. Ideally, we'd all wean ourselves off the need for sweet things and leave the honeybee with the food it has laboured hard for. If we want to preserve biodiversity, we would be much better off undertaking what is known as natural beekeeping, a much more bee-centric approach to beekeeping.[182] It is easy to provide habitat for other species of bees, and one of the best ways to do so is to make them a bee hotel.

Simply create a small three- or four-sided frame out of untreated planks that are around 10-15cm in width, before packing it full of bamboo canes or old flower stems that are cut to the same depth as the box you've just made. This box should be fairly small but big enough to fit 10-20 canes or stems (making sure they are as straight as possible) along each side, and should also include an overhang to protect it from the rain. Once it is packed well enough that it feels solid, simply hang it up on a south-facing wall that isn't exposed to the worst of the elements. You can also use bits of rotten wood with woodworm holes in them, or old air bricks, for a similar effect. Come spring you'll have some new neighbours move into your humble accommodation who'll start working for you and the rest of life on Earth – for free.

One note about 'local' honey: if you're taking all of your honey, as opposed to just any excess they produce, and then replacing it with sugar, not only is it unfair to the honeybee but it is also misleading to say that it is local; embodied in it are the food miles of the sugar you imported into your system.

Storing your produce

If you live in a temperate climate such as the UK's, storing your summer and autumn produce is something you really should consider if you don't fancy eating kale and the like for every meal during the winter. Various methods are at hand, including making jam, chutney, juices, drying, pickling and dry storage (for things like potatoes). How to store each fruit and vegetable is a book in itself, and the best I have found on the subject is Piers Warren's aptly named *How to Store your Garden Produce.*[183] Again, Freecycle is very useful if you're looking for the containers to store your food in.

If you ever need glass jars or bottles of various shapes and sizes, just do the rounds of the recycling bins of some street in my area on the morning the recycling gets put out each week – you could start a jam factory from the amount of jars you can find during one morning's stroll.

Be careful not to fall into the trap of thinking that you need to import lots of food stuffs into your own food system in order to preserve that which you grow or forage – people have been storing their food in the UK long before industrialised processes and fossil fuels came along. I recommend making jam using nothing more than plums (which you can grow or forage) and apple juice (that hopefully you've picked and pressed yourself) – the stones in the plums already have all the pectin you'll need, whilst the apple juice is a good and healthy replacement for sugar. What is important is to slowly learn the skills you'll need to preserve food – the best way to do this is by asking some of the elders of your community who hold so much unappreciated knowledge that needs to be tapped before it is lost. Doing so also re-establishes our elders as having the deserved and crucial role in society they once had and still ought to have, and the social benefits of this are very much underestimated.

Community orchards and the Abundance project

Community orchards are simply orchards created and maintained by local people, for local people. All you need to set one up is a bunch of enthusiastic people, some land (local councils often have land they are willing to allow community groups to look after) and a legal structure of some sort, which the *Community Orchards Handbook*[184] has lots of usefulness information to help you with. Such projects aren't just a great way of growing food such as fruits and nuts, they get local people together, growing food for themselves and each other, for workshops and courses designed to keep traditional skills such as tree grafting and planting alive, and for seasonal events such as wassailing.

Community orchards do take time to become productive, so it does involve holding a medium- to long-term perspective. If you're a bit less patient than that, there is no need to wait around while it grows. Abundance, a project originally created by a group called Grow Sheffield but which has since spread throughout the country, states that "each year hundreds of fruit trees go unpicked either because people don't notice them, may not be physically able to harvest them or [because] there are just too many fruits at one time". It was in response to this reality that they set up the first group in 2007. Its model is simple – a group of residents set up mutually beneficial links with other local people who have fruit trees they don't utilise, providing themselves with fruit and redistributing any surpluses to the rest of the community through cafés, nurseries, Sure Starts and other residents.

If you want food for free and an opportunity to get involved in something really positive in your local area, then why not find out if there is an established group in your local area? If there isn't, then contact the Abundance Manchester team[185] and ask them how best to go about it. To find a core group with which to start it, you could just send a group email out to your local Freeconomy group proposing such a venture. Alternatively, if you have a fruit tree whose harvest you want to share (and eat some of yourself), get in touch with them also. For more information, I recommend their book *The Abundance Handbook: A guide to urban fruit harvesting.*[186]

WATER

Even more important than food, is water. Water should be the easiest thing in the world to get without money, given its abundance on the planet. As hard as it is for us to imagine, there was once a time when we could cup it in our hands and drink it straight from a river or stream, tasting nothing like what most of us think water tastes like today. In a few remote, uncivilised places it is still possible to drink clean, fresh water. I had the pleasure of being able to do so once when I was living at the top of a mountain in the Mangamuka Forest in the Northlands of New Zealand. We were the first people downstream, and there wasn't another human being in sight for many miles. The river that flowed next to my tent was so clear that, when it was still, looking at its bed was like looking through a pane of glass. It tasted sublime, unlike any water I had tasted before. The first time I drank from it I realised I had never drunk water before, the way it should be, the way it once was. We bathed in that river, but to ensure it stayed pristine the others who lived there (I was soapless by this stage) would lather themselves up on the bank and fully rinse themselves off before getting back in the water, to ensure that the next people downstream also had a pure water supply. In relation to our land, atmosphere and water, we would do well to think of the next generation as those neighbours who live downstream.

If you live in a rural setting, getting enough water shouldn't be too difficult if you know how and have the means. However, if you are in the city this is a lot trickier for obvious reasons. In fact, the water issue is one of the reasons why I believe cities to be inherently unsustainable, as the water needs of millions of people living on top of each other can only be met by highly industrialised means, involving processes that are polluting our host and destroying it's ability to home us. Therefore, complete moneyless living *en masse* will only happen through land reform and a complete redesign of the way we live.

Nevertheless, there is much you can do in the meantime, and water conservation methods such as those I mention at the start of chapter seven, along with using a compost toilet, will all make important contributions. I will give you a menu of options that I hope are wide enough in scope to cover whatever your particular situation involves. With all the options below, I would get the water tested to make sure it is drinkable.

Water wells and bore holes

A well is created by excavating a piece of land for the purpose of accessing the groundwater of underground aquifers – the depth and radius of the excavation depends on how close to the surface the aquifer lies. Boreholes are similar, but are more like a narrow shaft and require drilling of one form or another. These can be expensive to create in the first instance unless you can tap into a spring that is near the surface. However, once you've done it it is there for life, as long as it doesn't run dry, providing you with a source of clean, non-chlorinated water. To find the right location for either of these, ask around your neighbours to find out if one of them is a water diviner with an unquenchable thirst for dowsing.

Until the last few hundred years, water wells played a hugely important role in hydrating the people of many rural areas, and in some parts of the world this is still very much the norm today. But because so many of us now dwell in urban areas, it's not something we have to think about anymore. Water comes from a tap. But what would happen if the economic mechanisms that facilitated such centralised and complex water systems ground to a halt, and those chlorinated water taps eventually ran dry?

Wells are still used even in the global West, but most are now created using high technology techniques such as boring, drilling or driving, and involve electrical pumps in their daily use. If you are intending to live off-grid on a piece of land, there is a temptation just to design in an electrically pumped well, as a decent solar panel would power it. Yet again I ask the question – what would happen if the global infrastructure, which manufactures the parts of the leisure batteries and photovoltaics that power your pump, collapsed? You'd be left with a well that had been designed for a level of technology you could no longer support.

It is for this reason, along with the fact that they are packed full of embodied energy and ecological destruction, that I argue against using electrical pumps. Many moneyless options are available, including everything from the age old (and my personal favourite, purely for romantic reasons) bucket to a very clever bicycle powered pump,[187] a device which not only builds resilience in your system but also keeps you fit and saves you a gym subscription as a bonus.

Rainwater Harvesting

Collecting rainwater is simple and the fact that so few of us bother to do it is yet another example of the wastefulness that comes with money's marriage to the principles of the economies of scale and division of labour. Rain falls from the sky, hits a surface (usually a roof), runs into some guttering, down some piping and into a water butt that is raised as high of the ground as is optimum for you. It can get more complex than that depending on what your needs are, but it really doesn't need to be. It has been happening since the days before Christ and we all really ought to be doing it, as part of a way of living which treats every drop of water with the respect it deserves.

Guttering and butts these days are usually made from plastics, but you can easily find suitable receptacles for the butts on Freecycle or from businesses (such as factories, warehouses and industrial-scale caterers) who regularly discard large storage containers that could fit the job. This is the only time you'll hear me say this but, in relation to water storage devices, big is beautiful, and I'd recommend finding yourself the biggest one that you can accommodate.

If you have another source of water, such as a well, then rainwater harvesting works as a supplementary source. Because the stored rainwater will often contain contaminants ranging from air pollutants to faeces, it is best not to be considered for potable uses and instead for things like watering the garden (not directly on edibles however), washing your clothes and water cannoning peaceful protesters at demonstrations.

There has been word of water companies contemplating charging people for this as they claim it is 'their' water – what on Earth gives them the audacity to claim such a thing, I don't know, but they are. My answer to them will be always be this: *don't worry, you'll get your water – it's just going to see the insides of my bladder on its way to you.* All roads lead to home, after all.

Springs, streams and rivers

For most of you who live in towns and cities, this will probably not be a realistic option. Springs are not unlike wells, the main difference being the fact that Nature brings the aquifer to the ground surface all by Herself. One example is a famous spring called Chalice Well in Glastonbury, and I've filled up my bottles and containers with its delicious water many times. There is no reason why nearby residents couldn't go there, or the white spring across from it, and fill their humble receptacles, and I know many who do. The water that comes out is full of iron and has a very unique taste, and is very good for you. With a bit of exploration, you may also find one near where you live, but this is obviously much more likely if you live rurally. Springs can sometimes need filters, such as a sand filter (which has no consumables and requires little maintenance), so testing the water is a wise first step.

Streams and rivers these days are very likely to be polluted, especially in and around towns and cities, or near industrial scale farms in the countryside. Again, test to find out. Regardless, as long as you have the means to boil and purify it, there is no reason why you could not use this water. Of course this isn't anywhere near as convenient as getting water from the mains, but this latter method is inherently unsustainable and therefore, by its definition, will have to come to an end sometime.

CHAPTER 9

WASHING

Whenever I begin Q&A sessions after talks I give on moneyless living, I already know that the first three questions will focus on something to do with cleanliness or hygiene – how I wipe my arse and the like. It's revealing how we seem to associate having no money with body odour, bad breath, dirty clothes, filthy bums and general stickiness. The extent to which we believe this to be true directly correlates to the extent our minds have been completely controlled and manipulated by the likes of Johnson & Johnson, Proctor & Gamble and Unilever, all of whom push their endless new products on us in what can only be thought of as a purely altruistic attempt to make our lives that little bit cleaner. Apparently, until they came along with their crystal clean brands – which by the look of their adverts I assume are made up of nothing less than roses, gold dust, diamonds, the pubic hairs of virgin angels, love, freshly squeezed lemons and sodium lauryl sulphate – we all stunk to the high heavens.

I gave up using any soap years before I gave up money, and my skin has never been more grateful for the reprieve. Skin is a little micro ecosystem in itself, and using soap is, in my book, on a par with cultivating the soil – I can see why people do it, but it's the shenanigans of a people who don't fully appreciate the intricacies of ecosystems, and the long-term damage we can do from what initially seems like harmless, innocent behaviour. Then again, I possess a terribly weak sense of smell, so it may be that I pong and that English people are just much too polite to tell me.

Since I've been *The Soapless Man* for many years now, my overriding advice on most things in relation to hygiene is to use water and little else. There rarely is any need for anything more than that, with a few exceptions. That said, receiving hundreds of post-talk questions has helped me understand that most of you will want something a bit more substantial – something more antibacterial, antifungal, antilife – than just water.

Some of my tips in this chapter will have come through personal experience from my presoapless days, others I'll have experimented with to some extent since going moneyless (clothes and teeth in particular), and the rest will have come from trusted sources.

Apart from cleaning agents, I'll also outline the moneyless infrastructure you need to keep clean. If you think staying clean and fresh without money is a step too far for you, consider lying back for hours in a wood fired hot tub, under a starry winter sky staring into your lover's moonlit eyes.

WASHING OURSELVES

We were washing ourselves a long time before the advent of money. So how did we do it? We used the water bodies as they are – seas, rivers and lakes. And these are still the only truly moneyless and sustainable options today, as they rely on nothing from industrialisation and its money dependent economies of scale and division of labour. The act of going for a swim in one of them sufficed at one point in time. Such methods are at the top of my POP model for washing.

For various reasons, from the fact that most of us will now live many miles from a water body to the reality that we're all a bit too soft to get into cold water, many of you may not consider this a realistic option. Not to worry, there are a few rungs lower on the POP ladder that would make a big difference to your ability to live with less dependency on money.

Showers

In terms of speed and water usage, showers have a lot going for them. If you live in a block of flats with no outside space, but have a south-facing window, your best bet to get free hot water (other than solar thermal, which I look in chapter eleven) is by using a solar shower, which you could leave by the inside of the window. A solar shower sounds technical, but is no more than a black plastic bag with a tube coming out of the end of it, with a valve at the end to control flow. The black colour will absorb the sun's heat and increase the temperature of the water inside. My advice is to put this out all day and have your shower in the evening. Non-coincidentally, you'll want a shower more often when the weather is hot, which are generally the type of days when you'll be able to have a decently warm shower from one of these.

Other than that, the best you're going to be able to do is conserve water – question how often you really need to wash, and then stay in no longer than you need to.

If you want a more year round solution to your showering needs, build yourself a wood-fired shower unit using materials you've obtained from gift economy websites such as Freegle or a skip. You'll need a couple of old radiators and a water butt ideally, all plumbed into a shower head in some sort of private cubicle, unless you are lucky enough to live in a part of the world that doesn't see the naked body as something filthy and repugnant to the human eye.

Baths

Hot tubs are one of my favourite things in the world. For it to be a moneyless tub, you have a range of options. Normal enamel tubs are easy to find in skips of recently decorated houses, and a quick post on Freecycle will probably result in more offers than you can reply to. If you want something a bit bigger, an old horse trough will also do a great job. For the less industrial feel, you could also copy the Japanese *furo*, which is a bathtub made from redwood planks, which swell as they fill with water and "seal the seams where the boards"[188] meet.

You're then going to need a water supply, a wood-burning system and ideally some cob to both insulate and beautify it. This is all a bit of an art, and to get yourself clued up I'd recommend Becky Bee's book *The Best Hot Tub Ever*.

BODIES

Facial and body soap

It is no coincidence that the same companies that sell you soap, sell you moisturiser. When you use soap, you strip away much of the goodness and moisture as well as what we think of as 'dirt'. The result being that we then become dependent on the same companies that sold us this moisture-robbing agent in the first place to put the moisture back in. They get to sell us two products when none were needed in the first place.

There is absolutely no need for soap, and the rest of the animal kingdom would attest to this. People who don't wash their hair for a few months are regularly quoted as saying their hair starts to clean itself. The same is true for skin. When I gave up soap many years ago, I'll admit it felt a little strange at first. I really wanted to just lather myself up in the shower. But after a week or two that craving faded. My skin is thankful for it too, as it is healthier than ever, and no longer addicted to something that it never needed in the first place to stay clean.

That said, the main reason I can live without soap is that I generally eat a very healthy diet: wholegrains, fruits, nuts, vegetables and clean fresh water, the odd herb tea and little else. All organic and fresh. If you put good stuff in, what comes out will smell fine. If you put junk in, what comes out will smell like junk. It's that simple.

If you drink a lot of coffee or fizzy drinks, smoke a lot of tobacco, or regularly eat processed food, then unfortunately you may need something more than water to stay smelling fresh and clean. I'd recommend using soapwort (*Saponaria officinalis*). It contains saponins, and it causes solutions that contain it to lather up, in a similar way to conventional modern soap. If you're of a foraging persuasion and know your local history, you may find this plant still growing wild near the sites of old Roman baths. When you stop and think about it, it makes perfect sense to grow your soap right next to where you'll need it. Today we call this Permaculture; back then they called it common sense. The problem is that we don't think like our forebears any more, as we can easily pick up something flavoured with the essence of jojoba and raw cocoa instead.

Failing having an old Roman bath nearby, you can also find soapwort close to streams and in damp woods and hedgerows. It's an easy plant to grow – it's a perennial, pest and disease free, likes rich soil but it can cope with dry and generally poor soil, and is very easy to look after. Keep a little eye on it however, as it can spread quickly in richer soils.

Soapwort can be used for all skin types (it's pH balanced for skin and hair, it's mild and has a refreshing feel about it). To turn your plant into a wonderfully mild facial and body soap, I'd recommend the following method:

- Chop 1 cup worth of fresh soapwort leaves, stems and root (if you have already dried and ground the root for winter use, use two tablespoons of it in two cups of water instead).

- Chop up about 5-7 tablespoons of fresh herbs, depending on how strong you want it. You can add other herbs to the mix, depending on your skin type. For dryish to normal skin, use lady's mantle. If your skin can be slightly oily, lemon balm and rosemary should do the trick. For very oily skin, yarrow, mint and sage work well. Regardless of what your skin is like, you can add lemon verbena, nettles, comfrey, chamomile or elderflower. Add this to the soapwort and soak in 1 pint of water overnight.

- It is common practice to then boil this mixture the next day, which is what I have done in the past. However, herbalist and author Jekka McVicar[189] recommends not boiling it as it can decompose the active ingredient. Therefore heat it up very well until it suds up a little (because it thankfully doesn't contain sodium lauryl sulphate, it won't have the level of suds you normally expect in soap – a very good thing).

- Once it has cooled, strain the liquid using muslin, and bottle it. It should keep in a cold place for up to about a week.

- Never take internally as it is mildly poisonous.

This recipe is also the second best makeup remover I know of. Realising that you're absolutely beautiful just the way you are tops the list. Soapwort can also help heal mild acne, especially if you add some marigold to it. If you really want to cure acne for good, I would highly recommend finding a Chinese herbalist in your local Freeconomy group. I tried every conventional facewash as a child, but it wasn't until I took Chinese herbs for it that I finally got rid of it. Considering that your skin is your body's biggest organ, it goes without saying that eating fresh organic fruit and vegetables (something I never did as a child) will help keep your skin healthy also.

Hand soap

Wood ash and water is an old tried and trusted method. Again, it's counter-intuitive to us today, but it works. Don't leave it on too long though as it will make your hands dry, and remember to rinse quickly. If you don't have that at hand, I'd chop the leaves of either New Jersey Tea or Mock Orange[190] (two shrubs that I'd recommend for your forest garden) and soaking them for a few hours.

Deodorant

Personally, I like the natural smell of people. Deodorant is used to mask the symptoms of an unhealthy diet. If you do want a moneyless deodorant, however, you can grow bay leaves and hyssop, make a herbal infusion out of them and smear it over your filthy body until your heart is content. I'd prefer to smell you though.

Moisturisers and toners

Aloe vera juice and gel, which naturally contains salicylic acid, is great both as a toner and a moisturiser, and is renowned for its uses in dealing with sunburn. Aloe plants grow fine indoors in the UK, and my advice is to keep as many plants as you can fit on your windowsill. Always harvest the biggest leaves first. There really is no need to fork out for expensive aloe vera based moisturisers from your pharmacy or health food shop.

Bums and toilet paper

The first question you should ask yourself is – do you need it? I've no doubt that almost everyone will say yes! But many cultures use water to clean their bums, and considering we use water for all other parts of our body, there would seem to be a lot of logic in that. If you do prefer to have a wipe, then there are a number of options.

First, you can approach your local newsagents and ask them if they're happy for you to take a couple of copies of the previous day's papers that they have to normally throw out. For bum wiping, I'd recommend the broadsheets as you get a long strip out of them, or ironically, last week's *Trade-it* magazine, partially for the beautiful irony, partially because it's full of shit anyway, but mainly because the paper they use just feels nice.

If that's all a little too industrial for you, then there are methods that were normal and worked well for thousands of years. Similarly to your dishes, pine cones (choose the softer, decomposing ones from the forest floor) and big clumps of grass work well. Anything broadleaved is good, though take care not to use any leaves that are toxic or poisonous to humans; a dock leaf will suffice, its anti-inflammatory qualities are particularly soothing if you've been on the curry the night before. If you are striving for Enlightenment and want to transcend the mundane material world, then use a bunch of stinging nettles and that will test your mettle. Surprisingly, smooth rocks with no sharp edges also work well, and the more porous the better. If you're lucky enough to have moss at hand in an emergency situation, go for that. If it's winter and all of the above are covered in a icy white blanket, then I'd advice using that blanket. Snow certainly isn't the most appealing option at 6am on a winter's morning, but that's sometimes what living ecologically means, so man-up and deal with it!

I've no doubt some of you will feel horrified about some of these options – I did to begin with – but that's more of a reflection of our odd culture than the methods themselves. Remember one thing: it's only poo, and it came from you in the first place!

TEETH AND MOUTH

Most people are concerned about keeping their teeth healthy and clean. Yet we get our toothpastes, toothbrushes and mouthwash from the supermarket or chemist, and it is hardly controversial to say that these are not sustainable methods of doing so. In cleaning our teeth today, we pollute our rivers, air and land. The good news is that there are moneyless, localised solutions available. Whether or not you'll actually want to use them is a different question, but the options below are the types you'll use if you want absolutely sustainable forms of mouth hygiene. With all of these, take further advice about whether they are suitable for you from an expert if you are concerned. You may come up with your own solutions the more you explore it.

Toothpaste

I've used a mixture of ground up wild fennel seeds and ground out cuttlefish bone (acting as the abrasive) as a toothpaste. The latter you can find on beaches, so if you don't live near one stock up on it the next time you go to the coast. Do check for sewage outfall first before gathering it. You can also grow fennel in your garden if foraging it is out of the question.

Such is the success of monetary economics that none of us can now imagine how we brushed our teeth before it paved the way for industrialisation. But for those of you who don't want to wash your mouth with fish bone, there are other moneyless options. Counter-intuitively, crushed charcoal has also been used as a toothpaste in the past but the idea of using this has, admittedly, never appealed to me thus far in my own experiment. Similarly, aubergine ash mixed in equal parts with salt has also been used regularly.

Toothbrush

Thomas McGuire, dentist and author of *The Tooth Trip*[191] gave me a number of excellent suggestions for your toothbrush. He recommends using either marshmallow roots or alfalfa roots, two plants with "good bristles". To make alfalfa root toothbrushes, gather alfalfa roots that have a thick diameter. Strip down the outer layer, and let them dry out as slowly as you can at normal room temperature. Once fully dry, slice them into 3-5in lengths, before whacking both ends with a hammer to loosen the fibres. Fold the roots in half so that all ends are now facing the same way. *Voilà*, your own toothbrush. Soak in warm water before brushing. Depending on where you live, other plants may be more appropriate for your toothbrush, including liquorice root, eucalyptus, bay, neem, fir and juniper.

Mouthwash

Kirsten Anderberg, in her book *Oral Health, Naturally*,[192] suggests making a rosemary and mint mouthwash. Boil 2.5 cups of water, then take it off the heat and add 1 tablespoon of fresh mint leaves, 1 tablespoon of rosemary leaves, and another of anise seeds if you can get your hands on them. Let the herbs sit in the water for at least 20 minutes. Once it has cooled, strain it using muslin and bottle. You can make herbal mouthwashes from rosemary, thyme and lavender – just make a tea out of it and then rinse as normal.

HAIR

Washing

Possessing, as I do, a head on which the hair on its chin is the same length as that on its crown, I don't feel very well placed to advise on shampoos. Thankfully I do have a few female friends with luscious long hair who have experimented with different recipes for the cause. And they've come up with some great combinations.

The first is one I'd never have thought of. Get yourself some rye meal flour, nettles and burdock (or one or the other). Boil the latter, strain it through some cloth and then add a couple of teaspoons of rye meal. Mix this together really well so it has the consistency of watery porridge, leave it in your beautiful mane for a few minutes and then rinse out.

The same soapwort recipe I recommended for soap earlier is even more suitable for hair. Just as you would with a conventional, commercial product, massage the solution into your hair, leave it for a minute or two, and rinse out.

This can also be tailored to your hair type: add fennel for greasy hair, chamomile if you have light hair, rosemary if you have darker hair and sage for an itchy scalp. As a treat you can also add a handful of lemon verbena or lemon balm to give it a citrus smell, and some catnip to promote its healthy growth. Both of these you can cultivate in your back garden, just keep the cat away from the latter.

Haircutting

One of the biggest surprises from Freeconomy members was the amount of people who use it to get their haircut. Given how preciously some people protect their flowing locks, it certainly wasn't one of the skills that I thought would be shared most frequently on the site. So if you fancy a new look, or its all become a bit unmanageable, search for a hairdresser in your local group and get it done for free.

Failing that, you could go and get a free semi-professional job. I often see signs on the windows of hair salons asking for brave volunteers who are willing to let their apprentices practise on them. Your other alternative is to, like me, have done with it and shave it off – as well as being incredibly low maintenance and saving you time making weird shampoos, it also means no one will notice when you eventually go bald.

Shaving

That said, if we had any sense, none of us would bother shaving. I go through phases of doing so, and have sometimes let it go all Giant Haystacks. I do like having a shave though, and I must admit it feels simultaneously both refreshing and stupid. Other times I'll do it if I am trying to look my best to impress a young lady – having the same financial status as a caveman is one thing, looking like one is another.

To shave without money or electricity, a cut-throat razor is your best bet, unless you want to go palaeolithic and use flint. If you don't have one, you should be able to find one on a gift economy website, as many people have them lying unused in this age of multi-blade razors, convenience, David Beckham billboards and disposability. If you are vegetarian or vegan, use the leathery surfaces of a foraged birch polypore (non-coincidentally also known as a razorstrop fungus) instead of leather to sharpen your razor.

I've had mixed reports from female friends that simply using friction can remove leg hair permanently from your body (it's also good for removing dead skin and calluses). The best tool for this job is a pumice stone. This can be done dry, but it is advisable to at least soften the area you are about to use it on with warm water and/or oil. I have personally yet to try it for my bikini line, you'll be disappointed to hear.

Instead of shaving foam from a can, you can use a soap made from a mixture of lye and either vegetable or animal fats (please use roadkill, as both wild and domesticated animals are having a tough enough time as it is without you killing them for a shave). This is time consuming, but then again, so is watching the telly. To make lye, all you need is a bucket or barrel with holes in the bottom, under which you place a large enough receptacle to retain the run-off. Line the top container with straw, and then the ash of a hardwood. Next pour rainwater over the ash a number of times – the more times, the more concentrated it gets. Each time the water is leached out of the top container and collected in the receptacle below, before being poured back over the top of the ash again. To test whether the lye is ready, you'll need an uncooked egg (ideally from one of your own chooks). Drop it (the egg, not the chicken) into the lye. If it floats with a quarter of it above the water, the lye is perfect for making soap; below that and the lye is too weak and needs a few more repetitions of the process above; if it shows more than a quarter, it's too strong, which can be remedied by just adding water until only a quarter shows. The water should get fairly hot, so allow it to cool.

Now it's time to add the fat or oils (which should be the same temperature as the lye after it has cooled) to start the saponification process. Stir it until the mixture begins to thicken, add any of the beneficial herbs that are suitable for your skin type (which I mentioned above), pour into a mould and allow it to 'cure' for a month or two.

By which time your beard or leg hair will be very much ready for its application!

CLOTHES

The best moneyless option for washing your clothes isn't a lot different to washing your body – down by the bank of the river. Similarly, if you want to use soaps of some sort, take utmost care not to pollute the river for those downstream. Considering that this option is just as impractical as sea bathing for most of us at the moment, there is a need for other options on the moneyless menu.

Washing

Hand washing in a sink or bathtub is still a realistic option, and it's a rather good way of getting some exercise in first thing in the morning. If that doesn't tickle your fancy, the washing machine is always an option. What type of washing machine you use will be the big question. Conventional machines eat electrical energy (not to mention water) for breakfast and so are a big draw on your photovoltaic or wind-powered system if you have one, especially in the winter, which unfortunately is the time when you'll need your clothes washed most.

In terms of purely off-grid clothes washing, the best (and most fun) that I have seen is the wooden hand-crank washing 'machine'. If you combine this with a bicycle powered spinner, to get your clothes fairly dry, then you've got yourself a really useful moneyless contraption, and a gym bicycle to boot for all those winter days you don't want to go out in the rain. If you want to seduce your partner into a romantic night in, tell him or her that they could first shed a little of their extra flab you've noticed by washing and spinning your clothes for you first. Smooth.

In terms of saving time, movement and labour, you could combine this washing machine with a mangle. Depending on how good this mangle is, you would use it either before or after the spinner – if it is very good, then use it after, and vice versa.

Drying

Getting your clothes dry without the spin cycle of an electric machine is the tricky part. Hand-wringing your clothes just doesn't do quite the same job, and is fairly tiring if you have a big load or are washing your bedsheets. It's good enough in the summer when there is plenty of sun, but I've found that in the winter hand-wringing means that clothes can take a whole week to dry out.

Enter the mangle. I found one on Freecycle, and they appear quite commonly there as few people use them any more; most people use electric washing machines and dryers. A mangle is a fantastic device where you feed your clothes in one end through two or more tight rollers, fed through using a rotating handle. This process squeezes out every millilitre of excess water, and while it obviously doesn't completely dry them it does drastically reduce their drying time. Once it comes out of the mangle, stick it on a long stretch of cord which can be suspended between two trees, ideally somewhere south-west facing so that it gets the sun for the best part of the day.

Alternatively, take the double-hard bastard option, which I once proposed to a woman who subsequently thought I was bonkers: put the clothes on wet, get to work, and let them dry out on your body.

Detergent

Some of you may have seen a product called soapnuts in your local or health food shop. I have used them for years. They have been utilised for washing clothes in India and Nepal for centuries, so there is nothing alternative or kooky about using them. There is absolutely no need to buy them, however, as you can grow them, but they are difficult to get started and like any tree will take time before your labour bears fruit.

If you aren't using boiling water in your wash, I would recommend boiling up the soapnuts (*Sapindus mukorossi, Sapindus detergens* or *Sapindus drummondii*[193]) first on your rocket stove in order to leach out as much of the saponins as you can, creating a soapnut liquid. You can still then put the nuts in the wash along with it, but doing this just means you maximise their cleaning potential. The quantity to use depends on how concentrated you make it – the best way to find out is by trial and error, but don't fret, you won't go too far wrong.

Best of all, you can take the used shells, blend them in your bicycle powered smoothie maker and turn them into an exfoliating scrub – add some herbs, coarse oatmeal and water to make into a paste if you want to be extra good to yourself!

Failing being able to grow soapnuts, there is always a soapwort recipe that will be more than adequate for getting your clothes clean, and it won't smell anywhere near as toxic as the conventional supermarket brands that claim to have extracts of patchouli and fairy poo in them.

HOME

I must admit, despite being anally tidy, I've never been much of a cleaner. I like a bit of bacteria, it's good for the constitution and I put the fact that I almost never get ill down, in part, to my repulsion of endless scrubbing and sweeping. Cleaning is an odd endeavour, and the fact we feel we have to highlights how linear the processes of our homes have become. I've yet to see a squirrel, bird or badger inventing concoctions and recipes with which to clean their homes. They just live, without the oppression of endless cleaning to weigh them down.

Nevertheless, I'm fully aware that I am out on my own with this one, and that most of you would like a clean house, and not a nest or den in the ground. Thankfully there are others who know how to clean their homes with nothing other than the plants that they can grow in their garden.

CLEANING USING 100% LOCAL INGREDIENTS

Steph Hafferty, organic no-dig grower, teacher and speaker[194]

Making your own cleaning products is empowering, creative and fun. It not only keeps you out of the loop of consumerism but also creates a home environment free of toxins and pollutants. Simple and a joy to make, these potions will ensure your clothes and home will be hygienically clean and fresh, smell fantastic and have the vibrant energy which comes from feeling fully connected with Nature and your home environment.

To make these recipes, you will need some old rags for filtering and cleaning (I love using old pieces of denim as cleaning cloths) jars with lids for storage and some recycled squirty bottles.

Apple cider vinegar is excellent for making cleaning products. Firstly, make some cider! Creative homemakers have use dried corn cobs as fermentation locks when making homebrew in demijohns. When the cider is ready, strain into non-metal containers, filling to three-quarters capacity. Do not cover, and keep it warm and out of direct sunlight, stirring daily. Natural bacteria in the air will turn the cider into vinegar in around 3 to 4 weeks when it will smell vinegary. Filter through cheesecloth to remove the 'mother' (the mat at the bottom of the container) to stop further acetic acid fermentation. Store in glass bottles with lids on. You can also use wine and malt vinegars in these recipes too.

Wonderful, powerful herbs to grow or forage for cleaning the home are rosemary, all mints, pennyroyal, thyme, lemon balm, pine needles, sage, lavender, eucalyptus, tansy and southernwood. They have antiseptic, antibacterial, disinfectant or insect repellent qualities, as well as smelling fantastic and making one feel amazing.

A handful of these herbs tied firmly together and added to hot water will add fragrance to most cleaning jobs and lift the mood. Simmered on the stove, they will cleanse the air and lift the spirits, especially useful if there is illness.

To make a cleaner for floors, paintwork and all indoor surfaces, make a soapwort (see page 184) preparation but add two handfuls of a fresh (one of dried), fragrant herb. Choose from mint, lavender, pine, rosemary, lemon balm, thyme or lemon verbena.

Potato water is an effective cleanser for carpets and fabric stains. Wash and grate two potatoes and add to a pint of water. Swish about for a few minutes then strain, pressing down hard to release all of the potato water. Add a further pint of water, mix and leave to settle. To use, dip a sponge or cloth into the liquid. Wash or wipe with cold water.

Woodash, mixed with water to form a paste, cuts through grease and grime as a scouring powder on woodburner glass, pots and pans (including the burnt underside), oven doors. It removes limescale from showers, brass, silverware and, when mixed with sand, for scrubbing stone floors. Woodash paste is brilliant for washing up when camping. Rinse well after use, of course. Always use ash from natural wood fires and wait until the fire is cool before collecting and storing in a lidded metal container. To help reduce damp and mould in cupboards, punch holes in a tin can and add pieces of charcoal.

Horsetail is full of silica and incredibly useful for the home, body and garden but as a gardener, I am very aware of its invasiveness and have mixed feelings about this extraordinary plant. Exceptionally difficult to eradicate, it is definitely better foraged rather than grown at home.

Traditionally horsetail is used to scour pans to a high shine and as a fine 'sand paper' for polishing wood. After gathering, leave in the sun for an hour or so before tying together and using. Wear gloves when scouring because the silica can make it sharp.

To make a liquid, simmer 50/50 fresh horsetail to water (or 25/75 dried plant) for 5 minutes then rest for at least 6 hours before straining. This liquid can be sprayed on mildew and added to herbal decoctions to aid the cleaning properties when cleaning floors, worktops etc.

A handful of chopped dried mint, rosemary, thyme or lemon balm mixed with a cup of salt makes an effective, all purpose aromatic scrub for the kitchen and bathroom. Store in a jam jar. After using, rinse with water before wiping down with herb vinegar spray for extra cleanliness and sparkle.

An alternative abrasive is washed, dried and crushed egg shells. Leave to dry in a warm, airy place and when dry crush further using a rolling pin. Add some finely chopped dried mint, lavender or pine for enhanced cleaning properties and fragrance.

To make a cleaning herb vinegar, shake the herbs gently to remove insects. I usually use equal quantities of rosemary, thyme, pine, lavender, mint and lemon balm. Fill a large jar with the herbs, then add vinegar, stirring to release any air. Seal and leave for at least two weeks, shaking gently daily. Strain and store.

This can either be used neat for stubborn limescale and cleaning the loo, or diluted in equal quantities with water or horsetail liquid for cleaning.

Mint and lemon balm window cleaner is not only excellent for cleaning glass (includin windows) but also works well as a general multi-surface cleaner. Mix 2 cups of lemon balm and mint decoction with vinegar and put in a spray bottle.

Pennyroyal is disliked by ants and fleas (and, apparently, rattlesnakes!) – scatter the herb either fresh or dried, or simmer a handful of the herb in 2 cups of water for 30 minutes, cool for at least 6 hours before straining and adding to a spray bottle. Pennyroyal is toxic and it is strongly advised that pregnant women should not use pennyroyal for cleaning.

Dried rosemary, tansy, thyme, mint and southernwood, chopped and put into bags made from muslin fabric scraps, keep moths and fleas from cupboards and clothes.

Dish Scrubbers

Humanity didn't always have throwaway Brillo pads or dish sponges to clean up those burnt pots after they were left too long over the camp fire. Back in the good old days, when life was supposedly "solitary, poor, nasty, brutish and short",[195] people used what they had growing at hand in their local area.

In the UK, this could be a pine cone of some variety, depending on what you are washing. If the mess is tough, use a tough cone. If you wanted to wash your bowl straight after eating, then a softer one would be more apt. Another option is to take a ball of dried grass and use as a normal scrubber. You'll be surprised by how effective it is.

An option requiring slightly more effort is the loofah (often referred to as a luffa in the UK). Whilst native to the warmer regions of the US, you can grow them in the UK if you have a sunny room, greenhouse or polytunnel. Whilst they are growing they look like a cucumber (they're from the same family), but after you dry them out you will be left with that fibrous internal structure that most of us recognise from the shops. One plant should keep you in sustainable, moneyless dish scrubbers for a year or so, and you can even use them as sponges for your body also. Remember to save seed for the following year's washing up.

CHAPTER 10

TRANSPORT AND HOLIDAY ACCOMMODATION

Broaching the subject of moneyless transport is a difficult task, as so little of what we conceive of as transport today could be done without money, and certainly not in ways I would consider truly sustainable. As I attempted to illustrate in one of the POP model examples I used in chapter three, the ultimate in moneyless transport – in sustainability terms at least – is walking barefoot (see page 199). One part of the reason I say that is because this mode of transport requires zero resources, meaning that you get an A+ on your ecological impact assessment. That's the lesser half of the argument.

The more important element of walking barefoot is that it fully connects you with the planet. I believe that shoes are like condoms, in a way. Of course, we wear them both because they protect us from various things – one from the cold, thorns and their urban relative, broken glass, the other from sexually transmitted diseases (STDs) and unplanned pregnancy.

But we pay a heavy and massively under-appreciated cost for having made ourselves dependent on both these forms of protection. Anyone who has ever made love to someone they deeply love and care for *with* a condom, and *without* a condom, knows the difference between both experiences. Both are still beautiful experiences, but with the latter the strength of connection between both partners is greatly increased, and in my experience it has been the closest I have ever come to feeling a complete merging with the whole. (I will look at forms of, and issues around, moneyless contraception in chapter thirteen).

The same I feel is true with shoes. They act like a barrier between us and the whole, creating yet another degree of separation. I went out with a friend and bushcraft teacher Malcolm Handoll on a survival weekend once, and the first thing he made me do was take off my shoes. I resisted a bit

(OK, a lot) at first – it was winter, about 2°C, rather muddy and we were on the windward side of a north-facing hill with a stiff December breeze coming face on – but I finally gave in to his coaxing. And glad I was for it too. Instead of trampling over everything in my big boots, I had to take care where I walked. I could feel the Earth beneath my feet, and it felt right to connect with Her in that way. It slowed me down. I had to look, feel my way along, and not race through the day at my normal speed. And as long as I kept moving I was warm. Of all the useful skills Malcolm taught me that weekend, simply taking off my shoes was probably the most important.

AN ODE TO WALKING BAREFOOT

Malcolm Handoll, bushcraft teacher
and founder of Five Senses[196]

You may think of thorns, gravel and gooey stuff when you think of walking barefoot. But to walk with bare feet is to feel your way just like you do with your hands, and just as you'd avoid a branch hanging in front of you, so you'll walk around any dangers on your path.

You may think of cold feet. Maybe your feet are cold due to inactivity, dehydration and reduced blood flow. But I tell you, a foot is happy when its muscles are working and flexing, blood pumping, and is soon warmed by exercise. Your circulation improves and your nerves tingle. It feels good to be alive, massaging your feet with every step, just like reflexology.

So maybe the coldness you fear won't last, as you warm up? There is one way to find out – try it.

Yes, it requires us to move differently, with conscious steps treading sensitively, but that is how we need to live, with Nature, not trampling over it disconnected by rubber. I want to connect so intimately with my world, like a tree with its roots deep into the soil, so I with my toes wiggling in the mud.

By contrast, imagine a life wearing boxing gloves on your hands.

That is how my feet feel in shoes; hot, useless, unable to touch. With my feet cut off from the world I lose track of where I am as it all passes by, step after step the same.

Try cleansing your soles on dew soaked lawns or an exfoliating foot rub walking over warm sand. There are also barefoot walking parks with sensory paths to explore. There is your own garden to dance in. Try it and have fun!

While I personally feel that barefoot walking is the ultimate in moneyless transport, it is by no means the only option on the menu, you'll be relieved to hear. There are many ways to get around, both long- and short-distance, in urban and rural settings, and at all sorts of speeds. All you have to do is pick the options that best suit your unique situation and ideologies.

My only advice: when you can, take the option that allows you to go the slowest and still get there on time – leave earlier if need be. Modern life is so fast that we're likely to wake up when we're eighty and realise we spent our entire lives racing through it, never stopping to talk with our neighbours, smell the flowers or listen to the birds sing their merry little tune. This pace of life is a significant contributor to our high levels of stress today, which in turn is widely accepted as one of the major factors underlying many illnesses and diseases.

One thing I would add before looking at the moneyless menu for transport is that you will be correct in observing that some of the options involve using cars (and other such things) that are made in the monetary, industrial economy. Criticisms on this point are perfectly valid, and I am often the first to do it myself. If you look at my POP model for transport (see page 55) you'll get a fuller understanding of my position on it – some of the options are stepping stones and transitional strategies to help us get from A to B in the journey towards absolute sustainability.

Despite understanding them, I sometimes find such blanket criticisms too simplistic. For a start, for someone who has driven a car every day since they were seventeen, walking barefoot for twenty miles is much too big a step to take. Whilst ecological sustainability is a major motivation for my version of non-monetary economy, my only aim with this book is to provide options that empower anyone, regardless of their intentions, to diversify their own personal economy and make steps towards living an ecologically sustainable, physically healthy and connected life.

There is another point regarding this over-simplification. We've all been born into a globalised age, whether we like it or not; the result of this means that from an early age (before many of us had even heard the words 'carbon footprint' or 'climate change') we all dispersed to the four corners of the world, leaving family and friends behind or somewhere else completely. Over the course of our adult life we set ourselves up in these far away places, making new friends and establishing social networks that we really value, meaning that many of us are very reluctant to give that all up and return home for good. Yet we don't want to never see our family or oldest friends again either. What do you do in that circumstance? Like all in life, it is never black and white, there is no right or wrong answer, which is why I want to share all the moneyless options I know of, even if some do stink of hypocrisy, just so that everyone has a chance to make steps towards their ideal.

TRANSPORT

Moneyless shoes

Apart from walking barefoot, the next step down on my POP model would be to make your own shoes. One simple solution is a pair of flip flops whose sole is cut out of an old car tyre (you can cut it around the shape of your foot). This sole can be clad with previously-loved carpet, and the straps made from melted and reformed plastic bags.[197] I wore something to this effect for many years, replacing the plastic bag straps with old bicycle tubes.

However, flip-flops, especially ones made from the detritus of the transport industry, are hardly ideal for all occasions. For something a bit more protective and strong, why not make a pair of my favourite moneyless shoes, the Dutch wooden clog. These have long been associated with farmers and workers because of their protective properties, but for the more creative they can also become a work of art. They are still widely used by Dutch farmers today. Interestingly, the French clog, known as the *sabot*, has Luddite connections, making it my personal favourite. During the eighteenth and nineteenth centuries, French workers threw their wooden shoes into the machines to damage them, simply because these machines were replacing their skilled crafts. The act became so common that it gave rise to the word *sabotage*. Clogs can be hand-carved from woods such as willow, alder, birch or poplar, making them the ideal footwear for the British moneyless contingent.

I've told friends that when I die I want them to make a pair of shoes out of my hide – willow soles with my bum as an upper would be my ideal. I haven't had any takers yet, so get in touch if you are interested.

You probably think I am wise-cracking, but I'm not. This is something very important to me. I want to be of use after my death, not thrown in a box where my flesh will just rot, while those six feet above me continue to import cheap shoes from China and Taiwan. We're no more special than any other animal, and if using their hides for footwear is acceptable then I can't see why it shouldn't be acceptable to use my arse too. Edward Abbey took this perspective a step further when he said "if my decomposing carcass helps nourish the roots of a juniper tree or the wings of a vulture – that is immortality enough for me. And as much as anyone deserves".[198] It is with humility such as this that we need to live our lives again.

Hitchhiking

Hitching is one of those famous moneyless arts – the picture of the free soul on the open road with nothing but a sense of adventure. Yet this depends on someone else having a car and all the costs and consequences of that, and therefore moneyless living's most common symbol is relatively low down my POP model for transport.

However, to completely disregard it would be just as foolish as thinking of it as a long-term solution. Hitching allows more efficient usage of finite fossil fuels, it facilitates connections between travellers and locals and all the mutual benefits that come with that, and it allows at least a few people to have a proper travel adventure, of a type diametrically opposed to the concept of a package holiday. It is a transitional strategy, not an ideal, and it's a tradition we would do well to keep alive for now. I have been hitching since I have been able to stand up, back in the eighties. In those financially humble days, there would be queues of hitchers at every exit from a town.

Now I can hitch the length of the country – from the south-east port of Rosslare to Donegal in the north-west – and not see one other hitcher along the way. It's a sad sight, and one which highlights the effect of money on our lives. Most cars that fly by have only one person in them. Regardless of ideologies, this is simply a terribly inefficient culture, which (as we seen in chapter one) it has to be in order to stay afloat.

As I mentioned in *The Moneyless Man*,[199] my tips for hitchhiking also apply to life in general: smile; keep baggage to a minimum and only take what you really need; be friendly; trust your intuition and instinct; and most importantly – have a route in mind but allow the adventure to take you where it will if a good enough opportunity arises!

RULES OF THE ROAD

Kath Kelly, author of *Thumbing Through: Hitch-hiking Tales from my Diaries* and *How I lived a Year on Just a Pound a Day*

Is hitching dangerous? I've been hitching alone for over thirty years, and the number of horror stories I've heard hasn't been high. Some people waited ages for a ride, and some, male and female, got propositioned, but that can happen anywhere. I've never been physically threatened while hitching.

It's important to exercise your prerogative to agree to, or turn down, a lift. If it isn't to the right place, the driver smells of drink, or you just don't get a good feeling from him or her, *you don't have to get in.* I believe plenty of people could have avoided trouble if they'd just said 'no' at the right moment.

What to wear and carry

a) A sign: A4 size card b) A marker pen c) Brightly coloured, clean-looking clothes d) Bad weather gear e) Small compact luggage: it may have to stay on your knee f) Wrap the stuff inside in plastic bags, in case you get soaked g) A mobile phone h) A road map i) Something to eat and drink, including something to offer to the driver.

Where and when to hitch

- In daylight: it's much safer if people can see you and read your sign.
- Just in front of a lay-by or other open area: drivers need room to get off the road if they decide to stop for you. When they do pull in, run! Don't keep them waiting while you stroll over.
- In front of motorway signs on a slip road: the big blue sign that says 'M6' shows where the non-pedestrian area begins.
- At petrol stations: They're nice light places to wait, with good facilities, and drivers come out of them feeling relaxed and refreshed, so they're great for hitching.
- Outside the city centre: walk to the outskirts of town where you're clearly visible and your destination is obvious.
- Outside a truck stop or industrial estate: good for long-distance traffic.
- At the car park exit after a public event: lots of cars will come pouring out. There will surely be someone going your way!

Happy hitching!

Bicycles bits and pieces

You didn't get a book on moneyless living to learn about bicycles. Even David Cameron, Prime Minister of the UK at the time of writing, cycles to work the odd time, albeit with his chauffeur in tow carrying his briefcase.[200] If I was a transport advisor to the PM, which I hasten to add I probably won't ever be, my first counsel would be around the subject of panniers – a rack on the back of the bike, coupled with two clip-on bags, would have saved him (or in this case, the taxpayer) the cost of a driver and all the expenses that go with a car – an MOT, road tax, insurance, bad health. I got my pair of panniers by posting a message on the Freeconomy website. Admittedly, they looked like they were teleported out of the nineteen eighties. The upside of this, however, is that twenty years later they are still in great condition, having been built with the quality and strength that was common in stuff back then, and lacking the built-in obsolescence incorporated into much of what we make today.

If you need to cart around something bigger than David Cameron's briefcase – which is a common reason cited by people who say that cycling isn't pragmatic for them – I'd highly recommend a bicycle trailer. These you can make yourself out of bits and pieces you may already have lying around the home – old kids bike wheels, storage containers, planks of wood and the like. There are many different designs available on the magnificent Instructables(.com)[201] website.

There are some other useful tips in relation to moneyless cycling, however. First, use money one last time in relation to transport (this would be somewhere half way up my POP model for transport) and get yourself a pair of GreenTyres(.co.uk).[202] These creations, which are as common as marijuana in the Netherlands (we could learn a lot from the Dutch), are puncture-proof tyres made out of recycled plastic and micro-pockets of air. Before I gave my bike, and the green tyres that were on it, away to someone on the Freeconomy website (Freecycle and Freegle are better set up for doing this but I am a little bit biased), I had one set of punctureless tyres for four years and they looked almost like new – that was after doing anywhere between 30-100 miles a week on them during that time. They're not quite as comfortable as normal tyres, but you get used to them in no time. On a side note, three months after giving away my bike on Freeconomy I received an even better one right at the moment when I needed one again. Give without any expectation of receiving, without a moment's thought of credit or debt, and you will receive whatever you need when you need it – if I have learnt one thing from the last fours years, it is to trust that.

In terms of lighting, you can often find old dynamos on Freecycle and Freegle, and these are a great moneyless replacement for battery powered lights, as you power them yourself.

Ideally you'll also be powered by your own home-grown produce. If you fuel your body using food imported from all over the world, cycling is no longer an ecologically neutral option, and it has been argued that it could even be worse than driving a car and consuming fewer calories that you've sourced locally.[203] That perspective is much too simplistic and reductionist, but it certainly is food for thought.

For the ultimate in moneyless biking (though, admittedly, not the ultimate in speedy biking), check out the Splinter Bike,[204] a 100% wooden bike made by Michael Thompson of the Eco-shed[205] in Norfolk. They even set a land speed record for it in 2011, clocking in at an impressive 18.11kph. Such designs are in their infancy, but bikes made from locally grown wood may be commonplace in the localised economy of the future.

Liftsharing

In my POP model for transport, this is near the bottom. It lacks the adventure of hitching and the sustainability of walking. Nonetheless, it still has a role to play in the transition to a new economy, and in your POP model for transport it may be near the top. As I mentioned earlier, my years on the road have shown me that out of every ten cars that will pass, there will be on average twenty two free spaces, even though everyone is going in roughly the same general direction.

It was in reaction to such ecological lunacy that a host of liftsharing sites grew up in tandem with the internet. The best of these is *lift*share(.com),[206] a site which matches together people who are taking the same journey. They have a very large database of members, with lots of journeys offered up, so if you are going somewhere that requires punctuality (meaning you can't chance hitching) then I would check them out. This website is especially useful if you make the journey regularly, as many liftshares can be an ongoing thing. Other similar sites, though all a little different, include NationalCarShare(.co.uk),[207] Freewheelers(.com)[208] and MyLifts(.com). Pick the one that best meets your needs. If you haven't got money to offer in terms of sharing the cost of the fuel, why not offer some of the food you've grown instead, or something you've created out of locally grown materials that the driver would like?

Freebus

If you live in a city and feel that you or others need a bus service in order to get around, then why not pioneer a free bus service in your area. If you're looking for inspiration and more information, one not-for-profit organisation called Freebus[209] did just that in Bristol (UK).

Because of its dependency on fossil fuels, insurance companies and lots of machinery, this would again appear somewhere in the bottom half of my moneyless POP model for transport. However, it is free at the point of service so, depending on your reasons for being moneyless, it may make it near the top of yours. It would be wise not to see it as anything more than a transitional strategy, helping those handicapped by this broken economy in which we find ourselves. Its illusory freeness shouldn't distract us from embarking on a relentless drive to create a new economy, one that works in harmony with the real needs of humans and the rest of Nature, and the reorganisation and redesign that will have to come with that.

ACCOMMODATION WHEN YOU GET THERE

Before you hit the road, you're going to want to organise some accommodation for when you get there (unless you want to be ultra-adventurous and trusting and leave it up to serendipity). In our culture that has almost always meant staying in a B&B, hotel or hostel, all of which are becoming increasingly expensive and impersonal.

There is absolutely no reason to have to pay for accommodation anymore if you are on the road. There are many projects now flourishing, some with millions of members in every nation of the world who have signed up to host you when you are in their neck of the woods. The even better news is that there is something for everyone's style and taste.

Couch-surfing,[210] free hospitality websites and ... just showing up

Couch-surfing is my favourite travel community, and out of all the free hospitality projects out there, it is certainly the one with most critical mass – at the time of writing, they have 3.7 million members throughout the world with 150,000 members in the UK alone, all willing to let you stay in their homes for free whilst you are on the road. That's a lot of beds and couches to choose from, regardless of whether you're going to stay in London or New York, Craggy Island or Pala.

Not only do you get a free couch (or often a bed) for the night, you get to make new friends into the bargain. If that wasn't enough to convince you, couch-surfing also means that you instantly get plugged into all the local knowledge about the best places to go in that area, getting you off the tourist trail and into the little gems that only locals know about. You also get access to a kitchen, meaning you don't have to eat out. What makes the couch-surfing project stand out is that it has evolved beyond just being a free accommodation website, and now actively facilitates fun activities that people on the move can get involved in with locals. *Time* magazine went as far as saying that couch-surfing isn't "just a means of accommodation, it is an entirely new way to travel," whilst the *New York Times* has remarked that it "takes an ancient notion of hospitality and tucks it into a thoroughly modern paradigm".

WarmShowers[211] is a very similar project to Couch-surfing, but specialising in hospitality for cyclists who are touring around the country. This way you get to meet other cyclists who understand what you need after sixty miles on the road – a warm shower – and who may become a cycling buddy in the future. If you're very lucky, you might even get some wacky form of cream made from wild plants that will sort that saddle rash of yours out for you. A couch-surfer called Jim, who came and stayed with me for a couple of nights while I was writing this book, had been using the WarmShowers website throughout his journey, and had some excellent tales to tell from it. Most of these wouldn't be appropriate for a family book such as this, but one involved him staying with a very financially rich family who insisted on plying him full of expensive champagne for the night, causing him a hangover that took him three full days of cycling to recover from.

Other similar sites include Hospitality Club[212] (which grew out of a desire to facilitate international peace and which also has a huge membership), Global Freeloaders[213] and Servas.[214] If you speak a little Esperanto,[215] an international auxiliary language first created by the writer L.L. Zamenhof through a book titled *Unua Libro* in 1887, you will find yourself an international network of people happy to host you on your travels, enabling you to learn more of this neutral, international peace promoting language in the process. Another option is to just show up in town and start engaging with the locals in as positive a way as possible, and see where it takes you.

Whereas Freeconomy fulfils the role of Department for Skills and Labour in the gift economy, and Freecycle and Freegle the Department of Stuff, websites such as these look after the Department for Temporary Accommodation.

Wild Camping

For the more adventurous amongst you, I recommend putting your tent or tarp on your back and pitching up wherever you like. If you want to go truly moneyless (i.e. not using a tent that was produced using industrialised processes) on your journey, I'd highly recommend learning how to build your own shelter from what's around you. The woods is a great place to stay, as much for the scenery and its ability to keep you hidden as for the shelter-creating materials it presents you with.

Bushcraft Shelter

If you really want to experience a taste of how it is to live in the wild, then I'd highly recommended learning how to construct your own bushcraft shelter using whatever is at hand. A large part of learning this art involves identifying what qualities and properties you actually need in order to stay warm, dry and comfortable for a night, and then knowing how to find the materials that contain those requirements. There are many styles of shelter to choose from, and again I would recommend Ray Mears' *Outdoor Survival Handbook* for those of you who want to see the complete menu of options for truly wild camping.

Long-term free accommodation

If you want to stay in a place for more than just a night or two, Stay4Free[216] is a project which allows you to have a house all to yourself. How it works is simple – you sign up, list both your home and your desired destinations, and contact anyone on their database that could potentially fit the bill, requesting a house swap. If they fancy coming and spending some time in the part of the world your house is in, then you can agree dates and details between yourselves. All that is left to do is to organise getting there, which you can do by any number of the means I examined earlier.

CHAPTER 11

LIVING OFF-GRID

Whenever you try writing about off-grid, the biggest challenge you face is actually defining it. Back in the day it was easy. It meant no electricity (and therefore no gadgetry), a well or a clean stream or river for water (once the norm), rapeseed oil candles for lighting and fields of produce. Except they didn't call it 'living off-grid' back then. They called it living.

In today's globalised and ubiquitous monetary economy, the lines have become blurred. The term 'off-grid' refers to homes which could survive by themselves even if civilisation collapsed around it; or, more technically, homes which are autonomous and do not rely on public utilities such as electricity, gas, water and waste management, by using systems and technologies that allow them to produce everything their inhabitants need.

In reality, it's not quite so clear-cut. A house which uses solar photovoltaics (PV) for electricity, a bore hole and rainwater harvesting techniques for water, and a passive solar design and a woodburner for heating is generally considered off-grid; and by definition that is correct. The debate surrounds the issue of whether or not people who rely on the grid to produce the things that allow them to then live off-grid are still reliant on the grid, albeit in a marginally less direct way. Many of the component parts of guttering systems and PV are made by processes that require a vast global network to come into existence. It can be argued that these products are just a proxy for the physical grid networks they've been produced to replace. Over the last decade the lines have become even hazier with the introduction of wireless mobile phones and internet dongles – if these networks are intangible and invisible, are they still part of the grid or not?

This is a debate that could go on long into the night, and in the absence of a bottle of raspberry wine I'd suggest that we leave it there. In the end it doesn't really matter how you define off-grid. The reasons you do it may be completely different to the reasons I do it. My passion for off-grid living stems from a fascination in designing systems that allow us humans to live in harmony with the bigger organism we are a part of, instead of being perpetually at war with Her. I want to explore what a truly sustainable way of living is. You may want to live off-grid to regain some peace of mind, or because you want to reduce your carbon footprint, your bills or break free from the shackles of the monetary economy, at least for large portions of the year. Another reason to be 'free'.

If I was asked to clarify the blurry lines of off-grid living, I'd explain it something like this: in the event of an apocalyptic scenario that caused all industrialised systems to magically evaporate in an instant (one can dream, can't one?), I would say the extent to which you were off-grid would be equal to the amount of years you could survive afterwards. If you could live the rest of your life in the same manner, that's ten out of ten. If you got into trouble after year five because your leisure battery died and your electric pump would no longer send you water, then I'd personally say you weren't as far off-the-grid as you could have been. Therefore the key to truly off-grid living is keeping it as simple as possible, reducing your reliance on an economic system you have no control over, so that if the shit ever does go down, you could be unaffected by it all. The further off-grid you go, the more resilient you will be to external shocks, whether it be hikes in oil prices, complete financial meltdown or the landing of aliens in London, Washington and Beijing. The purest form of off-grid living is the fully localised gift economy.

To help you make the choice that works best for you and the biosphere at this moment in time, I suggest you choose from the menu of moneyless tools below and then draw yourself a POP model so that, over time, you can evolve to the way you ideally want to live.

ELECTRICAL ENERGY

There is no way to produce electricity that is completely moneyless in the truest sense of the word (requiring zero money at any stage of the process). Even the most relatively sustainable forms aren't sustainable in absolute terms – the minerals and materials used are all of a finite nature, and our acquisition of many of them wreaks a lot of destruction on the Earth. And anyone who has tried to make a monocrystalline silicon wafer from scratch quickly realises that the global infrastructure, with its high economies of scale and fine division of labour, is needed for the job.

I used solar panel to generate electricity for three years whilst claiming to live moneylessly, and whilst in practice and spirit I was, I still felt it tainted what I was trying to achieve. I chose to use a solar panel to power my laptop, and an incoming calls only (pay as you go) mobile phone to enable me to communicate what I was doing and why, so as to make my experience a resource for anyone who may have been interested. This was a compromise of course, and tinged with hypocrisy, but such are the decisions we sometimes have to make in this perfectly imperfect world we live in.

If you do want to live moneylessly and have electricity, then you have three main options: micro-hydro, solar and wind. Which one is most appropriate for you will depend on where you live. If you're in the south of Portugal or Greece, solar is a great option. On the other hand, if you find yourself on a hill in the Highlands of Scotland, wind may be more appropriate, unless you have access to a body of fast-flowing water, in which case a combination of hydro and wind may be best. It is also difficult to advise which of these gives the best return per kW of energy they produce, as it is regularly changing depending on government policy and new technologies. If you're really interested in learning what the best options are and how to install and use them, I'd recommend *The Renewable Energy Handbook*.[217]

Having to buy a wind turbine or solar panel to begin with may not be the necessity that it would first seem that it is[218] – projects such as Open Source Ecology[219] (see page 222) are now paving the way for such machines to be made DIY.

Lighting

One of the basic reasons most of us *need* electricity today is for lighting. Our lives no longer beat to the rhythm of the seasons or the rise and fall of the sun, partially due to the incremental discovery of increasingly factory-dependent forms of human-induced lighting. In another horrible case of chicken and egg, the 24/7 culture this has created has convinced us that we now couldn't live without such lighting.

Be clear about this – the most ecological and non-exploitative way of lighting your house is to not at all. This doesn't merely result in you using zero resources. It also stops you from doing all sorts of other stuff, including working long into the evening, and can instead force you to relax or maybe even have some people-centred fun. I've little doubt that this will sound, at best, an impractical solution to the majority of people. But there would be many grossly unappreciated benefits of doing so. Turning off the lights could be utilised as a pathway to resynchronising with the rhythms of Nature, something we drastically need to do if we are to create a new, more expansive and holistic story of self. Other benefits are more obvious. Before the popular use of electrical lighting in Ireland, people would gather in each others moonlit living rooms – a time when these rooms were actually living – telling stories, reciting their own poems or the works of Patrick Kavanagh, Brendan Behan, W. B. Yeats, William Allingham, James Joyce, Oscar Wilde and the like from memory, singing songs, dancing and generally creating their own entertainment. You couldn't do any work because you couldn't see very much. And without other powerful distractions, such as digital television, computer games and films-on-demand, people connected a lot more with each other and co-created their own fun.

However, if after all that you've decided that you're still in favour of human-induced illumination, you don't necessarily need electricity, or even petroleum based candles, to light your house. Beeswax is a great alternative, and you can produce it in your back garden in collaboration with a swarm of honeybees. Using the model of beehive I footnoted in chapter eight, you can acquire a fair amount of quality beeswax with which you can make candles that only require some simple everyday equipment in their construction.[220] Incidentally, beeswax can also be used for a whole host of other purposes including furniture polish, lipbalm, wood-filler and for sealing on jams, making it a very versatile substance to help produce.

If you think this is all a bit too much hassle and that an electrical switch is easier, then take inspiration from a twelve your old whom I met at a talk I gave for him and his classmates at the Malvern Spring Gardening Show one year. Apart from trying to convince his architect dad to build an Earthship at the time, he told me that he also made his own candles from beeswax and – wait for it – sold his excess candles so that he could raise money for charity. If we adults can't even be bothered to take responsibility for our own lighting needs, then we really need to question whether or not the hot air that comes out of our mouths about climate change and resource depletion are just a bunch of empty words.

The next level down on the lighting POP model would be using energy you created using a wind turbine or solar panel, both of which can keep you bill-free but which also keep you one notch more reliant on an industrialised system that is destructive and that will not last forever. But if this is a step you can realistically do now, it is still very worthwhile.

COOKING

Most modern cookers run on gas or electricity supplied by the national grid. Despite the convenience of having such easy energy sources on demand, neither of these are particularly efficient or sustainable ways of cooking, and they certainly aren't moneyless. According to Greenpeace, the UK's "centralised model of production and transmission wastes an astonishing two-thirds of primary energy inputs, requiring us to burn far more fuel and emit far more carbon dioxide than necessary".[221] Out of every 100 units produced in this centralised system, 61.5 are "lost through inefficient generation and heat wastage at the source", while 3.5 units vanish in distribution on their way down transmission lines. But the wastage doesn't stop there – because this energy seems infinite to its end consumer, coupled with the fact that we have to take no personal responsibility for producing it, we waste another 13 units (of the remaining 35 units we have left of the original production) through carelessness and the inefficiencies that come with not really caring.

How we choose to cook our food matters. Not just to the state of the biosphere and those who live on top of these resources we like so much, but to ourselves. Cooking on a conventional gas or electric cooker gives us no sense of a deeper connection to the Earth, our holistic selves, whereas there is something about sitting around a camp fire, gazing into the flames, which triggers something primal in us. It makes us acutely aware of the cycles of life and death and the power of Nature, and it intimately connects us to what we consume.

The Campfire

If you live somewhere that allows you to have a campfire regularly, I'd highly recommend it. This option is certainly not the most efficient way of cooking, as a relatively high proportion of the energy created is inevitably lost to the atmosphere. Despite this, the fact that it has zero reliance on industrialisation and its flotsam scores high in terms of ecological footprint and moneylessness. All you need is some tinder, wood and a spark. To cook the food you can make a simple tripod (three straight and sturdy rods tied with some cordage will suffice) from which you hang an old pot. However, my preferred method, due to its simplicity, involves supporting the pot with a horizontal rod that is suspended over the fire by the use of two vertical branches with V-shaped ends staked into the ground.

If you have the stones available to hand and want to make the most efficient use of the heat generated, I'd recommend creating a keyhole fireplace. You start your fire in the main ring area. As soon as it gets really hot you transfer some of the coals into the smaller rectangular bit at the bottom. This allows you to have good control of your heat source, and a pot (or a large skillet if you have one) will get all the support it needs from the surrounding stones, whilst still allowing air to circulate.

Rocket Stove

For the first two and a half years that I lived without money, I cooked on a rocket stove come rain, hail or shine. They are easy to make, taking only an hour or so to construct if you have all the materials, and they can be made completely out of consumer waste, of which there is much to choose from. All you will need is an elbowed flue pipe (you should find one at the tip), some catering sized tin cans (15kg olive cans are good for a large rocket stove, ask your local café or deli for these), and some insulating material (ashes are the ideal from a permaculture perspective). To make one,[222] go to www.permaculture.co.uk, type 'rocket stove' in the search box and choose the model best suits your needs.

The main problem with these stoves is that you only have one ring – I like to minimise that problem by steaming my vegetables on top of the pot that I am boiling my potatoes or barley in, or by using a hay box.

Hay box

The hay box is a very useful tool for anyone serious about living without money, or at the very least cooking without bills. Think of it as an energy-free slow cooker, which you can use inside or outside the house. It is free to make (though dependent on the waste of civilisation), and once constructed it is the perfect complement to a rocket stove, as it will save you a lot of wood, time, and effectively gives you an extra ring.

All you need is a box of some sort – this can be a wooden chest or a medium size cardboard box (24 x 18 x 14in is good). Insulate this first with anything that is at hand and not being used – tin foil or old tiles are good. Once that is done, you can create the majority of your insulation using polystyrene, shredded paper, or as the name suggests, hay (the latter is my preferred option as you can produce this yourself). To keep the hay from going everywhere, I recommend shoving as much hay as you can squeeze into some small string onion bags (ask your local greengrocer for these), but this is by no means necessary. Leave a space in the middle of your insulation for a large cast iron pot, one with a lid and two small handles on each side if you have it. And that's it.

In terms of cooking with it, it's equally simple. Bring your pot to the boil on whatever it is you use, or at least to the stage where you would normally simmer it on a conventional cooker, depending on the food you're cooking. Making sure the lid is on securely, stick it into the space left in your prepared hay box, cover with as much hay as you can pack in, and close the lid of the box. For extra insulation, you can put a rug over it or bury it in a hole in the ground.

How long it then takes depends on the food – barley takes about four hours, vegetable soup about an hour, whilst fish will take at least an hour and a half. If you use this method it is necessary to plan ahead, so if you want barley or rye for lunch you should bring it to the boil at the same time you make your morning tea. Once it's fully cooked, you may want to slightly reheat it again, but this isn't necessary.[223] The good news is that if you forget about it, the food will never burn.

Earth Ovens

Cooking is one thing, baking another. If you fancy moneyless bread, pizza, foccacia and the like then you are going to need a wood-fired oven, which can be fuelled using locally grown or scavenged wood. If this sounds like it's the best thing since wood-fired rye sourdough, I'd recommend reading

Build Your Own Earth Oven[224] by Kiko Denzer before going any further.

The key to making an earth oven is ensuring that you give it enough time to dry; depending on the season, this may take weeks. To speed up the process, you can light little fires in there regularly. The good news is that it will not only give you years of great, moneylessly baked food, it will become an attraction for many people in the local community who fancy making their own pizza or bread from it. Why not make its construction a community event in the first place, drawing on the skills, knowledge and resources of all involved? An earth oven will not get used very often by one family, so sharing it with everyone in the community is a beneficial act on every level – personal, social and ecological.

HEATING

Staying warm in temperate climates does not have to heat up the biosphere, and there are many moneyless solutions to heating bills out there, ranging from the simple to the technical. Which one you use will depend on your situation and needs.

Jumpers (and long johns)

It's a lot easier to insulate yourself than a house, but I'm always amazed to see how many times I visit friends in the city who are sitting indoors, with the thermostat up high, in a T-shirt. I appreciate that we all like a little comfort, but a jumper or two in winter isn't too much to ask of a population that lives in a temperate climate. If we had to go to the trouble of chopping wood we had to grow ourselves to heat our homes, there is no way we'd waste so much energy for the want of a warm jumper and a pair of long johns.

Gas bottle wood-burner

To heat my moneyless caravan for three years, I used a wood-burner converted from an old gas bottle. What design you will want to use depends on your circumstances, but there are a number to choose from[225] – I used a 13kg bottle.

Two pieces of advice: first, burn off all the paint and zinc from the gas bottle somewhere outside, as the fumes from both could make you very ill

(I strongly recommend doing it with an experienced/qualified person the first time). Second, I would strongly advise that you consider putting a baffle plate in it. A baffle plate is a piece of metal that is usually fitted inside the stove. This baffle stops the heat going straight up the chimney, meaning that the hot gases produced have to stay in the burner longer before they find their way out. This gives the flue gases more chance to mix with the air and fully combust, meaning more heat for you. Depending on how efficiently they burn and whether or not you incorporate this into a grander design for your house, you may also be able to use this wood-burner for cooking and water heating.

Once you've made one yourself, and tested it out for a few months to see if it works efficiently, why not organise a local Freeskilling event (see page 236) and show others in your local community how to make one too?

Masonry stove

If you want something more efficient than a gas bottle burner (which despite being potentially free to make has only an efficiency of around 50-60%), Patrick Whitefield recommends fitting a masonry stove.[225] Whereas conventional wood-burners, such as the model above, heat by convection (warming up the air as it burns), these function by burning very quickly during the day, storing it in the masonry walls and tiles which often clad it, before releasing it slowly as radiant heat throughout the rest of the day and night.

These work particularly well if installed in a passive solar house – building one of these, or converting to one, is probably the best thing you can do in terms of heating your house for free. If you are building a new house, build it with the masonry stove in the middle, as this one stove could then "heat all the rooms in a medium size house, upstairs and down".[227] On a moderately cold winter's day, you could get away with only needing one 45 minute burn for the entire day. If used in a passive solar house, this may also suffice for very cold weather.

Another benefit, as Whitefield points out, is that masonry stoves also allow you to "make good use of prunings, brash [and] slabwood" which you may otherwise struggle to use. And because of their efficiency, they are almost certainly fit for use in smokeless zones. The bad news is that these will not be moneyless in the first instance, and can be quite expensive.

Sources of wood

Whether you are wanting to cook dinner on a rocket stove, or fuel your fancy new wood-burner, you're going to need a source of wood.

For kindling, I find old vegetable boxes excellent as they light very quickly, and once you break them up they are already the ideal size for this stage of the process – no need for fiddly fine wood-chopping. Wholesalers and retailers of fruit and vegetables usually have to spend time and money breaking up and dumping these, so if you ask them nicely they'll be more than happy to give you a load.

For burning, you're going to need something much more substantial. If you're very lucky you'll have some ash, hawthorn, maple or hazel growing around where you live, as all of these are very good for burning. If you are scavenging wood that has already fallen, always try to identify what type of tree it is, as each will have different qualities which will affect how well it burns – knowing someone experienced is useful, but don't worry if you don't as you will learn through doing it yourself. I stumbled upon this following wonderful little old poem by Lady Celia Congreve[228] (believed to have first been published in *The Times* on March 2nd 1930) which, if you can remember it or keep it handy, offers a brief guide to the qualities of each type of wood you may be contemplating burning.

THE FIREWOOD POEM

Beechwood fires are bright and clear
If the logs are kept a year,
Chestnut's only good they say,
If for logs 'tis laid away.
Make a fire of Elder tree,
Death within your house will be;
But ash new or ash old,
Is fit for a queen with crown of gold

Birch and fir logs burn too fast
Blaze up bright and do not last,
it is by the Irish said

Hawthorn bakes the sweetest bread.
Elm wood burns like churchyard mould,
E'en the very flames are cold
But ash green or ash brown
Is fit for a queen with golden crown

Poplar gives a bitter smoke,
Fills your eyes and makes you choke,
Apple wood will scent your room
Pear wood smells like flowers in bloom
Oaken logs, if dry and old
keep away the winter's cold
But ash wet or ash dry
a king shall warm his slippers by.

As a general rule, any wood you collect should be seasoned well before burning. If you are chopping wood down, please do plant more, remembering that the next generation's ability to live moneylessly, in terms of their heating at least, depends on you thinking many years ahead.

If you live in the city and don't have much access to trees or fallen wood, you can approach your local joiner and carpenter's workshops, if you have them, and ask them if they're happy for you to come and take their off-cuts away – do not burn any painted or treated wood, chipboard or MDF. Whilst you're there I would also recommend getting as many bags of sawdust as you can possibly transport, as this will be useful for lighting your fire. Simply stick a little sawdust in the newspaper you use as a starter and watch it catch fire very quickly, and last for much longer. If you have extra, it is also ideal for covering your poo in the compost toilet (see page 142).

Solar Thermal

One of the few things that even my more hardy friends want is hot water, at least in the winter. Which is understandable, given the climate in the UK. That desire doesn't mean that there is a magical solution that matches both the desire for true sustainability that we pay lip-service to and the levels of comfort that our pathetically soft rear-ends have become accustomed to, but it is the reality of where we are at in terms of expectation.

There may be a middle ground. Instead of buying a solar water heater, you could build your own. Nick Rosen, in his book *How to Live Off-grid*, describes how some of the houses he visited at Townhead, near Sheffield, use what he describes as "the simplest form of DIY solar heater": a system involving "old radiators painted black and fixed to their south-facing walls." Black is used as it absorbs heat. Rosen explains that the water from "their well, or rainwater tanks on the roof, passes through the radiator, is heated by the sun,"[229] and eventually makes its way onto your skin or dishes.

OPEN SOURCE ECOLOGY

This is a project that consists of a collaboration of farmers, engineers and supporters whose goal is to build a Global Village Construction Set (GVCS)[230] that they claim is "a modular, DIY, low cost, high-performance platform that allows for the easy fabrication of the 50 different industrial machines that it takes to build a small, sustainable civilisation with modern comforts." The machines they are working on include everything from 3D printers to wind turbines and aluminium extractors from clay.

Given my philosophical beliefs, machines such as these find themselves near the bottom of my POP model for the appropriate level of technology in my life, despite the generous spirit behind the project and the intentions and ethos of those involved. Yet given that "open-source, low cost, modular, user-serviceable, DIY, closed loop manufacturing" are stated key features of all the things they've built and intend to build (the designs of which will be freely available to me and you), I felt it was appropriate for me to include it here as their work may be very beneficial in helping you, and us collectively, to make the transition from the monetary economy we live in now to a decentralised, fully localised gift economy in the future.

OPEN SOURCE TECHNOLOGIES AND FREE COMMUNICATION

Considering that the levels of technology that I feel are appropriate make Luddites look like Silicon Valley entrepreneurs, promoting open source software such as some of those below probably seems a bit odd. Despite my beliefs that the existence of such logistically complex technologies are the root of many of our personal, social and ecological crises, I agree that they can play a transitional role in getting us out of the mess the stories behind them got us into. In fact, many of the transition tools I mention throughout this book have an online aspect to varying degrees, despite the fact that their ultimate goal is to get people participating in outdoor life again.

What technologies – both software and hardware – we do use, and how we acquire them, is very important, especially in relation to moneyless living and activism. Open source technology is not only free for everyone to use, its philosophy is very much in keeping with the principles behind Freeconomy.

Computers, mobile phones and other communication devices

I got the last three laptops I've used from members of my local Freeconomy group who had upgraded to a newer model. Of course these only came into existence because other people continue to buy newer ones, and that is a valid point. Regardless, it is no argument against making full and complete use of every resource we have, especially if we can utilise them to help the transition to post-industrial and non-monetary economies. If you can't find a computer on either Freecycle or Freegle, then you will certainly be able to find the component parts for one from different members of the network – a screen from one, a keyboard and mouse from another. All you then need to do is put them together, which someone from your local Freeconomy group should be able to show you how to do.

Whenever I tell someone I don't have a mobile phone, someone always tells me that I can have their old one. This I find very kind and generous – the problem is, I don't have a mobile phone because I don't want one, not because there isn't an endless pit of them lying around! Unless you have a fetish for new, shiny things, there really is no need to ever buy a mobile phone again. If you get one with a pay-as-you-go SIM card in it, you'll be able to receive calls for free – I used one like this for three years.

Once you have your computer, you then have to decide what operating system and programmes you want to run on it.

Free Communication

As you may have guessed by now, I'm not a fan of mobile phones, for any number of reasons – their reported effects on bee populations, the fact we're instantly contactable at any hour of the day or night for both work and pleasure, and the way they have cunningly convinced us that we can no longer live without them. On the surface, they look off-grid, as they are not connected to anything, especially if you power them using solar. However, the grid they are connected to is an invisible one – the fact we can't see it doesn't mean it isn't there.

Skype

I'm often surprised by how few people use Skype,[231] which enables people to talk to each other for nothing. It isn't as convenient as a mobile, and because of the cheap calls you can make on the latter its appeal is diminishing. However, if you want to live moneylessly and still communicate with faraway family or friends, I'd suggest using it for all telephone and video calls, at a location where you can get free access to the internet.

Linux

This is an open source computer operating system that forms the foundations for free alternatives (such as Ubuntu) to other operating systems sold by Microsoft and Apple, such as Windows. I've found Ubuntu to work better than any other operating system I bought in the past; it is much quicker during start-up and ongoing use, it is secure (you don't need any costly antivirus protection), and very much in keeping with the philosophy behind Freeconomy and the gift economy. Due to its increasing popularity over the last twenty years, more and more software is now compatible with it, meaning that it is the operating system of choice for anyone who wants to take the control of technology away from the large multinational corporations and give it back to the people who use it.

OpenOffice and LibreOffice

OpenOffice[232] is to Microsoft Office what Linux is to Microsoft Windows. It is the free and open source alternative to the expensive word processors, spreadsheets and presentation tools that are ubiquitous amongst computer users today, which I can only assume is due to a lack of awareness that tools such as OpenOffice exist (it works with either Linux or Windows). In my experience these work just as well, and this book was written on OpenOffice.

In 2010 some of the OpenOffice team set up a new organisation called The Document Foundation, in order to protect OpenOffice from potential external factors. The result of this is that LibreOffice[233] (meaning 'Free Office') came into existence and, like OpenOffice, it is compatible with other major office suites and platforms. Why not try both suites and then choose the one that suits you the best.

INFORMATION SECURITY

It is an unfortunate fact of today's culture (at least in the UK) that anyone living an unusual lifestyle – especially one that questions the dominant cultural stories – is liable to find themselves under observation by the authorities. Recent media revelations have covered everything from phone hacking to undercover cops infiltrating environmental groups for years at a time. The government campaign slogan declared, "If you've got nothing to hide, you've got nothing to fear", but this is an argument that is long since discredited in academic and philosophical circles.

I'll assume that you, dear reader, have nothing to hide. Does that mean that you are happy to send me your address and credit card bills for the past year? Or your health records? Or nude photos of yourself? Probably not. Our desire for, and right to, privacy does not imply that we have done something criminal or shameful, and our status as decent human beings should not mean that we are obliged to show everything to every authority who wants it. This is especially true when we consider how frequently these official databases are hacked and/or leaked to the world, and how inadvertent errors in such secret databases have led to people being jailed or having their bank accounts frozen without even being able to find out why.

There are valid arguments on both sides of the transparency/privacy debate, but they rarely seem to cut both ways. Are Google, or the police, keen to reveal all available information about themselves? No.

This book is not the place for a lengthy discussion on privacy, but my personal belief is that people should have the ability to decide for themselves how much of their information is tracked and stored. Accordingly, here are a few useful free tools for keeping your data secure.

DuckDuckgo and Startpage

If you don't like the idea of corporations storing your information for any of a number of reasons then DuckDuckGo[234] is the search engine for you. It never stores IP addresses or user information and only uses cookies when absolutely necessary. Not only does this protect your privacy, it has two other benefits. First, you won't get bombarded with advertisements that the algorithms constructed by those whose motto is 'don't be evil' have worked out will appeal to some vulnerable aspect of your psyche. Second, you will be able to escape your 'filter bubble'. Many people assume that everyone's results on Google search are the same, but in fact the results it returns for each search you make are personalised based on over fifty indicators, including your search history and click history. So if you tend to click on things you agree with, Google will gradually demote (effectively filter out) more and more opposing information and differing viewpoints, leaving you less informed.[235] DuckDuckGo and other alternatives do not do this.

However, if you like the advanced search algorithms that Google uses, but don't like them having so much information about everything you look at, Startpage[236] is an excellent compromise, as it allows you to utilise Google's search results without allowing them to track your searches or record your IP address.

Hushmail

If you currently use a normal email account, you may as well just cc. in the police and MI5 to your emails, such is their ability to access your account if they suspect you of doing anything *untoward* – and remember, the authorities seem to classify almost anything that is helping to protect the community of life on this planet from the interests of corporations as *untoward*.

In truth, the only really secure way of sending email is to not send any, and use the more old fashioned methods instead. The woods, without your mobile phone even on you, is probably the only fully secure place left in this country to discuss something you want to keep private.

Below running off to the woods, on the scale of information security, is running your own server to host your email, but this isn't sustainable in any sense of the word. The most realistic option is to get yourself a Hushmail[237] account. Hushmail encrypts your email before it is sent so that nobody other than those who are the intended recipients can read it, after they themselves have decrypted it by one means or another. In Hushmail's words, "a typical email message is no more secure than a holiday postcard sent through the public postal system", whereas with their system it is more like "a letter in a sealed envelope". Hushmail doesn't operate outside of the law, so do use it with that in mind. But privacy is central to everything they do, so they will fight for it all the way. They don't, under any circumstances, release customer information unless they are issued with an order that is legally enforceable in British Columbia, Canada, where their servers are held.

TrueCrypt

If you like Hushmail and DuckDuckgo, you may also be interested in TrueCrypt.[238] This uses on-the-fly encryption to allow you to protect any files on your computer that you don't want anyone else to obtain access to. As the government cracks down more on activists campaigning for a more sustainable, just and free world, tools such as TrueCrypt can play an important role in keeping those who have the courage to stand up to this system out of its prisons. It's incredibly secure. The FBI spent a year trying to obtain access to TrueCrypt protected disks owned by Brazilian banker Daniel Dantas, who was under investigation for financial crimes, and were unable to decrypt them. If the bankers can protect themselves with it, activists may as well also. Just make sure you don't lose your password, otherwise it could take the world's greatest hackers years of work to enable you to access them again.

CHAPTER 12

EDUCATION

> *School is the advertising agency which makes you believe that you need the society as it is.*
>
> Ivan Illich, *Deschooling Society*

It goes without saying that education is crucial to our wellbeing and happiness. But what type of education is best? Before we can answer that question we have to first consider and define what exactly we are educating ourselves for. If it is for a life in the wage economy and the repetitive conveyor belts of industrialisation, administration and consumerism, then our current education system has a lot of merit, considering its unparalleled success in factory farming the human bodies and minds required to keep the Good Ship Economic Growth afloat. Its prowess in simultaneously stamping out our ability to question the cultural stories that form the hull of this ship shouldn't go unrecognised either. In contrast, if education's aim is to give us the best opportunity to live happy, deeply connected, sustainable, creative, free, holistic, compassionate and adventurous lives, what form would it take and how would it look?

If we believe that there is more to life than packing plastic or coming up with some technical innovation that makes cleaning the carpet easier, then we may want to rethink how we view education. Learning is something we couldn't avoid even if we wanted to. Every moment of life is an opportunity to learn something, even if we are only doing it on a subconscious level. Therefore is it something we must necessarily do in a classroom, formally teaching children the skills they'd realistically need to get jobs in the global economy as it functions now? Or would we be wiser to educate ourselves for life through actual living, integrating our education into the fabric of daily life in the context of a community whose primary focus is to create a habitat for happy, healthy and creative people?

The next generation of humans undoubtedly going to inherit a world is very different to the one you or I grew up in, like it or not, considering the converging challenges we're faced with. It is on that basis that I would argue that we must rethink how we do education. If our children's future concerns revolve around how they are going to eat, or produce the panoply of other things that make up their basic survival needs, then is teaching them the advantages and disadvantages of Just-in-time inventory systems, or the Ten Key Rules of Retail Marketing, really the wisest way forward?

I'm not for a moment suggesting that all of the current educational system is wrong. Given the stories we've convinced ourselves of, it is probably the best we could have, and compared to many other countries we're very lucky to have it. But there is an opportunity cost to this current system, one which I believe is too high a price to pay. We're learning skills for an economy based on specialised division of labour in a high technology society, without any thought for the very basic needs of human life.

I was 22 before I planted my first seed. Bar the occasional blackberry, I had never been wild food foraging either. I didn't know one tree from the next, let alone have any clue about which ones would be good for making chairs and which for making houses. I'd no idea how to communicate my feelings to girlfriends without it inevitably blowing up into an argument. I knew there were some 'environmental' problems in the world, but I had no understanding of how utterly important microbes, fungi, algae, earthworms and death were to the health of the entire biosphere and all that lived within it. I could produce profit and loss accounts for businesses with consummate ease, but I hadn't the faintest idea of how to love someone unconditionally. In *Last Child in the Woods*,[239] Richard Louv talks about 'nature-deficit disorder', which he claims has led to epidemic obesity, depression and attention-deficit disorder, amongst other things. Growing up in semi-rural Ireland, my symptoms weren't quite as extreme as that, yet I am still only beginning to feel a full respect for the rest of life, such was the deep impact of my separation from Nature.

As I mentioned in chapter four, the reality of educating their kids is one of the most commonly cited reasons why parents tell me they couldn't live moneylessly. And it is impossible to disagree with them, for all sorts of obvious reasons, within the context of how we live today. Yet if we changed the rationale behind education and learning, and consequently the ways in which we share skills and information with one another, whilst co-creating new designs for living that reflect this new perspective and which integrate learning into everyday life, then I see no good reason why it wouldn't be possible.

Can you imagine a world where a child, instead of going to a suburban school, grows up in a community of people who want to educate their children for a life of creativity, connection, freedom and – heaven forbid – fun? Where one day little Benny goes out picking ramsons with his mother in the morning, before helping his father cook them up for lunch. A world which offers him the freedom to then go off and play with his friends in the afternoon, before coming back to read with his big sister in the evening. A way of life where the next day he is outside helping his neighbour Jim make a chair out of the coppiced willow that his uncle planted three years earlier. An educational system where Benny can come or go whenever he pleases, but almost always comes, whether it be to help his mum make plum jam from the fruits of their forest garden as she teaches him maths, to help his father plant some seeds, or to chase the ducks and chickens around the pond after collecting a basket full of eggs. Such a system chimes with the Nigerian Igbo's saying, *Ora na azu nwa,* meaning: *it takes a village to raise a child.* If you can imagine anything resembling this, then keep reading, and resolve to do everything you can to educate your child in a way that rings true for you.

EDUCATION FOR A NON-MONETARY ECONOMY

In this chapter I am not going to ramble on about the types of learning systems we could dream up and put into action. There's no need. People are already out there making them happen. Some of these are options which are already being done without any money, taxpayers' or otherwise. Others, whilst currently functioning with the use of cash (and sometimes lots of it), have been included because a) they could quite easily function on a moneyless basis if we constructed gift economies for them to operate within and b) they are already actively encouraging their students and teachers alike to question the way we live today, and to dramatically change the spirit in which we do so. Therefore I include them all to highlight the range of transitional teaching methods we already have available to us, from which the educational forms of the future may spring.

Home education

Despite it being the method by which we have educated our children for most of our time on the planet, a few centuries of classroom schooling have made home education an idea that seems radical to most people today. Indeed, people often need reassuring that the law is clear on this matter, which it is – while education is compulsory, attendance at a school is not. It was in response to the vulgarities and ineptitude of modern day education that home schooling experienced a rebirth in the 1960s, following the publication and popularisation of books such as John Holt's *How Children Fail*[240] and subsequent *How Children Learn*,[241] along with others such as Ivan Illich's *Deschooling Society*.[242]

THE OPTION OF HOME EDUCATING

Ross Mountney,[243] author of
Learning Without School: Home Education[244]

Of all the alternative choices there are in life, the choice of home schooling is probably one that worries people the most. But thousands of parents in the UK are dissatisfied with the way schools are educating their children and are now successfully home educating. Hopefully this will give a little insight into how, and alleviate some of those worries.

We decided to home educate ours for two basic reasons; our increasing distaste with a conveyor belt style of pushing children towards results with disregard for the development of the individual. And secondly, more importantly, because they were unhappy. They became unwell as a consequence and we were shocked to watch their pre-school desire to learn squeezed out of them by an over-prescriptive curriculum.

Now, they are launching into the world beyond their school years and they, and many others like them whom we home schooled with, are proof that home education works extremely well. You can provide a stimulating and individualised approach to learning that equips your child with what they need to live their lives productively. It can cost as much or as little as your budget allows yet still be a good education. Your children can build valuable social skills by mixing with a wide range of people and a high proportion of adults, in contrast to the inhibiting and sometimes questionable social climate found in schools. You can successfully enable your home schooled children to go onto higher education or into work as they desire without disproportionate pressure.

How does it work?

The approach to home educating you adopt can be completely up to you and the needs of your child and family. We are all very familiar with a school-style approach to education and many parents start out using that as a model. There are books with academic exercises in them which you can find in most libraries and online, and there are many, many learning websites, games and activities online (like BBC Learning). You can find out almost everything you need to know on the web including the National Curriculum.

But as your confidence grows you discover that there are many ways to learn other than by academic exercises and this familiar school approach. For example; you probably learnt to use your new mobile phone by exploring what it does and using it, not by reading about it. Children can learn in the same way. Education does not have to be complicated.

Many children learn to read just by being read to and enjoying books with their parents. Many children begin to understand number and maths in the same experiential way, just by using numbers and counting. Physical and practical everyday activities (shopping is a good example) that involve discussion, observation and explanation, can teach children enormous amounts. In fact many parents don't realise that they have already taught their children so much before school just by incidental conversations, by engaging with them, by giving them time and attention. This style of learning can continue as you home educate.

All experiences teach your children something. By making those experiences varied, stimulating, proactive and relevant, your children will be learning. Sitting in a classroom at a desk, listening to a teacher and writing stuff down is no guarantee there is learning taking place and, despite what we've been conned to believe, it's not the only way to learn either. If children are involved with what they're doing, whether it's enjoying *Horrible Histories*, creating, growing food, or visiting a nature reserve, they will be learning from it, even more so if there's an engaged adult chatting with them about it.

Children learn best from practical involvement. The beauty of home educating is that you can make much of your child's learning practical, from experimenting, making up stories, dissecting a chicken, to exploring materials or pairing the gloves (good start to times tables). Equally, children learn just as well lying on the floor, or lolling on the settee, out in the garden or even on the beach, as they do sitting at a desk. They can also be fiddling and not still, they can be noisy or use music if it helps, they can learn later in the afternoon not early in the morning (which is no good for teenagers). If it works, you can do it that way.

Just to give a typical day as an example; we may have started the morning by studying a book based in Victorian times, followed that up with a web search, discussion and a trip to our local museum where there was a Victorian classroom, researched a Victorian recipe to cook at a later date, had a swim for recreation and exercise usually with other home schoolers, visited the library. This gives you an idea of how you could vary the day and approach learning in a different way. You can have as much or as little structure as suits.

Thus, through home educating you can strip away many of the unnecessary school-style structures like tests, time and age limits, subject and timetable restrictions and learn in a way that truly suits your child's needs, rather than the needs of an institution which requires to teach masses with as little teacher input as possible.

Home education can give your children a thoroughly enjoyable experience of learning. If they're enjoying it, they will learn. In fact, one of the things that moved our children on the most was the discovery that, rather than something being done to them by other people, often in uncaring ways, learning was actually something that they could have some charge of and enjoy. That feeling remains with them in their older lives now.

How do your children mix and make friends?

There are many home educators' blogs on the web and organisations to support and help home educating families; the community grows daily. So there is no need for anyone to home school in isolation – kids or parents. Networking on the web and joining organisations will soon find you other home schoolers.

We joined several home educating groups. These varied in what they provided. Some were for social purposes; meeting for sport or at play centres where parents could swap concerns, ideas and get support whilst the children were active. Some were for educational outings, perhaps a field trip, visit to a gallery or site of specific interest. Or sometimes for an organised activity or learning session.

Through these groups both parents and children form relationships and make friends. The children also make friends in the same way all children make friends, through clubs, sports and social activities. Schools do not have exclusivity on friendships. In fact some of the relationships there are formed under threat and anxiety, not through care, mutual interest and respect.

Within the home educating groups there is usually a high proportion of adults to children. So children have an adult example on which to base their own behaviour. This makes them far more skilled in their interaction, conversation, compassion and care for others. It also makes them far more employable.

Far from being 'weird', which is a myth about home schooled children, they are in many ways much more able to fit into society than school children. The social setting in school, where you rarely interact with anyone outside your age group, is highly unnatural and forced. Home schooled children are socially skilled because they have learned in more natural social groupings, mixing with people of all ages, who wear normal shoes not just designer ones, who interact out of friendship and support rather than one-upmanship, bullying and tension and who don't have to fight to get their needs met.

What about cost?

Schools try to impress us with their glittering resources. But it's not resources that educate the children, it is the people with whom they learn and the experiences they have.

Many children sit in schools surrounded by the latest technology, books and qualified teachers but remain totally switched off. Because it's not the gadgets or the teacher status that get children learning, it is encouragement, stimulation, care and attention; not always in abundance within schools.

We, and many others, home educated on a very tight budget. But we were able to give our children a rich educative experience by using the resources that were around us and the experiences in our everyday lives. For example, we didn't need costly equipment, we could improvise with what we had. We didn't need expensive workbooks to learn about history, we visited local places of historic interest, mostly for free, museums included. We have a home full of things to use in mathematical calculations. We used recycling centres. We extended language and vocabulary by talking, reading and writing. The world around them became the children's biggest learning resource, particularly for science. A caring, interested adult, the best resource of all. These are free. You can't really buy education; you have to nurture it.

What happens as they get older?

Parents tend to think it gets more serious as they get older. In actual fact the foundation years of a child's education are the most important. As they get older their education develops naturally outside school.

Through discussion with them about what they might like to do in the world, ours made their own choices and with our guidance worked towards finding the right path for them. Our children decided to go to college to gain qualifications for university. Some of our friends studied for GCSEs and A Levels at home using study packs. Some did neither and went straight into work. You can choose the route you want. You can take it in any direction you want, any time scale you want, according to your child's needs and preferences.

A different understanding

When you home educate you begin to develop a different understanding about what education is, far removed from the the grade-greedy culture of schools. Education is to help equip children for life in the world outside school, not to force them to gain grades just to push schools up League Tables.

Education is not only about knowledge, it's about what you do with that knowledge in the light of being a caring, responsible, respectful human being. Kids learn about that in an atmosphere of being cared for and respected themselves, not in a place where they have no choice and no voice. Education is a personal and individual journey, not a by-product of politicians trying to win votes.

Home educating allows you to turn the education of your children from a political, conveyor-belt process into a personalised journey of self discovery and growth. It gives you the opportunity to demonstrate the importance of care, responsibility and respect. And it gives you the chance to make love and fulfilment an important part of that journey. For it is loving and fulfilled citizens, not necessarily qualified ones, who make a loving and fulfilled society. Which is ultimately what education is for.

Freeskilling

A child of the Freeconomy movement, Freeskilling organically grew out of its parent's success, adopting its ideology, utilising the database of skilled and kind people it accumulated, and applying it in a way that made the most efficient use of its members' time. A small group of people, including myself, set up the original group in Bristol in 2008, and since then the Freeskilling format has spread to many countries around the world.

Freeskilling is hardly rocket science (though rocket science could be taught using this model), and for us it began with a simple question: what if everyone in our local Freeconomy group took turns to teach everyone else who was interested – children and adults alike – one skill that they possess, completely for free? If the woman who knew how to carve wooden spoons taught that to everyone who was interested one evening, and if the man who knew how to make great bread taught local loaf lovers how to make a fantastic sourdough?

The answer: you'd have a community of highly skilled, economically resilient people, all of whom would become increasingly self-sufficient by the week and much less reliant on money to meet all of their needs. It would also create a growing database of available skills which, in turn, could be passed on to others in the wider community on either a group or one-to-one basis.

The Bristol Freeskilling evening takes place one evening each week (in other areas they have day long events, whilst others organise it once a month). One person from the local group, knowledgeable and skilled in a certain field, comes along to a free and regular venue and spends anywhere between 30 minutes to 2 hours teaching others in the community how to do that skill. The venue hosts the evening for free, the member of the community teaches for free (and often gets a valuable lesson and experience in public speaking in the process), and the attendees get to come for free. No funding is needed, and everyone has the opportunity to learn, regardless of their financial status. Skills shared range from bicycle maintenance, basic DIY and plumbing to wild food foraging, knitting and tutorials on using open source software and platforms. Within this model, the teacher one week is the student the next.

The Bristol group, as well as many others, has been a huge success, and despite not having a penny of funding it continues to attract anywhere between twenty to two hundred attendees per week. But that is only part of the story. It also attracts a diverse group of people and this inevitably leads to many friendships being made, strengthening the community and sometimes even resulting in further collaborative social projects being created by those who meet there. It's a perfect example of the gift economy in practice, and proves that people don't need the incentive of monetary reward to want to teach other people in their community the skills they've been able to acquire.

If you like this concept but haven't got a group near you, then why not set one up? All you need to do is gather a small group of people who are willing to volunteer an hour or two of their week to help organise it (you can put a shout out for such people on your local Freeconomy network), find a venue that is willing to host it for free (cafés and social centres are often happy to), and then ask the local members of your community (whether it be through Freeconomy or as a poster on your various local noticeboards) if they want to fill one of the weekly/monthly slots on your schedule and play their part in the great reskilling of society. All that is left to do then is to promote it on the plethora of free networks that people in your area use, whether it be word of mouth or online social networking – you could even set up a website to this effect.[245]

FREESKILLING IN PRACTICE: SOURDOUGH BREAD

Richard Andersen, a Freeskilling teacher some weeks, a Freeskilling student others

Freeskilling always appealed to me as a step towards what we need to open up to in society: sharing knowledge and resources in our local community without needing to involve money, a false resource that will only become more and more scarce. In a close knit community like a village or a local interest group this sharing might happen more spontaneously, but with half the world's population now living in cities it is imperative that we try and facilitate community exchange on a wider scale.

A friend of mine taught me the simple steps involved in making sourdough bread and gave me some starter culture to keep. This was three years ago and the culture lives on in my fridge, having spawned several offshoots for friends and fellow Freeconomists. It is a joy to teach such a simple process and watch people go away with a bit of starter that could live to see their grandchildren make their own bread.

There is a sense of freedom in not having to use commercial yeasts, and a poetic beauty in working with wild fermentation as our ancestors did generations ago. You can make better bread than anything you see in the shops or supermarkets, and if you go skipping for flour, or grow and grind your own grain, it is totally free.

For the sake of ease I recommend getting hold of a starter from someone, rather than making it yourself. It's more fun to share and less hassle! Here's a basic recipe:

3 cups of flour (your favourite stoneground spelt or rye, or whatever is in the skip!)
2 teaspoons of salt
1 cup of starter (see, it's as easy as 3-2-1)
Water
Optional: seeds, herbs, spices, fruit, onion – literally whatever you fancy putting in your bread. Experiment to your heart's content.

Mix the dry ingredients (flour, salt and seeds/spices/etc.) first, then add the sourdough starter and a cup of water. Mix well together with a wooden ladle first, then squeeze it between your fingers for maximum mixing and enjoyment! You want a fairly wet mix, so add some more water if it feels a bit dry.

Let the mix stand in a bowl for an hour or so at room temperature with a towel over it to keep flies and dust out. Whilst you wait, grease a bread tin with some butter and dust it lightly with flour. Take the bread mix out of the bowl, drizzle a bit of oil on the kitchen surface to prevent it sticking and fold the dough onto itself a few times. No need for heavy kneading! Shape the dough to fit the tin and put it in the tin. Cover the tin and let it sit at room temperature for 5-10 hours. I usually set my dough in the evening and bake it the next morning when I wake up. If you have a wood-fired oven and are skilled in using it, then bake your bread as you would normally do the first time, then simply alter your technique as you experiment with this variety.

If you are using a normal cooker, heat your oven to about 220°C and bake the loaf for 40 minutes. You'll have to experiment because all ovens are slightly different, but this is a good starting point. If your loaf comes out a little too hard or soft, just adjust your temperature accordingly. If the loaf is slightly undercooked in the centre turn the temperature down a little and lengthen the time. Take the loaf out of the tin, let it sit on the counter with a kitchen towel over it to cool slowly. And that's it!

The Khan Academy and Instructables

The Khan Academy[246] is a sort of online Freeskilling, and is a powerful tool both for parents who are considering home schooling and those who want to learn – or for their children to learn – in their own way and at their own pace.

Imagine you were teaching cycling to some kids, who, after a month or two of trying, still hadn't mastered staying on without using their stabilisers. They show up for your next class as normal, both excited and nervous about the prospect of taking the stabilisers off. But you tell them that was last week's lesson, and that this week they are going to have to ride a unicycle, just because they should have learned to cycle by now given that others in the class already have. This sounds like an absurd way to run an education system, and it is, but it is exactly the way education works in many countries.

The Khan Academy works on a completely different understanding of what education is about. It allows students to master one thing before moving on to more difficult aspects of it. Used in conjunction with home schooling, children could develop at a rate they enjoy, and not one that is stressful and unhelpful to them.

Founded by Salman Khan[246] as a not-for-profit organisation, it is an ever expanding collection of videos (2,800 different tutorials at the time of writing, which have already provided over 120 million lessons) that teach the viewer, in an easy and fun way, everything from algebra and arithmetic to art history, economic theory, biology and even how the money and banking system works. All is available for free.

Instructables(.com)[248] is a very similar project with a huge database of skills, mostly practical, such as how to make a cantenna,[249] your own solar panels, and how to knit or walk on stilts (which I am not entirely convinced is practical but sure is a lot of fun). Again it works as an online version of Freeskilling. If you know how to make something, you can either film yourself doing it or write step-by-step instructions, before uploading it onto the website. From that point onwards anyone can search for that skill and learn how to do it. Similarly, if you want to learn something, go to their website and search for it. My advice is to view a number of different options – and there is always a choice – before deciding which instructions to follow.

While both of these depend on access to a computer and the internet to exist, I see them as powerful transitional tools that will enable us to skill up for a different future and learn in different ways. If you are completely moneyless and have no internet access, you could use both for free at your local library. Given that libraries are free only at the point of service and currently rely on taxpayers money to exist (though they could be run on a non-monetary model and examples of this do exist), it would be good if you then put these skills to use in some way that was beneficial to the rest of the community in your local area, and not just yourself.

The Barefoot College

As noted earlier, the majority of schools today are designed with the needs of the monetary economy in mind, and not the people they were once intended to serve. Schools today certainly aren't run with localised living as the goal. It was in response to this that Sanjit 'Bunker' Roy[250] set up the first *Barefoot College* in India in 1972. Since then it "has been providing basic services and solutions to problems in rural communities, with the objective of making them self-sufficient and sustainable".[251] Throughout the day and night it teaches young and old, literate or illiterate, the skills they need to be of use to their local community in a way that ensures they are as self-sufficient as they can possibly be.

The skills they teach can be roughly categorised into "solar energy, water, education, healthcare, rural handicrafts, people's action, communication, women's empowerment and wasteland development". They regularly train people to be such things as teachers, solar cooker engineers, hand pump mechanics, blacksmiths, water testers, doctors, midwives, dentists, artisans and water drillers, all of whom can then serve their community in ways that work for them. The school has five 'non-negotiable' values: equality, collective decision making, decentralisation, self-reliance and austerity (simplicity I believe is a more appropriate word), all of which I believe ring true to the value system of a moneyless economy.

This college currently only exists in India, but there is no reason why it couldn't be replicated in other countries around the world, as the functions it serves are universal, as are its guiding principles.

Other alternative schools

There are many other forms of alternative schooling, but to outline them all would be a book in itself – Fiona Carnie's *Alternative Approaches to Education: A Guide for Parents and Teachers* is a good start for those of you who would love to explore more. I would encourage you to check out other educational models such as the Steiner (Waldorf) schools,[252] Sudbury, Montessori,[253] the Small School,[254] Schumacher College[255] and Summerhill.[256] None of these models are currently moneyless (though they can be free at the point of delivery), but I include them because I see no reason why moneyless versions couldn't be devised and implemented in the future if the will and commitment is there. I also believe that their approaches could help prepare the soil from which the seeds of moneyless economies can grow, as they (to varying degrees) encourage their students to think and live freely and in a sustainable manner.

EDUCATION IN A GIFT WORLD

Charles Eisenstein, author of *The Ascent of Humanity* and *Sacred Economics*

What would education look like in a world in which our connections to Nature and community were healed? Some would say that school itself will wither, its artificial separation of the young from adult activities being a primary engine of youth alienation and disconnection. Perhaps so; on the other hand, young people have always had their special realm, a kingdom of childhood neither rigidly set off from adult society, nor identical to it. And there have always been some adults temperamentally drawn to interact with this realm. I think, then, that even in a future where self-direction and apprenticeship take on a bigger role, there will still be something that we could call school.

Obviously, though, such an institution will be very different from schools today. Far from being an agent of social and planetary healing, today's school system is deeply implicated in maintaining the status quo. Who would consent to perform the mindless, tedious, degrading, dangerous, or immoral jobs necessary to make the world go round, who had not been so conditioned by school?

If not to condition us to do trivial, degrading, or unpleasant work for external rewards (now grades, later money), then what could the purpose of school be? Our naïve response, 'to learn', cannot be it. Children learn automatically; they are like sponges. The question is never whether they will learn; the question is what they will learn. In most societies, they learn the attitudes and ideologies that justify and perpetuate that society, and they learn the habits of complicity, obedience, and dependency on authority. Reacting to this, some philosophers of education propose that a child's learning should be guided solely by his or her own curiosity; that teachers should never pressure or guide a student toward a topic of study, but merely be resources for a child to come to, instruments of a child's self-education. There are schools designed along these principles – the Sudbury model schools – and doubtless they have a place.

Yet, there is also such a thing as a great teacher. I've had the good fortune to experience several. They infected me with passion for something I might not otherwise have known to exist, they pushed me to achieve things I didn't know I was capable of, they initiated me into a new world. There is a fine distinction between pushing knowledge on someone who is not interested in it, and recognizing in someone an interest that they themselves are not aware of. Wary of arrogance, some people say that a teacher should not teach, nor a healer heal, without the explicit invitation of the recipient. A great teacher or healer, though, might listen to the silent asking.

I have spent several paragraphs arguing that there even should be something called 'teaching' and 'school', because that is not at all obvious to those indignant at the awful and sometimes violent colonisation of childhood by school. School has been an instrument of oppression. But what could it be?

Because the nature of school is so intertwined with the nature of money, perhaps the economic future that is possible offers a glimpse into what is possible for school as well. The modern economy forces most people to do things they don't fundamentally care much about, or even that they hate, for an external reward (money) that they associate with their comfort, security, and well-being. So also for school and grades. School is practice for life. Well, suppose we create a different kind of economy, one in which the primary question of *Homo economicus* is not, "How do I make a living?" but rather, "What am I best able and most willing to give to the world?" In other words, what would school look like aligned with an economy of the gift?

In such a world, school will be a place where, first, children discover what their gifts are and what they care about, and second, where they practice and develop those gifts. School today already does that, a little bit, if you are lucky enough to have gifts that the system recognizes and condones. If your gift is for writing or mathematics, you might indeed discover and develop it in school.

But if your gift is improvisational acting, or emotional intelligence, or the sensing of human energy fields, or for growing plants, or almost anything involving the hands or the heart, it is more likely that school will suppress your gifts than develop them. In a way this is understandable: after all, such gifts have been of little use in achieving a secure place in the society of the machine. But that society is changing, and of such gifts the world is now in crying need.

"School is a place for children to discover and develop their gifts." From this principle, a diversity of pedagogic methods and educational models can spring. Many exist already in the margins and crevices of our educational system, in the alternative schools and the classrooms of maverick teachers. In a gift-based future, what today is alternative, maverick, and marginal will become the new normal.

CHAPTER 13

HEALTH AND SEX

First, there's the question of resource consumption ... Second is the failure to accept limits, of which overpopulation and overconsumption are merely two linked systems. Beneath that is our belief we're not animals, that we're separate from the rest of the world, that we're exempt from the negative consequences of our actions, and that we're exempt from death. Beneath these beliefs is a fear and loathing of the body, of the wild and uncontrollable nature of existence itself, and ultimately of death.

Derrick Jensen, *Endgame Volume I*[257]

Debates on all aspects of moneyless living can get lively, with opinions as strong as they are divided. No aspect of the subject gets more heated, however, than the interconnected topics of money-free health and sex. Which will hardly come as a shock to you, as both are extremely emotive issues. However, as Wendell Berry poignantly points out, "if you are going to deal with the issue of health in the modern world, you are going to have to deal with much absurdity. It is not clear, for example, why death should be increasingly looked upon as a curable disease, an abnormality by a society that increasingly looks upon life as insupportably painful and/or meaningless."

Because of their emotive nature, it is very difficult to get any serious, objective debate on the subjects of sustainable health and sex which examines them at a level they deserve and require. I fully appreciate the sensitivity of the issue and the fact that we all have loved ones who have, on the face of it, only survived because of industrial-scale medicines. But I feel that taking the utmost care not to offend anyone has to be weighed up with a bit of a reality check, given that the health and procreational abilities of our entire species hangs in the balance. After a few hundred years of the story of industrialisation, the direction we now take will decide the fate of ourselves and many other species. I feel that each of us has a duty to ask each other tough questions, instead of burying our heads in the sand hoping that the problems will magically disappear. If we don't create healthcare systems which also care for the health of our host organism, then such pontificating won't matter much anyway, as we'll all have lost the ultimate debate. Nature will always have the final word.

Some of what I speak about in this chapter will be hard to contemplate – I say this on the basis that I find it somewhat difficult myself. There are no nice, easy ways out of the pickle we have gotten ourselves into, but we must at least be honest with each other. Our entire civilisation is unsustainable, and that includes our methods of producing healthcare and contraception. Take one dialysis machine, syringe or catheter, examine the raw materials and production processes involved, and you suddenly see a global industrial system unfold. People often ask me "but can we not just have industrialised healthcare and abandon other, more superfluous industrialised products?" No. Such an understanding is fantastical, ludicrous. If you want high tech healthcare, you have to accept the spectrum of industrialised goods. To make just one syringe you need someone working on an oil rig. But an oil rig would be unfeasible if society was only demanding syringes and a few other healthcare products; it only becomes feasible when we want billions of litres of oil and tonnes of plastic, used for all sorts of journeys and useless (often harmful) stuff, every day. Not only that. Specialised workers have to have some way to get to their place of work (cars, trains, buses), and the software and hardware to make them, which require yet more factories. These factories need quarries and parts that are produced in yet more factories requiring even more parts which need further factories and quarries. You can easily see where this leads.

It is important to remember that the very industrialised system that we cling to for our medicines is also the source of many of today's biggest killers. And that beneath all of these arguments for modern industrialised healthcare, lies the unquestioned premise that this is in fact the best, or only, option available to us. As with everything else, we need to fundamentally question the stories that lie behind our approach to medicine. Take just one example: the myth that antibiotics and vaccines saved us all from succumbing to such miserable diseases such as measles. This simple tale, designed to celebrate and exemplify the birth of modern medicine, digested and accepted by even the most 'radical' of us – is simply untrue. According to Ivan Illich, "the combined death rate from scarlet fever, diphtheria, whooping cough, and measles among children up to fifteen shows that nearly 90 percent of the total decline in mortality between 1860 and 1965 had occurred before the introduction of antibiotics and widespread immunisation."[258] So how have we all come to believe the opposite?

On a superficial level, it is not in the interests of big pharmaceutical companies, or the governments they lobby, to have facts such as this widely known; moreover, it suits them down to the ground for us all to believe that our health is dependant on the highly scientific (i.e. inaccessible) knowledge of outside authorities. The version of history we are told is often distorted to whatever story will make the most profit and bring in the most taxes. But in itself, however problematic, the behaviour of these institutions is simply a symptom, a reflexive action against a much deeper root cause. For on a fundamental level, the story of Western medicine chimes so strongly with – and indeed is utterly dependent on – the idea of the self separate from Nature that to question it requires a complete shift in our conception of humanity. This is perhaps why this subject is the most sensitive and controversial of all, because how we deal with the health of our selves is a huge reflection on how we understand them – and mirrors can be immensely uncomfortable.

Some points I make in this chapter will bring up strong feelings in you. If they do, try to view these arguments from the point of view of the whole, or a species on the brink of extinction, instead of the anthropocentric and egocentric view we normally default to, and see if that changes your perspective. The issues involved aren't just emotive, they are also intricate and complex. I will leave the over-simplification of them to others. I want to know what a sustainable way to live – and die – is. If you're easily offended or believe that as many humans as possible should live at all costs, then I'd recommend skipping this chapter and move onto whatever chapter will be of more use to you.

Philosophical discussions aside, I will be outlining all the options that I believe will enable us to make love and have full and healthy lives in a way that also acknowledges the needs of the whole. There won't, unfortunately, be any tips on how to give your partner multiple orgasms. I, being moneyless, prospectless and aesthetically unpleasant, need to keep a little ammunition to myself, otherwise I'll be restricted to the two most sustainable forms of sex there are: chastity and masturbation.

HEALTH OF THE EGOCENTRIC AND HOLISTIC SELVES

A personal anecdote

I'd like to start this with a very personal anecdote, one which I hope you will appreciate isn't easy for me to write publicly about, but one I feel is important enough to justify the loss of my privacy regarding it. At the beginning of 2011, just over two and a half years into living moneylessly, I realised that I didn't want children and took the decision to have a vasectomy. This, unless I was prepared to do a DIY job (which, my dear reader, I wasn't), would involve going to the tax-funded National Health Service (NHS) to get it done. It was a difficult decision for me – I'd been living in the UK for ten years (the first eight as a taxpayer) and hadn't been to a doctor or hospital in the UK before.

I had a few reasons for choosing not to have kids. First, I decided a while ago to dedicate my brief time on Earth to doing the little I could to try and help change the cultural stories that guide our lives, and to help co-create more sustainable ones. If I was going to be a father, I wanted to be a good one, and to be a good one I feel you need to spend lots of time with your child. But I knew that I didn't have that time spare, and I realised it was going to be like this for a long while. Aside from that, I also didn't feel an overpopulated island and over-stressed planet needed another mouth to feed and body to clothe. This latter point is a very personal opinion, and I say it merely to be honest and transparent about my reasons. I am in no way saying that having babies in an overpopulated world is *wrong or right*, to do so would be absurd, and the issue is much too complex for such simplified perspectives.

On the basis of that logic, I took a big decision and went for a very simple fifteen minute procedure that would mean that, from that point onwards, my sperm would no longer be able to enter my seminal plasma whenever I had an orgasm. Sperm are like the rich, they only make up 1% of the total, while the other 99% – the plasma – carries them along. This I had researched and knew. What I didn't know was that in some small percentage of cases things can get complicated afterwards.

A few days after the operation I started feeling a strong but dull pain in the lower sides of my back, the place where men's testicles originally descend from. After reading many horror stories on the internet, that hub of fear-mongering, I started to panic, worried I'd have to live a life of testicular pain and with the libido of a captive panda.

After days of it getting worse, I gave in and went to the doctor. He said I had an infection, and that a prescription would clear it up. This posed any number of dilemmas for me. I am completely opposed to animal testing, and these antibiotics would undoubtedly have been tested on animals. I was also moneyless, with no back up funds or bank account. But I was scared – really scared – that I was going to allow an infection to spread and all that would come with that. So I took the weak, easy option and went for the prescription.

Whilst prescriptions are free for anyone on jobseekers allowance, they aren't free for moneyless people who don't claim benefits. So I asked a friend if she would help, and to cut a long story short she refused, along with correctly accusing me of being a fraud, which I was. A very scared, vulnerable-feeling fraud, but a fraud nonetheless. I asked another friend, an animal rights activist who was even more opposed to animal testing than me, and she said she would help me unconditionally in whatever way I needed it. Looking back, this unconditionality was more medicine for my soul than anything a doctor could give me.

As it turned out, the antibiotics didn't work, and the infection came back. My doctor advised me that another round would do it, and my activist friend offered to pay for it again. I accepted. That was up until the last minute. I was cycling the eighteen miles from my caravan into the city (which wasn't ideal for the testes at the time, I can assure you) when I had a voice inside of me telling me to trust in my beliefs, to trust the Earth to cure me, and to show just a liitle glimpse of some balls, pardon the pun. So I thanked my friend but told her that I was going to do this the way I should have in the first place. I got some sage and drank gallons of sage tea. I got some fresh comfrey, ground it up, made a poultice out of it and sat with it on my testicles for hours on end. And as the infection started to dramatically reduce, I made love to a friend who I had been intimately connected to. And with the blissful explosion that came at the end of what was an uniquely beautiful experience, all pain left and never came back.

When I look back I deeply regret not having stood up for what I believed in when it really came to the crunch – that time when it's not easy to stand up for what you believe in – and for asking someone to use money to buy me something during a period of my life when I was claiming to be completely free from money. I feel a slight sense of redemption for having eventually come round to what my holistic self knew, and I thank the universe for giving me a second test, another chance to show if I really believed in what I was talking about or not. What would I do if I was faced with the same situation again? I would hope something similar to the second choice, but again I don't know. The egocentric self has such a hold on us that it acts in fear whenever faced with its own mortality, and within such a story it is completely natural to want to survive.

What I am trying to say by telling this story is that these issues are certainly not black and white. I want to illustrate how I've also made hypocritical choices I don't agree with, which put my narrow egocentric self above that of the whole. Through it I also want to express my feeling that we need to love each other unconditionally, even when we see each other making decisions we feel are hypocritical, because in the end we're all hypocrites. Loving unconditionally, however, doesn't mean that we need to stop challenging each other, and my friend who said no was right to challenge me, no matter how hard it felt at the time. That said, my other friend who decided to help me unconditionally was also right to do so, as by that point such unconditional love was what my fragile soul needed. Both helped me in different ways.

That is not to say that challenging each other and acting unconditionally towards each other are always mutually exclusive. They are not. I believe that we can do both simultaneously, if we understand both balance and compassion. If we have differences of opinions we can say, "I don't agree with your choice, and this is why, but if it's your ultimate choice I will respect that, and if you need my help I will give it in any way that also allows me to stay true to my own beliefs." Unconditionality creates powerful bonds between people, and it is these bonds that will be at the heart of a localised gift economy.

I also feel that this story highlights how pervasive the "industrial medicines are the only option for many illnesses" story is. I, someone who had been looking into alternative practices for years and who was utterly opposed to modern medicine, defaulted into choosing that option when the heat was turned up, not trusting Nature who, in the end, was the one who provided me with everything I needed.

At what point do we stop?

We're all aware of the idea that industrialised healthcare, dependent on the marriage of money to the ideas of high economies of scale and fine division of labour, has extended the average human life considerably over the last few hundred years (though given the amounts of energy we still continue to pump into it, the benefits have become increasingly marginal and are approaching zero). There almost isn't a person I know who doesn't think extending human lifespan is a good thing. How could it not be, as long as those extra years are healthy ones, not miserable ones strapped to life-support machines? Whenever I question it, I am asked if I would rather see people die of preventable diseases and illness; you can see how this debate gets emotive from the beginning. But whilst I can truly understand anyone's desire to use money-dependent healthcare in order to stay healthy and alive, it does originate from the delusional story that our health is independent from the whole, and vice versa.

To illustrate this, I want to ask you a series of questions. Through industrialised processes we've found medicines that can keep our bodies functioning in this world for an average of eighty years,[259] up from thirty three years in the Upper Palaeolithic age (though during this time if you did make it past fifteen you would, on average, make it to fifty four, a fact that is also regularly and conveniently left out). I can see why everyone would view this as a positive – who wants to die, after all, when you live under the tyranny of a story that leads you to believe you are not part of the whole?

So my first question is this: what if science found a medicine tomorrow that would enable us to live, with a healthy body, to one hundred years on average? Or one hundred and fifty years, or three hundred? Would we accept it? Many would of course say *yes!*, why not? But when one considers the implications of this on the Earth's ability to sustain us, and its astronomical effects on population, the answer is not so clear-cut. Even with current healthcare systems as they are, population is skyrocketing, as this graph so dramatically illustrates:

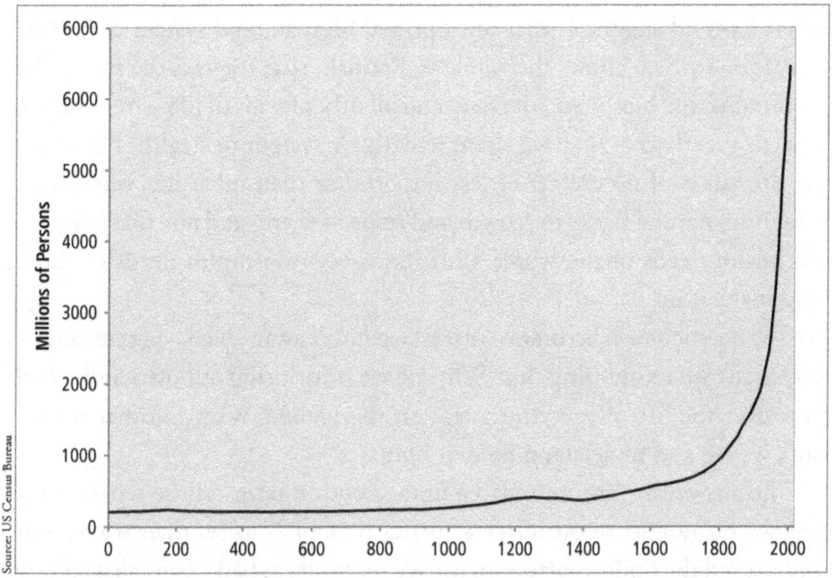

Growth of human population since AD 0

When I was born, in May 1979, the world population was 4.2 billion.[260] By the time I started writing this book, a mere thirty two years later, the seven billionth child was born, a 67% rise in an already large population in less than half a generation. Though not all of this increase is due to people living longer, take a moment to consider what the great global push towards longer life expectancy is going to achieve. Through both our numbers and, especially, our consumption rates, we are already pushing the planet's ecosystems over the edge – can you even imagine what would happen if we all started doubling or trebling our life expectancy again?

Considering this objectively, it becomes clear that when it comes to life expectancy, more is not always best. As always, there's a fine line between maximum and optimum, and the difference is key to our future. So this raises a crucial question – what is the optimal life expectancy of a human on Earth? In fact, the question is more precise than that – what is the optimal average life expectancy of a human in each geographical region and locality on Earth? If it's not three hundred years, is it actually eighty years either? Or was it fifty four?

I've no precise answer for this, and I don't expect you to have either. What I would suggest is that our optimal lifespan, and system of healthcare, is one which allows the whole to flourish, that respects the rivers, the mountains, the biosphere, the trees and all other forms of life – from honey bees to meerkats – that we share it with. A system of healthcare where the human is of no greater or less importance than other life, one which recognises natural limits to growth and respects them, and one that balances the health needs of the whole with the egocentric health needs of those who make it up.

The question then becomes – as intelligent, self aware, life-loving creatures – why aren't we recognising this? Why are we prioritising our own individual lives over the life of everything else on the planet? Why, in other words, can't we see and understand natural limits?

The answer to this can only be understood in terms of the separate self – if we do not sense ourselves as being part of Nature, then we cannot understand the limits it places on us. We see limits as bad – capitalist culture has made unlimited growth the be all and end all, and that is reflected in our understanding of our selves as well. We are economic people, after all. But limits, in fact, are absolutely integral to healthy systems. A child without limits runs out of control and is not happy. Pathogenic bacteria, left unchecked, destroy their host. So ourselves, and so our ecosystems. Without limits we are a disease on the Earth, mindlessly consuming our host, with thought only for our own survival. But after the host dies, what next?

Death is our biggest limit, and one we have come to fear the most. A fear of death, and of loss, is healthy and understandable, but the lengths to which we as a culture have taken this is not. Around the world, and even in our own pagan ancestry, death and regeneration were, and are, celebrated as vital elements of the natural cycle. Out of death comes life.

Yet, as always, we are trapped in linearity. Not part of any bigger system, we must always go forward, and at the end point there is nothing. We can never come back in, and so the finishing line terrifies us. We are so removed from understanding ourselves as rotable, decayable, decomposable beings that the thought of becoming one repulses us. We deny death, deny ageing, deny degeneration. We must be young and beautiful forever. And modern medicine, of course, is the epitome of this. Life must be prolonged at all costs – and at the cost of all life.

A bizarre attitude towards death is not the only unhealthy aspect of our healthcare system. Consider also our War on Germs. I do not have the space here to examine Western humanity's obsession with germs. It is everywhere and all pervasive – in our relationship with our food, with our children, and, most fundamentally, with our selves. In our thinking, a 'healthy system' is one in which there are no germs – 'invaders', from the 'outside', hostile to our body. There is no appreciation of the integral interplay of all life; simply protect your skin-bag from everything that is 'else' and you will be fine. As Eisenstein points out, this attitude extends also to our understanding of healthy ecosystems – widespread tree death has been attributed to fungi, but why, he asks, "are the trees susceptible as never before?"

The War on Germs assumes and reinforces the fundamental premise of industrialised medicine – the idea of the separate self – which in turn leaves unquestioned the methods we use to both heal it, and, crucially, keep it healthy. If disease is caused by germs, and germs are controlled by technology, how much importance is going to be placed on eating well, on having enjoyable, relaxing lifestyles, or on maintaining healthy relationships, and how much is going to be placed on ensuring that more and better technology is available? It is also important to recognise that many of the illnesses and diseases we're faced with today – such as cancer, obesity, diabetes, autism, ADHD and the plethora of conditions related to stress – are created by the same industrialised economic model that produces the medicines we use to treat them. As Thomas Berry points out, "you cannot have well humans on a sick planet". Eliminate the source of the disease and you eliminate the need for an unhealthy cure.

This is not a treatise on 'alternative' medicine. Modern medicine has much to teach us – I simply want us to question some of its basic assumptions. Is it healthy to fear, and avoid, death? Is it accurate to see and treat disease simply as the result of an invasion of 'foreign' bacteria? Are we right to value technological fixes over maintaining much more natural lifestyles? Are we really understanding 'health' in the right way? If not, then we need a different system of healthcare, one which reflects and reinforces an understanding of ourselves as inseparable from the ecology around us. This is the essence of the solutions I am proposing in this chapter. The medicines and sex products listed below can be produced in a localised, moneyless manner, using methods which embrace both our old traditional methods but also integrate all the information we've learned through this monetised period of human history we've been through.

If you just want free healthcare (free, that is, in its delivery as opposed to its construction), then all I need to say is use the NHS (if you live in the UK). It goes without saying that I am no healthcare specialist, so take nothing I say as expert medical advice. Anything I do say will be based on my own personal experience and sources of knowledge which I personally trust. Please do not mindlessly follow any of them without speaking to someone trained in that particular field first, as your body and medical history is uniquely yours.

LOCALISED HEALTHCARE OPTIONS

Some people ask me why we need localised healthcare. This idea is hugely important, in a number of ways. First, and most importantly, we need to find ways of rediscovering our connection to our immediate environment, not simply develop an abstract identification with the romance of the rainforest or the oceans. Shrubs and hedgerows and roadside brambles can seem uninspiring, but Nature is real and alive there too. What's more, take one artificial pacemaker, deconstruct it, and you'll notice thousands of components, all made from finite minerals and materials from every geographical region of the world, all requiring highly toxic and linear processes to come into existence and finite resources to get to our localities. Not only that, they also depend on the destruction of habitat for both human and non-human life, the exploitation of people who live on top of these 'resources' that we believe we have the right to acquire, and the politics that go with all of that. It is self-evident that you cannot continue using finite materials forever, therefore it should be self-evident that you can't continue with the healthcare systems that depend on them. Non-localised healthcare systems are simply not sustainable. As Dr. Dan Bednarz and Dr. Kristin Bradford reported in their 2008 article *Medicine at the Crossroads of Energy and Global Warming*, "through our unrestricted use of energy and resources in the healthcare industry, as well as our production of greenhouse gases, we are actually contributing to the ill-health of our planet and ensuring future suffering of the Earth's inhabitants".

If healthcare is to be healthy for the whole, and not solely for a human culture that now perceives itself as separate from everything else, it must be localised, as hard as that is to conceive today. We've created a huge mess for ourselves, with most of the Western world now dependent on one form of mass-produced medication or another – antidepressants and the like for our decline in medical health and all sorts of toxic concoctions for our myriad modern physical problems. Yet localised healthcare offers some inspiring examples. For example, in *The Transition Timeline*, Shaun Chamberlin notes that "Cuba today has similar life expectancy (78 years) and infant mortality rates (0.5%) to the UK, but uses a far lower energy, lower cost system. It is very much community-based, with a much higher doctor-patient ratio than ours providing a small surgery in each village, and giving doctors the ability to diagnose on the basis of the social and psychological factors affecting the patient, as well as physical symptoms. It is also based far more on preventing illness rather than treating it after the event. Here in the UK we often hear laments for the old 'family doctors' who used to provide a similar service."

This reminds us that despite the sometimes overwhelming challenges we face, there are many options still available to us. If we combine all we have learned from The Industrial Age with new stories that value meaning, fulfilment and happiness over financial growth and Gross Domestic Product (GDP), and mix that together with a redesign of how we live, then anything is possible if we roll our sleeves up and get to work. Our greatest challenges can be transformed into our greatest actions.

Herbalism

Herbal medicine has somehow become described as an *alternative* approach to healthcare, despite the fact that, for obvious reasons, "herbal medicine is the original medicine".[261] Both humans and animals have been using herbs to maintain health and cure themselves throughout their history. The brilliant thing about herbs is that you can cultivate them using very little space in your garden by, for example, creating a medicinal herb spiral. Medical centres too can take advantage of this, as demonstrated by the Ruskin Apothecary in Gloucestershire, who are developing the concept of the 'One Mile Pharmacoepia', aiming to source as much of their medicine as possible from within a one mile radius.[262] Many useful herbs still grow wild, meaning that you can pick them as you go for a stroll. As with wild food foraging, make sure you consult an experienced forager or other reliable source before using wild plants as some of them can be toxic and poisonous to humans. *(Disclaimer – do check with your qualified health practitioner before taking any of the remedies stated in this book, especially if you are on other medication.)*

WILD DRUGS

Zoe Hawes, author of *Wild Drugs*,[263]
medical herbalist and teacher[264]

The UK has an amazing range of medicinal plants that can be gathered or grown for free. Don't waste your money on well marketed, imported exotics.

Understanding disease is crucial. Illness is a sign that your body is out of balance. It doesn't occur spontaneously, your body isn't letting you down, it means it has been adapting its normal function to cope with restrictive things in its environment.

Our bodies evolved to run away from, or fight off, things that are life threatening. When the dangerous thing has gone, the body rests, replenishes energy, absorbs nutrients required for repairs and eliminates all waste materials and toxins.

We are each uniquely programmed through our DNA and emotional patterning to unconsciously perceive what is dangerous or safe. The unconscious brain then instructs the body to respond via the nervous system and hormones to ensure our survival.

If you want to become proficient at using plant medicine to prevent disease or to help your body to recover from illness, then identifying things that inhibit 'normal' functioning is essential.

Basically, medicinal plants work on the body in four main ways, via stimulation, relaxation, nutrition and elimination. You choose appropriate plants that support the processes the body is struggling to achieve. These actions do not suppress symptoms – they are supporting what the body is trying to do naturally. Herbal medicines take time to work as they facilitate the body to heal itself.

Try not to think "I'll take this herb for this ailment". Instead consider "What does this body need to be balanced and functioning optimally".

Identification

When foraging for plants that you intend to ingest ensure that you have identified them correctly. Find your local wildlife group or botany club or see if your local qualified Herbalist is doing any guided walks. Take a good plant key with you. Check and double check. If in doubt don't use it. Take a sample home or photograph it and look it up in as many sources as possible.

Harvesting

There are general rules that apply to harvesting. Herbs that have special requirements are discussed in their entry.

General guidelines

- Handle plants gently to avoid damaging them.
- Collect on dry days, after dew has dried but before the heat of the sun.

- Don't harvest by obvious sources of pollution.
- Reject diseased or damaged plants.
- Do not over-harvest or gather more than you can prepare in one go.
- Take gloves, a digging tool, secateurs and something to carry your harvest home in.
- Get permission from land owners.
- Be sustainable, only harvest when the plant population is strong and try to encourage plants by scattering seeds, replanting root crowns etc.

Preparation

The most basic methods of preparation are:

- Infusions (tea) using water and fresh or dried herbs, made as you need them. Use externally or internally. Put 1-3 heaped teaspoons of herb in a teapot, soak with a mug full (200ml) of boiling water. Cover. Leave for 5-10 minutes. Strain and drink hot or cold or use as a compress or skin wash.
- Tinctures are alcohol based, they preserve the properties of fresh and dried herbs and are taken as required. Pack the chopped herb into a jar, just cover the herb with strong alcohol (vodka). Put the lid on, shake daily for 2 weeks. Strain. Bottle. Take 1 teaspoon up to three times per day.
- Infused oils are for external use. Pack dried herb into a jar and cover with sunflower oil. Leave in a sunny place for 2 weeks. Or heat it gently over a *bain-marie* for 2 hours. Then strain and bottle.

- Syrups are made with honey or sugar. They can disguise unpleasant tasting herbs and can be frozen or kept in the fridge for a few months (see elderberry).

I have described my preferred method for each plant but these aren't hard and fast rules. Experiment and find what works for you. My essential herbs are:

Yarrow – *Achillea millefolium*

A common meadow plant flowering in late summer. Gather the entire stem and flowering head and dry for tea or use fresh for tincture. It relaxes blood vessels, allowing blood into areas of tension. The bitter taste helps the liver eliminate accumulated wastes. It is also anti-inflammatory. Take a strong hot infusion to promote sweating and reduce high temperatures, or for urine infections. Make a tincture to take regularly for irritated skin problems(eczema), period pains and heavy bleeding, before food for indigestion and sluggish bowels with piles. For toothache dig up fresh root, chew it into a pulp and pack it round the affected tooth. While you're waiting for it to work, dig up a few more for later and a couple extra to dry for another time.

Elder – *Sambucus nigra*

Commonly found in hedgerows; flowering in May/June and ripe berries in August/September. Gather the flower stems, snip off as much of the green stems as you have the time or inclination for. Spread the flowers on paper to dry. Take them as a tea to tone up mucous membranes in the ears, nose and throat. They reduce catarrh and ease hayfever. Drink a hot tea to promote sweating and cooling of the body, perfect for colds and flu. People with hot, dry skin conditions that don't sweat easily will benefit from this tea too. The infused oil of elderflowers is moisturising for dry skin.

Elderberry inhibits the flu virus. Collect bunches of purple berries and strip them from the green stalks with a fork. Dry them for tea, use them fresh for syrup or make a tincture.

Nettle – *Urtica* spp.

Nettles are a super food. Collect fresh young plants in early Spring. Cook and freeze in batches, dry to use for tea or in stews or soups.

To make nettle vinegar: chop fresh leaves and stems into in a jar and cover with cider apple vinegar. Shake daily for 2 weeks, strain and bottle. Use in salad dressings or add to vegetables, soups and bone broths.

Nettles inhibit histamine and reduce allergies. Drink daily before and during hayfever season. They are rich in minerals: iron, potassium, calcium and vitamins: C, B complex and beta carotene. These are all antioxidants. They promote urination and removal of inflammatory wastes from the blood, good for skin and joint disease like eczema, gout and arthritis. They also stop bleeding and their iron levels benefit new mothers, women suffering from heavy bleeding or anyone with anaemia. They also increase the flow of breast milk. The root is used as a treatment for enlarged prostate in men with problems urinating.

Dandelion – *Taraxacum officinalis*

Dandelions thrive everywhere. Harvest young leaves to eat in salads, chop into cider vinegar (see nettles), dry for teas or to tincture. The leaf increases urination and elimination of wastes. They are rich in potassium. Eat them daily for high blood pressure, joint disease or water retention. Dig up the roots in winter for fresh root tincture or dry them and gently roast until brown, to grind and use as a coffee substitute. The roots help the liver process wastes and toxins and improve digestion. Use them to cleanse a sluggish system that shows up as skin disease, PMT, hormonal imbalances, headaches, irritable bowel, gallstones, constipation and indigestion.

Pot Marigold – *Calendula officinalis*

Once you've grown Calendula it should self-seed every year. Pick the flower heads regularly to encourage more flowers. Use the fresh petals in salads and dry petals for teas.

Pack dried flowers in a jar, cover with sunflower oil and leave for

2 weeks. Strain, bottle and use it to heal itches, rashes, scratches and sore skin. Melt some oil and beeswax together for a salve.

Make a tincture with the flowers and take teaspoon doses regularly to promote healing, reduce scarring and inflammation, and to support the immune system. Calendula is antifungal, viral and bacterial. Its bitterness supports the liver, digestion and regulates menstruation.

Garlic – *Allium* spp.

Wild garlic (*A. ursinum*) grows wild but cultivated garlic (*A. sativum*) can also be used. Gather wild garlic leaves in spring for salads, soups and for pesto that can be frozen. Cultivated garlic bulbs store well. Garlic is a powerful anti-infective against virus, bacteria and fungus.

Infuse a chopped clove in oil for 12 hours, then strain and use for ear drops or rub on athlete's foot or ringworm. Store the oil in the fridge and make it fresh every week. Chopped garlic on toast, or a salad of the leaves, fights infection anywhere in the body. Eat it till you smell of garlic, then keep eating it, until you are better. The smell is the anti-infective part. Chop cloves into honey and take a teaspoon every 2 hours for coughs, sore throats and colds. Garlic has powerful antioxidant properties protecting the heart and blood vessels from damage that leads to high blood pressure and heart disease. Include it daily in your diet for all its wide ranging health benefits.

Peppermint – *Mentha* spp.

There are many wild and cultivated mints in the UK. They are all medicinal. Peppermint relaxes spasm in the muscles of the intestines, skeleton and blood vessels in the head. Take a strong tea of fresh or dried leaves for colic, wind pains, irritable bowel, nausea and headaches, or to decongest sinuses and mucous coughs. It combines perfectly with elderflower and yarrow for colds and flu.

Make a cooling poultice for painful muscle injuries, aches, itchy bites, rashes and sunburn by moistening 4 tablespoons of dried herb with hot water and folding it into a clean cloth. Allow to cool and apply to the affected area for 30 minutes. Repeat as required.

Thyme – *Thymus* spp.

Cultivated thyme has the strongest medicinal effects. Wild thymes are smaller and difficult to gather in good quantities without affecting the population. You can gather the whole plant all year round. Thyme is anti-infective against viral, bacterial and fungal infections. Drink a strong tea of fresh or dried herb for infections in the mouth, throat, lungs, bladder or intestines. Dab thyme cider vinegar onto fungal feet daily for at least 3 months. Thyme is also antispasmodic and relaxes the airways and intestines. Take a tea or tincture regularly if you have asthma or irritable bowel.

Chamomile – *Matricaria recutica*

I have rarely found true chamomile in the wild. Those that look like it are usually mayweeds. The smell of the flowers and the hollow yellow centre of the flower is how you identify it.

It grows easily from seed. I have successfully grown it from an organic tea bag emptied into a seed tray! Scattering seedy flowers in late summer ensures baby plants in Autumn that will flower next year. Harvesting a decent amount of flower heads is a long job. Bunch together large flowering areas and cut them, green bits and all. The green bits are also medicinal. Dry it for tea or make a fresh herb tincture. Chamomile calms and comforts distress. Drink the tea for upset tummies, irritable bowel, stress and anxiety, insomnia and agitation. Use weak tea to settle teething, colicky or feverish infants and children.

A selection of local remedies

Migraines and headaches

If you suffer from headaches or migraines, feverfew is a herb you ought to grow. It's an anti-inflammatory, and got its name from an age-old belief that it helped people suffering from fever. Today it is used mostly as a preventative measure for people wanting to relieve or stop migraines coming on. A survey of people suffering from migraine in the UK found that "more than 70% of them felt much better after taking an average of

2-3 fresh feverfew leaves daily".[265] Chewing on a bit of white willow (*Salix alba*) bark will also help with any headaches, as it contains chemicals that work in the same way as aspirin.

One important note: herbs (or any painkillers) can be very effective in dealing with the pain and discomfort, but they are not cures, and therefore it is crucial that you begin to understand what is causing such pain in the first instance. Diet, levels of exercise, stress and digestion issues (amongst many other factors) will all play a role.

Cold sores

As well as hayfever, I get cold sores from time to time. There are a number of pharmaceutical brands that admittedly do work quite well (though I've no idea what the subsequent health consequences are of using them in a system as complex as the human body), but they really are unnecessary. I switched over to using lavender when I began living moneylessly, and if I use it early the cold sore doesn't even get its foot properly in the door. It's free, it's natural and it's an easy win.

Hayfever

Being allergic to grass is a weird ailment to have. I've suffered many summers with it in the past, and because higher concentrations of carbon dioxide in our atmosphere lead to higher levels of pollen,[266] many more of us are suffering too. As anyone who has tried to ease the symptoms using pharmaceutical products will attest to, they simply don't work very well, and in my experience they just made me feel worse.

The great news is that there is a solution, and it requires zero money and only five to ten minutes of work. The remedy is a weed that grows as commonly as grass (you will find it amongst it) called plantain, and you'll find it in plentiful quantities in both urban and rural settings. It's a natural antihistamine, and turning it into the most potent hayfever remedy I know is easy:

- Harvest 10-30 leaves of this plant (depending on how acute your hayfever is), after using a reliable friend or book to help you identify it correctly. If you want to save time, pick as much as you can in one go and dry the rest in a pillow case on the radiator.

- Put the leaves in a saucepan, pour some cold water on them (so you don't scald them) before soaking with boiling water. I'd recommend one or two litres, again depending on how potent you want it to be.
- Allow it to cool down before putting it in the fridge.
- If you want to sweeten it up, add some apple juice to it, but I find it fine as it is.
- Drink about 200ml twice or three times a day, as needed. Start before your hayfever normally starts, and keep it going throughout the hayfever period, or until it stops.
- Get outdoors and make up for all those summers you couldn't fully enjoy.
- Tell any other hayfever sufferers about it if it works for you.
- Alternatively, make a fresh tincture from the leaves and take 1 teaspoon 3 times per day. It is also good for long-term allergies such as eczema and asthma. It also cools and calms hot, sore and irritated tissues in the bladder, stomach, intestines and airways.

I hesitate before telling you the next part of this story, for fear I'll be labelled a bit kooky, as I've zero scientific evidence for it bar the empirical evidence gained through living my own life. After having spent a summer using plantain, which drastically reduced my symptoms, I decided that I was no longer going to do this silly hayfever thing. For over twenty five years I'd done it, and I'd had enough. It was stupid to be allergic to something as ubiquitous as grass. So around January of 2011 I decided to stop having hay fever. No drugs, no plantain, no nothing. Enough was enough. So everyday for the next six months I reminded myself that to be allergic to Nature was ridiculous, and told my body to stop reacting to harmless pollen in this way. It's my body, after all, so I should be able to instruct it to react in ways that are helpful to me, the one who inhabits it.

This is the bit I am worried about relaying to you – it worked. I should be excited about telling you that, but I'm not, because I have no scientific evidence of why. I just know it worked. The reason why I am concerned is because the war between science and religion is now over. *Science has become the new religion*, and its followers are stricter fundamentalists than any you'll find in Christianity or any conventional religion. This is not because I believe science has no place in the world – of course it has, and a very important one. But it is just one of a range of ways of understanding the world.

These are just a few examples from my personal experience of herbal medicines. For a much more comprehensive guide to herbal medicine, I would recommend Zoe Hawes' *Wild Drugs* and James Wong's *Grow Your Own Drugs*.[267] To learn how to cultivate natural medicines, *Jekka's Complete Herb Book*[268] is useful.

Other local forms of healthcare

Apart from herbalism, there are many other forms of medicine and healing that don't require complex technologies or infrastructure and that can be done locally. All that is needed is people with the right knowledge and skills, methods that were mastered in various parts of the world long before industrialisation. Options to choose from range from acupressure and chiropractic therapies to naturopathic medicines. Each one of these is a life's work and a book in itself, but if you want to get an overall picture of the menu you have available to you, then Goldberg's *Alternative Medicine: The Definitive Guide* is a very good place to start. I would also recommend asking members of your local Freeconomy group for advice, as alternative healthcare is one of the most frequently shared skills on the global network.

Plasters for cuts

The underside of a birch polypore (a bracket fungus that you'll find on birch trees) is a perfect moneyless alternative to plastic plasters. Simply mark out the shape of the plaster you want from its bottom side, using a knife. Peal away the outer layer of it, and place on your cut. It will often almost stick itself, but you can hold in place by twisting some grass together and tying it over the plaster and around the part of your body you've been cut on.

Women's health

Having never ovulated once in my life, I feel distinctly underqualified to speak about women's health. However, it is such an important issue, both personally and ecologically. Ecologically, tampons and sanitary towels are a nightmare. When you consider that every woman uses, on average, 22 items of sanitary protection every period (11,000 items in her lifetime)[269] and that these end up in landfill or our seas, the cost both ecologically and financially is obvious. Multiply those figures by billions, and you see the problem unfold.

There are solutions. One of these is the mooncup, which is a little rubber cup inserted into the vagina and held in place over the cervix to collect menstrual flow. It's reusable and should last you a lifetime. It comes with mixed reviews from different female friends of mine. Some say that it works great, while others report that it can leak a little, which is hardly ideal. If it works well for you, it will save you a lot of money and drastically reduce your ecological impact. How you would make one, I have no idea, and so unless you come up with a solution yourself it will involve buying one to begin with.

If you want pure moneyless menstruation, the options may seem less appealing. In a German book titled *Die unpäßliche Frau: Sozialgeschichte der Menstruation und Hygiene* (*The Indisposed Woman: A Social History of Menstruation and Hygiene*),[270] the authors suggest that women in Germany (and there is much evidence that this was also the case in many other parts of the world before industrialisation) either made their own reusable pads (designs are available in the book) or wore no pads or underwear and just bled freely. The former is entirely manageable, though I've no idea how comfortable it would be as I know no one who has tried this (and am unable to myself). The latter would require a total redesign of society, and a move away from tyrannical patriarchy.

Given that a total redesign of society is not likely before the weekend, the best thing our governments could do in this respect is to allow women the option of having some time off during their menstrual cycles, or at the very least the freedom to organise their lives around it. Considering governments and corporations are dominated by men, this is just as unlikely. They will simply say that such a move would be 'economically unviable' (which, remember, actually means 'financially unviable'), at which point all discussion ends, such is the hold that money has on our minds. This is a monetary economy, not a human economy, and so money-making endeavours will always triumph over those that create happiness and well-being.

WILD SEX

The only thing more taboo to question than the destructive consequences of money and modern healthcare is the ecological sustainability of modern sex. Moneyless sex seems like an odd conversation to have – few of us would like to think that our sexual practices were monetised, as it evokes thoughts of prostitution and the like.

Whether sex is truly moneyless, or sustainable, though depends on what products you use. I'm not talking vibrators and lube here, though they are relevant questions needing answers in themselves. I'm talking contraception. In a world without the industrialised large-scale factories that ecologists and environmentalist claim are destroying life on Earth, where would we get the sex products that we've become dependent on: the condoms, the coils, the pill (both *morning after* and *contraceptive*)? The vast majority of sex today involves industrialised processes which are not sustainable. Yet populating the world full of babies and spreading STDs is hardly ideal either. Thankfully, there are a few moneyless solutions out there. How willing you are to use them is another question!

Contraception

Once you rule out celibacy – which I am going out on a limb to assume most of us are – you descend a slippery slope of degrees. There is no 100% contraceptive. Out of all the options I have studied for birth control, I choose a vasectomy (the female equivalent is hysterectomy). Using current methods of surgery it is not moneyless or sustainable in its first instance, but it is a one-off act that then allows you and your partner (if you both are free from all STDs and are in a monogamous relationship) to enjoy condom- and pill-free sex, both of which when applied *en masse* are responsible for a lot of ecological issues.[271] Word of warning – unlike a condom, you cannot leave a vasectomy in a foil wrapper if you change your mind and do want to have a child. Vasectomies have some small risks too that you need to find out about, and though it can be possible to reverse a vasectomy, it should be treated as if it is not.

If that is all a bit too high technology for you, then you could look to the medieval times for some ideas. Back then animal's bladders and intestines were used to make condoms, tied up with a bit of twine. Such was the difficulty and time taken in making them that they used to get reused, regularly. They didn't know this back then, but plants of the genus *Sapindus* (also good for washing your hair, as we have seen) can make a decent spermicide. Scientific tests have shown that this isn't quite as effective at killing sperm as its chemical alternatives, but apparently it is less of an irritant. Instead, women sometimes used (or more accurately, were probably made to use) a pessary that was applied within the vagina – one such one was a substance made of honey, acacia bark and ground dates, all mixed together into a gooey paste that was then applied to a piece of cloth – usually linen – and put into the vagina. It is just a guess, but I would imagine this was a man's idea!

But please, don't all rush out the door looking for roadkill to dissect for their intestines (whether you choose deer or squirrel could be a little too revealing), or to plant seeds of the *Sapindus* family just yet – having never personally tried these, and with a distinct lack of previous research having been done on the subject, I cannot give you any advice on how reliable these methods were. My gut instinct: making a wish upon a star probably has a similar reliability rating.

Since those days a wide range of options have been developed. The Rhythm-, Knaus-Ogino-, Standard Days-, Cervical Mucus- and Basal Body-methods are other tools in the moneyless birth control toolbox, all reported to have varying degrees of success (and failure). None of these should even be considered without a complete understanding of how they work, and they will also require the woman to have a good understanding of her own cycles and body. Like any contraceptive, these are certainly not 100%, but they can be successful if combined with other methods (especially if the man practices non-ejaculation) at the same time. It goes without saying, but I'll say it anyway – none of these protect against STDs.

If you want to find out more about herbal methods for controlling fertility and aborting unwanted pregnancies, then three books are recommended: John M. Riddle's *Eve's Herbs: A History of Contraception and Abortion in the West,* James DeMeo's *Herbal Contraception and Abortion in Sex-Positive Cultures* and Rina Nissim's *Natural Healing in Gynaecology: A Manual for Women.* Anthropologists in the past, who have studied small subsistence societies, believed that no contraception existed for a long time. Why? Because for cultural, and possibly sexist, reasons they only ever asked the men. It turns out that if they had bothered to ask the women, they would have had an entire history of answers. The men in these times were clueless about it all, whilst the women knew exactly what they needed to do. Such knowledge was understood and applied widely until the Roman Catholic Church became powerful and decided it knew best for all the world's peoples, and forbade such preparations. They even tried women who used them as witches, such was the threat they posed to a male dominated institution. God forbid, quite literally, that women could have control over something as crucial as life.

This is that one area of moneylessness which is very complex. Like many aspects of the way we live, we've got ourselves into a right muddle. STDs are rampant, we've created a culture that is highly sexualised and population levels are already out of control. To stop using contraceptives now would be disastrous for the human species, yet to continue with the industrial economy will be disastrous for our home, Earth. One way or another, something will have to give at some point in the future, we simply cannot continue as we are.

Lubricants

Such extravagances as vaginal lubricant are a little less crucial than contraception in the exploration of moneyless sex solutions. But far be it from me to deprive moneyless folk of any pleasure they can sustainably have. Wild sex guru (self-proclaimed that is) and friend of mine Fergus Drennan has come up with a solution that is very close to my heart: *Chondrus Crispus,* otherwise known as carrageenan or Irish moss, a seaweed that is found on the west coast of Donegal, where I grew up in Ireland. Its scent still reminds me of home.

Making it is easy. Ideally, you would gather it in summer, wash it in fresh water before putting it out to dry on a blanket in the sun. Once dry, rehydrate it the following the day and put it out to dry again – repeat this drying process two or three times, until the colour goes from purple to lilac and onto the white creamy stage you are looking for (purple lube is probably not a major turn-on). Once this is done boil it, remembering to stir it regularly so it doesn't burn, before straining it off using a cloth such as muslin. What you will be left with is E407, a vege-lube. This must be used fresh to prevent getting any infections.

A tip for those of you who like sex to be a little more spontaneous than a four day build-up: if you reduce it on the saucepan a lot further, you can get it to set afterwards once it cools, meaning that you can cube it and stick in it the fridge (or a moneyless cool area) for a couple of days. Reheat as needed, but use within a few days. If your partner hates waste, reminding her (or him) that it is about to go off is a powerful argument for getting an extra bit of nookie!

Alternatively, a simpler method is to dry the carrageenan out as above, and when foreplay is beginning to stick it in some boiling water. This should take at least twenty minutes to be ready. If you've moved on from foreplay into sex before the lube is ready, you've been a very selfish lover and you should go and take a good hard look at yourself in the mirror.

Studies at the Laboratory of Cellular Oncology, of the US National Cancer Institute in Maryland, suggest that carrageenans might function as a topical microbicide, protecting you against sexual diseases, so this could be a good two-in-one product, a bit like shampoo and conditioner all in one bottle.

Aphrodisiacs

The best moneyless Viagra I know of is a plant called horny goat weed. Apparently its name is credited to a goat herder who once noticed a large increase in sexual activity amongst his flock after his goats had been munching on this weed. Whether this is true or not, who knows, but I prefer the story that I just made up involving a goat herder who ate the weed himself and then took a liking to Billy.

The good news is that this weed has the same effect on humans – it increases libido in both men and women.

Dildos

OK, I'm well informed by my female friends that the entire point of this ecological catastrophe that we call industrialisation was to produce the ultimate dildo – the vibrator. Apparently the entire cosmos has been unfolding in this way just for this product. So as a man I wouldn't dare suggest that its very existence is the spawn of Satan Himself and that using one is to be complicit in the rape of our Mother. The vibrator is, it appears, the fundamental flaw in my entire worldview.

But think again. There are many examples of dildos that existed long before the notion of money. The ancient Chinese used handcrafted wooden ones, and a dildo made out of carved antler bone was recently discovered at a Mesolithic site in Sweden.

These are by no means the most interesting examples. According to author Michael Pollan,[272] "witches and sorcerers cultivated plants with the power to 'cast spells' – in our vocabulary, 'psychoactive' plants. Their potion recipes called for such things as datura, opium poppies, belladona, hashish, fly agaric mushrooms (*Amanita muscaria*), and the skin of toads (which can contain DMT, a powerful hallucinogen). These ingredients would be combined in a hempseed-oil-based 'flying ointment' that the witches would then administer vaginally using a special dildo. This was the 'broomstick' by which these women were said to travel." Various accounts suggest that the broomstick that witches have been depicted riding came into legend because of their use of it as a pre-industrialisation dildo. So guys, if your special lady tells you not to come into the bedroom because she is 'sweeping it', you know what is really going on in there.

SPEAKING OF SEX

As Charles Eisenstein suggests in an essay titled *Rituals for Lover Earth*,[273] we might do well to move away from referring to our planet as *Mother Earth*, and instead term Her *Lover Earth*, remembering that the language we use is key to how we interpret the world.

Because our relationships with our own mothers, at least in infancy, are based on taking without concern for their needs (as is appropriate for an infant, where the Mother takes full responsibility for the setting of any limits), using the term Mother Earth can perpetuate the story that we can take and take from Her without ever giving back. Our relationships with our lovers are different, however. Here our ideal is to give as well as to receive, in a respectful, loving and ecstatic partnership. Eisenstein believes, and I agree, that simply referring to our planet as Lover Earth could be one little way of helping to bring about the urgently needed change in perspective necessary for the creation of a reciprocal relationship with our planet.

Culturally, the last two hundred years might be said to have been about 'having' sex, not making love, and the difference is crucial. As a species, we need to start making love to the Earth again, and to stop 'fucking' Her. If we do, our union could birth a new era of creativity, fulfilment and healthy ecosystems, so different from the one we see in front of us today.

A SIMPLE CHOICE

Our choice is this: either we change our ways and get real about becoming sustainable in all we do, including our healthcare and methods of having safe sex, or Nature will sort out the problem for us. We simply cannot have globalised and industrialised healthcare and a healthy, thriving planet with fresh air, clean water and fertile soil. The choice is ours.

CHAPTER 14

CLOTHING AND BEDDING

If there ever was an indicator of the sheer, utter stupidity of our species – aside from defecating into our water supply – it's the fact that we need clothing and footwear. What were we thinking when we took this evolutionary path? Out of one hundred and ninety three species of monkey and ape on the planet, only man is not entirely covered in hair (aka built-in unisex apparel).[274] To exacerbate the situation further, we've managed to create a cultural story that champions the idea that hairless is sexy. To then conform to these manufactured expectations, we shave most of the little bits we have left off, using one form of blade or another.

I sometimes wonder at the absurdity of a naked ape living in a country that gets reasonably cold for a part of the year, and rarely gets warm enough for lengthy nakedness. Given our anthropocentric view of the world, we take it for granted that *Homo sapiens* are native to the entire planet. We'd never take such a perspective with any other species. No one argues that banana plants or coconut trees should live in the Shetland Islands. Why is it then that we never question whether or not hairless apes such as ourselves belong in regions where they need to use up huge acres of land just to put their clothes back on?

Theories abound regarding why we have no hair, with no end of anthropologists coming up with all sorts of bizarre reasons why we decided to go naked. Whatever the truth is, the reality remains that most of us find ourselves in countries where the temperature drops below what our flesh seems to be able to cope with. The result of which is that we need clothes of one kind or another.

In order to produce moneyless clothes, we either need to use fibres that grow in the wild, grow crops (such as cotton and hemp) that are famed for their ability to be turned into garments, or kill animals for their clothes and skin. This wouldn't be so much of an issue if there weren't so many of us, but the fact that there are now over seven billion humans poses huge ecological, logistical and ethical problems in this regard. A bad situation is only made worse by the fact that the marketing departments in the houses of Armani, Primark and the like have convinced us that we need new skins every couple of months.

The challenge that we need to find a solution to is how to keep ourselves warm and protected throughout all the seasons in a way that doesn't strip the Earth of all of its natural fertility and resources. In this chapter I aim to outline both short- and long-term strategies for doing this, enabling you to take the option that allows you to have the least impact on the Earth in the short term, and with the aid of your own POP model for clothing, the maximum connection with Her in the long-term.

An important note: I've dealt with shoes in the chapter on transport, as I think of them more as a vehicle than fashion, which probably reflects my own mindset of shoes being functional rather than stylish. Now if a woman had written this book ... well, you know what chapter you'd find shoes in!

CLOTHING

In *The Revenge of Gaia*, scientist James Lovelock argues that we should give the Earth and its ecological systems a well-deserved break and allow it to catch its breath again. Whilst I disagree with many of his proposed resuscitation techniques, such as nuclear energy, I would echo his calls for 'a sustainable retreat'.

One area of our lives in which it would be easy to give the planet the weekend off would be clothing. Unlike food, we don't actually have to produce it relentlessly every day. The vast majority of the apparel produced goes to those of us in the global West, and we're not exactly walking around threadbare every day. We don't need any more clothes for a long, long time. We only continue to buy clothes at anything like the scale we do because we have become sheep, longing to conform to society's norms, as opposed to having any functional need for more and more. It is ironic that the marketing departments of many clothing brands encourage their targeted consumers to be unique, self-assured and confident in their own style, yet the entire industry is premised on the hope that everyone will mindlessly conform to whatever a small handful of elite industry heads decides is cool at any given moment.

The fashion industry, where clothes come in and out of style with every season that passes, has a massive impact on the ecological systems of the planet. The most common crop used for clothing is cotton. Despite it taking up only 2.5% of the world's cultivated land, cotton uses 25% of the world's pesticides. For every kilo of final cotton textile, 11,000 litres of water is used, meaning that for every cotton T-shirt we buy 2,700 litres of water have been consumed.

Cotton isn't the only culprit – most common fibres should be ashamed of themselves. It is hardly surprising that synthetic fibres such as polyester and nylon are no angels either. The manufacture of nylon creates nitrous oxide (no laughing matter) which is 298 times more potent a greenhouse gas than carbon dioxide. Polyester, the world's most popular man-made fibre weighed in at 17 million tonnes produced in 2001. It is made from oil, is very thirsty, uses over four times the amount of energy per tonne of spun fibre than hemp and its production is easily the biggest emitter of carbon dioxide of all the fabrics that we make clothes from.[275]

This constant damage to the planet makes even less sense when you consider that we have already produced enough clothes for the next decade; that is, if we could all just learn to share, mend, and swap those we already have. There are many projects established to make it as easy as possible to do so, all of which have the added benefit of you acquiring a new wardrobe without any additional cost to either your egocentric or holistic selves. Of course this is not a long-term strategy as all clothing will eventually wear out, but it is an important transitional strategy if we are to drastically reduce our water usage and the pollution of our water bodies, allow soil fertility to build up again, and avoid the very worst consequences of climate chaos. Long-term we need to grow plants that we can produce clothes out of locally, which meet people's needs, but maybe not their every desire.

Short-term clothing solutions

Clothes swapping and sharing evenings

Just because you're bored with some of your clothes, it doesn't mean other people would be. Instead of hoarding them in your cupboards, bring them along to a clothes swapping party, pass them on to others who like them, and pick up items you fancy from those who are participating in exactly the same spirit as you.

Swishing parties[276] are easy to organise, and help planning them is at hand. Lucy Shea, the founder of Swishing(.com), says they are a great way to "save money, save the planet and have a party," and are "for all those women who want to combine glamour, environmental protection and frugality". Shoes and jewellery are also on offer for free. These seem to be tailored to, and frequented by, women at the moment, but there is absolutely no reason why guys couldn't organise the same, other than the fact that they are perfectly happy with the two pairs of jeans and three T-shirts that they already own, and couldn't think of anything worse than trying on clothes all evening.

If you want to combine swapping with some DIY workshops on how to mend and alter your clothes, the Wendy Tremayne inspired *Swap-o-rama-rama* events take place in over one hundred cities globally. Both of these projects are perfect examples of how we can rethink the ways in which we can meet our clothing needs – in terms of both style and functionality – in the short- and long-term.

Make do and mend

This phrase grew out of the Second World War (the idea existed long before it), a time when all attention was on the war effort and clothes from industry were in very short supply. The *Ministry of Information* at the time produced a mini-book showing its population how to maintain and revamp their wardrobes, focusing on skills such as knitting, crocheting, sewing, how to deal with the 'moth menace', how to best wash your materials, darn socks and mend jeans. Stupidly, it didn't tell anyone how they could best erase the skid marks off the inside of their pants caused by thoughts of the Jerries flying overhead.

These skills will be very useful in the future, and it is essential that we collectively keep the knowledge alive. Organising events such as the *Stitch 'n bitch*[277] – where I hope more stitching than bitching goes on – and regular Freeskilling evenings focused on clothes reparation and alteration is a perfect way to keep the vital knowledge of that war generation alive.

We have a long distance to go to become truly moneyless for clothes. Most people today can't use a needle and thread with any proficiency, let alone know how to grow the crops that make the fibres in the first place. This is largely due to the economics of insanity which result in us now being able to buy a T-shirt on the High Street for a couple of pounds, coupled with the fact that we now have absolutely no part to play in any of the stages of our clothes production, meaning we have only a fraction of the respect for them we ought to have. Until we reconnect with the processes of making our clothes, expect the ecological disaster that is the fashion and textiles industry to only get worse.

Go freeshopping

The Freeshop (see page 98) is a great logistical system for the sharing of clothes on a daily basis. Don't forget that it also relies on stockists (that's you and me) to keep its shelves full, so if you do have some clothes that no longer fit, or an item that you know you will never wear again, do drop them in and let them be used by someone who needs them.

Reinvent

If you've had enough of some of your clothes, why not take them apart, see what designs you can come up with, before combining them in some weird and wonderful manner. Friends will think you've been on a shopping spree when all you've done is mix and mismatched some of your old stuff to make something unique. At the very least it's a lot more innovative and original than following the herd to High St.

Long-term clothing solution

A stitch in time will save nine, but there is a limit to how many times you can mend a piece of clothing before it is completely spent, especially when you consider the poor quality of mass produced clothes today.

For us to become truly moneyless in relation to our clothing in the long-term, we're going to have to get used to the novel idea of having only as many items of high quality clothing as we functionally need for each season. We simply do not have the acreage per person in the UK to have fashion collections any bigger than is necessary, once current stocks run out.

I appreciate that we all like to have a range of clothes to choose from for different occasions, but choice and absolute sustainability are quite often non-compatible, and at some point in our future we have got to decide whether we want a bulging wardrobe on an uninhabitable planet, or a couple of practical and well-designed outfits on a biodiverse and healthy planet.

Making your own clothes requires skill, time and experience, but by starting to learn how we can source the materials we need to survive today, we'll be well equipped for a time when it may be a necessity rather than an option. In doing so, we can get a great sense of creativity, autonomy and meaning from the knowledge that we've just made ourselves, or someone we love, a garment that will be very useful to them for years to come.

Below are a couple of options to consider. This is not a complete guide, but it should give you an idea of what it is possible to do in terms of moneyless, long-term clothing in the UK.

Hemp and Nettles

If you want to be moneyless for clothing in the UK by getting back to basics and making your own, one of the fibres on your menu has got to be hemp. One issue is that our government has a fetish for controlling as many aspects of our lives as they feel they can get away with; therefore, if you want to grow even the varieties of hemp that are only suitable for fibre production, you'll need a licence from the Home Office. If you even want to import its seeds for the purposes of sowing, you will also need to apply for a licence from the Rural Payments Agency (RPA). Such laws are inherently unjust, and as Mahatma Gandhi once said, "so long as the superstition that men should obey unjust laws exists, so long will their slavery exist". We cannot allow sustainability to be illegal.

Regardless of how you manage to get over this issue, there are many moneyless advantages to hemp. Hemp is one of the most crucial agricultural crops for a sustainable future, as it can easily be managed with zero imported inputs. Unlike other crops intended for clothing, it is very resilient and needs no pesticides; it adds nutrients to the soil and so can be intercropped with other useful plants who need what it supplies (therefore requiring no synthetic fertilisers); and the fact it grows quite thick means there is little need for weeding, meaning less work and more time to play chess or have hot tubs under the starry night sky with lovers and raspberry wine. Not only that – as if that wasn't enough – but according to Matilda Lee, author of *Eco Chic*, "it 'breathes' and so keeps you cool in hot weather, and is soft, comfortable and yet hard-wearing".

Hemp has no end of other uses, ranging from it being an excellent rope making material to producing very healthy seeds for eating.

Another very useful plant for making clothes is the stinging nettle (*Urtica dioica*). The fact it grows wild in huge quantities across the length and breadth of the country is a bonus, as it needs zero work in terms of cultivation. Suggesting to someone that they could make a pair of pants out of nettles seems almost akin to asking them to wipe their bum with a cactus, such is the seemingly absurd prospect of such an idea today. Yet we forget that people have been making their clothes out of nettles for millennia, and its popularity didn't fade until around the 16th century when cotton came to prominence.

Ray Harwood, a professor of textiles engineering at De Montford University (DMU) in Leicestershire, believes that nettles could be a very important fibre again in the future, and has set up a project aptly called STING (Sustainable Technologies in Nettle Growing). If you want more information about how you can best utilise nettles for clothing, contacting them would be a great place to start.

Once you acquire whatever fibre you are going to use, you will need to learn other skills too, such as how to spin a yarn and turn it into something that resembles cloth. I'd recommend spending some time working with somebody who has a lot of experience in using these skills, along with utilising every possible means to educate yourself in what could be a crucial skill of the future.

Braintanned roadkill buckskin

Before you make a drum out of your roadkill buckskin (see page 288), think about using it for your own clothing first. Buckskin originally referred to the leather made out of the hide of the male deer, the buck, but is more commonly used these days for any leather with certain characteristics and qualities, notably its softness and pliability.

If this is something you really want to learn more about, Matt Richard's book *Deerskins into Buckskins: How to Tan with Brain, Soap or Eggs*[278] is essential reading, though volunteering with someone who can teach you would be very beneficial to you mastering the art.

Here is a very brief introduction to the process so that you may get a very basic idea of the time, skill level and effort involved. The stages go something like this:

- Skinning – this involves removing the hide from the carcass, taking care to keep it as complete as you possibly can. Using a sharp, flat rock, scrap away the flesh and fat of the animal.

- Hair removal – there are two main ways to do this: the dry scrape method and the wet scrape method. The former involves drying and stretching it on a frame, and then taking a very sharp stone to it to remove the hair. The wet method involves immersing it in a solution of lye in water, before taking a dull stone or a split leg bone to it. Wet scraping is easier to do, but dry scraping can often lead to better absorption of the brains (a later step). An old traditional alternative, practised by American Indians, was to simply put the hide in a cold river or stream, weigh it down with rocks, and let the passing water erode the hair over time.

- Stretching – here the drying, tanned hide is stretched out, so that the dressing below can lubricate the fibres of the hide and keep it soft and pliable.

- Tanning – once the hide has been sufficiently scraped, it needs to be dressed with the animal's brain. This can also be done with egg yolk or an oil and soap concoction.

- Smoking – if every stage so far has been done correctly, you should have a buckskin that is supple and dry. At this point it should be smoked long enough that the colour of the smoke (which will depend on what wood you use) penetrates through to the other side of the hide, at which time the skin should be turned over again until it becomes your desired colour.

As a vegan who doesn't see veganism as the ideal but as a response to the Industrial Revolution and the notion of agriculture, I have only one issue with using roadkill buckskin clothing: it inadvertently promotes and normalises the use of leather to a population who will, in all likelihood, not then go out and make their own leather clothing themselves from roadkill, but instead go off to a department store which will undoubtedly have sourced their materials from supply chains that are incredibly cruel to the animals whose bodies they are profiting from. Such an outcome would be the antithesis of my intention.

That said, I believe that using roadkill buckskin is actually 'more vegan' than buying natural fibre clothing that has come from the global industrial-scale economy. I realise that seems an absurd, potentially provocative statement to make and it certainly isn't my intention to offend other vegans. But I do believe that vegans who think that buying cotton and other pesticide-ridden fibres produced on land that has, first, been relegated from Wild to agriculturally managed land before, subsequently, being shipped around the world using fossil fuels (which have been extracted in ways that inevitably destroys huge swaths of habitat and all that once lived in it – the Gulf of Mexico being but one example), are deluding themselves to some extent about how 'vegan' their lifestyles really are. Pesticides are not vegan, the clue is in the name. Neither are fossil fuels. This is not a criticism in any sense, as I have nothing but respect for anyone who lives as aligned to their beliefs as they feel they can, especially those whose aim is only to minimise cruelty. It is merely a challenge to those who already live with compassion to extend the boundaries within which they contemplate the consequences of their consumption.

Jewellery

Living moneylessly does not mean you have to go unadorned. There is no end of simple materials you can use to decorate yourself with, all of which you could find on a stroll through the woods, countryside or beach. Materials include cordage made from natural fibres (again, hemp is good), bone, shells, plants, seeds, wood, petals or anything that you find as you are out foraging. All you need is a little imagination and a desire to be creative.

BEDDING

Assuming that you don't want to sleep in a bushcraft bed of leaves and springy branches for the rest of your days, you will want a more long-term solution to bedding.

Peg loomed woollen underblankets

If you are vegetarian or vegan, using sheep's fleece poses more complex philosophical questions than buckskin from a roadkill deer, as it is a by-product of a method of farming that involves domesticated animals and which will probably not be aligned with your personal principles. Yet regardless of whether you agree or disagree with sheep farming in general, one of the many realities of our truly disturbing economic, industrial and agricultural systems is that a lot of smaller-scale farmers have no outlet for their sheep's fleeces and often have to give them away. Synthetic and non-organic, mass-produced fibres, which I've argued earlier are also non-vegan despite superficial appearances to the contrary, have destroyed the demand for fleeces. If this is a resource that, for whatever reason, you feel happy to utilise for its highly beneficial insulating properties, I would recommend engaging in a fair relationship with the farmer. This could simply mean bringing over some bread or other food that you've produced when you've got excess.

Fleece's have many uses, including clothing, but are particularly good for creating a very warm underblanket for your bed. In order to make one, however, you're going to have to first construct a peg loom. This is fairly simple and something almost anyone can do. To make the loom, all you need is a beam of roundwood (or planed timber if you have some handy), between 44-47 pegs (0.55in pine dowels are good), ideally an antique, manual hand drill to make holes for these pegs in your beam, some cord and a few spare hours. Once that is done, you'll have a low impact piece of equipment that will last you many years and on which you will be able to make all the underblankets and rugs you will ever need.[279]

Pillows

Once you've made your pillow case with your fibre of choice, you can stuff it with the fluff of a perennial herbaceous plant called reedmace (*Typha latifolia*), which grows in temperate and tropical climates alike. If you want to find it, your best bet is to look around ponds, lakes and sometimes rivers and other marshy land. If you've filled enough pillows with it, the plant can also be used for everything from mats and chair seats to making your casks watertight and even fireworks.

If you want to have more lucid dreams, add some mugwort to your reedmace pillow and expect your sleeping time to become much more interesting! Be aware that these dreams may instead be rather nightmarish, and that some people are allergic to mugwort. Experiment with a small amount first.

If you don't fancy lucid dreaming every night of the week, there are other plants which can affect the quality of your sleep. For pleasant dreams, for example, use chamomile and lavender. If you need a good deep sleep try valerian, but as always take all appropriate safety precautions.

Duvets

Duvets can be made by simply making two sheets of equal sized cloth, sewing them together using an old Singer hand-crank machine, and stuffing it with whatever material you want for insulation. I found all of these components on Freecycle over the years. If you don't want to actually make the duvet yourself, you'll find lots of already made ones on there too.

A material which would give you a great balance between insulation and comfort is wool. You could acquire this wool by keeping some woolly pigs (otherwise known as a Mangalitsa, that look like half sheep, half pig) who naturally moult their wool in the summer months to avoid overheating, meaning no shearing of them is required. Alternatively – if woolly pigs aren't alternative enough – you could collect the wool that gets stuck on barbed wire and save it up to make one foraged duvet – this may take you a long time but it would be a work of real art! This wool should ideally be washed and carded using a hand-carding machine, giving it the desired fluffy effect you will probably want. It is then ready to be quilted.

As is the case throughout this book, the ideas presented in this chapter are just a selection of the possibilities available to us. Undoubtedly many of you will have your own ideas on the production and maintenance of your clothing, and so I invite you to go to the website which supports this book (on which we have released a free online version the book) and post any ideas, articles, practical advice and questions you have on the subject of clothing, bedding, or any other aspect of life for that matter, in the relevant board of the forum you'll find there.

CHAPTER 15

LEISURE

They deem me mad because I will not sell my days for gold; and I deem them mad because they think my days have a price.

Kahlil Gibran

All this serious talk about social and ecological crises, obsolete cultural stories and resource depletion is a bit too much for my little brain sometimes. Questioning life, and exploring its mysteries, I believe is an inevitable consequence of having a healthy and relatively free mind, but it should never get in the way of the real point of life: loving every minute of it.

It is a common perception that a money-free life must be a dour, boring existence with little to do. I would argue the polar opposite – that living without money and creating your own fun and adventure is much more exciting than passively watching others do it for you. Reality TV is the posterboy of a culture that *consumes* instead of *plays*.

When you disconnect from the world of high technology and reconnect with Nature, you stop becoming a consumer of life and finally begin participating in it, like you did as a child. Is listening to an album on your iPod, taking in a movie at the cinema, or going to the pub for a bottle of ice-cold American beer really the fullest expression of the human potential that lies inside us? Imagine a society where we made our ales and ciders together, before drinking them around a campfire whilst singing, dancing and playing music together. A world where we spent our days meeting our needs in ways that integrated pleasure and creativity, where one day we'd be making a table, the next day planting some acorns, and in the evenings telling stories, learning chords, playing chess using pieces we hand-carved ourselves, and generally making merry. After all these years of being told moneyless living must be boring, I would love for someone to finally explain to me how participating in life could be less fun that just consuming it.

There is so much each of us could do in life, so much to experience and wonder at, yet we spend much of our time working around the clock just to pay for things that we don't really need and which eventually end up owning us. As Epicurus once pointed out, there are two ways of getting rich: increasing your financial wealth, or decreasing your desires. Every bill or expense you can eliminate from your life means that you get to spend more of your precious time here doing the things you really want to do and less of the time doing things that you have to do to pay the bills. Reducing your outgoings means regaining control over your life and it affords you the time to work on whatever projects you want. *It buys you* the time to get creative, learn something new or volunteer for a project you believe in. The closer you reduce these bills and desires to zero, the closer you are to complete freedom. Let go of your addictions and you will soon regain the freedom to spend your days doing whatever the hell you like.

Far be it from me to tell you how to have fun. However, because our cultural conditioning has lead us to the point where we now equate fun with the consumption of externally created entertainment, I've gently suggested a few examples of how you can put the DIY back into enjoying yourself.

LEARN TO PLAY (AND MAKE) AN INSTRUMENT

One of the most fulfilling things you can do is learn to play an instrument. It is a great gift to be able to share with others, and there is nothing like an evening of jamming to bring friends closer together. If you're musically challenged like me, take inspiration from the Happy Mondays' Bez and just be the guy or gal who dances in front of them playing the maraca.

It is even more fulfilling if you've managed to make the instrument yourself. One instrument that it easy to make from locally available materials is a log and buckskin drum.

- Go to the woods and find a dry log roughly the size you'd like your drum to be – both diameter and length are important considerations here. A drum can be any size but I'd recommend going for one at least a foot in diameter. Bear in mind that the bigger it is the more work you are going to have to do to hollow it out.

- Get yourself some buckskin. Given the amount of animals that die on our roads every year, the best of option here is to use roadkill. Learn how to create the buckskin you need if you already don't (see page 282) – asking your local Freeconomy group for help with it would be an excellent place to start.

- Decide how thick you want the structure of the drum to be, and mark it out. This needs to be strong enough to support the buckskin and not break from the pressure of the sinew thongs (see step 6).

- Hollow out the insides using a chisel and a hammer, and keep going until you've reached your ideal depth and width, emptying out the shavings and excess as you go.

- Take your buckskin and immerse fully in water, ensuring that it is completely soaked. As it dries it will reduce in size again and become tight.

- Stretch the buckskin across the log you've just hollowed out, and secure the buckskin with thongs of sinew (or thin leather). As with the main skin, soak these in water so that they secure the main skin tightly as they dry. Be careful not to tie these too tight.

SOUNDS FROM THE UNCIVILISED

Jess Pasteiner

It is no coincidence that as the towers of civilisation have gone up, the sounds of the drum have faded. Ancient, primal, raw – earthy rhythms are nothing less than battlecries, pulling us in to the very depths of our experience. They are an awakening, to the universal rhythms in whose breast we nestle: the tides ebb and flow, the seasons pass, the moon fades once more.

If we allow it to rise up out of its own time and place, music connects us, to the souls that created it and to the land that birthed it. If we do not seek to impose our will on it, it will immerse us, in our own temporary tempo, in the chorus of possibility. As the jungles screech and the prairie howls, the rivers thrash and the oceans moan, we dance in the call of the wild.

But civilisation is not one to sit back and let the wild be heard; civilisation cannot bear to relinquish control. Wildness scratches and bites and loves in the daylight; it catcalls at our conferences, and giggles at our governance. It entices us down darkened alleys into a consciousness where superficiality gleams like sickened neon. And so, of course, it is silenced. In an orgiastic worship of professionalism and production we take music from our campfires and place it on a stage, up there in front of us, showing off under the spotlight. In bright, air conditioned studios voices are botoxed and pedicured and coated in makeup. We are fed entertainment on a gilded plate; we are separated from our own song.

Reclaiming music is vital to us reclaiming our wildness. Humans on our cultural peripheries *inhabit* music: song as medicine, song as map, song as sacredness. Song as a place to live, a place to breathe, a place to join joyously with your brothers and sisters and writhe around in the first Om of the world. Song as a space to *participate*, in the melody of life.

But not us. *Harmony* is no longer something we seek, connection is no longer something we value. Participation is an adventure we have forgotten is available to us. But it exists, always, rhythm as wild time dancing always beneath the surface. All it needs is an awakening. Go play.

Tom Hodgkinson, author of *How to be Free* and general advocate of idleness (an art I fully agree with but have somehow seemed unable to master yet), suggests learning the Ukulele. I've no idea how you would make one using local materials that make anything close to the sound we are used to, but with a bit of patience you will be able to find one on Freecycle or Freegle. I've been told that it is much easier to learn than the guitar, and due to its diminutive size it is easy to take on your moneyless adventures. I've regularly noticed pianos and other instruments being offered for free on many of the gift economy websites mentioned in this book.

PAINTING

Even if you are as artistically latent as myself, painting is a magnificent way to spend a day whenever you can make the time. It's even more enjoyable if you can make the paints yourself first, allowing you to draw a landscape with the very materials that came from that landscape. A work of art isn't just about what it looks like visually – part of its beauty must come from how it has been produced, and its story.

Making paints from plants is easy, and what you want to use will depend on how much time you want to put into it. If you are going for the minimalist approach, you can make many colours simply by mashing fresh berries and flowers with a mortar and pestle. For yellow, three or four cups of marigolds (*Calendula officinalis*) should yield you a fair amount. For darker colours, such as blues and purples, you can go for plants such as blackberries and hibiscus, while field poppies will do a lovely red.[280] They don't keep very well unless you add industrial scale ingredients, so pick fresh and use quickly. There are worse ways of spending your time than harvesting your paint, making incredible colours out of them, before painting the very landscape these ingredients originated from (or the people who helped you pick them). If you're in the spirit you could even go on to share your finished work as freely with your community as Nature shared the materials with you.

Depending on where you live, many other materials can also be used – ochre clay for colours such as yellow/gold, purple, brown and red, chalk for white, black from soot or charcoal, and burnt apple seeds or ground rocks and bone for other colours.

Paintbrushes in medieval England were made out of animal hair, but because of the issues involved in modern day animal farming (unless you use roadkill squirrel hair) I prefer the Roman methods of using twigs, reeds and rushes. If you are an artist, you'll know what qualities you require from your brush for a particular piece; all that is needed then is finding something in Nature that already has those qualities.

The mushroom paper I spoke of in chapter five is good for watercolours, but in terms of painting in general, anything can be a canvas – a footpath, a cyclepath, your house front.

STREET PARTIES

Few of us know our neighbours anymore, a reality that perfectly symbolises the path that Western civilisation has led us down. It really doesn't have to be that way though. I'm not suggesting you should want to be best mates with everyone on your street, but being able to walk down it and at least give a smile and say hello to one or two can really benefit your (and their) life and sense of connection and community.

The best way to break the ice is to organise a big party. *Streets Alive*[281] is a national organisation that advises small local community groups, such as a gathering of neighbours, on how to throw one hell of a street party[282] in a way that doesn't alienate or annoy anyone. After having a few drinks together you'll suddenly notice yourself talking with them as you pass by each day, or who knows, maybe even becoming close friends. I heard about one case where people who met via a Streets Alive party organised a weekly dinner party evening, with each person taking it in turns to cook for everyone else. It is a bit like watching TV show *Come Dine With Me* except a) nobody has to win or lose b) you actually get to eat the food c) you actually get to meet the people d) you don't have an entire camera crew in your sitting room e) every word you utter isn't going to be feasted upon by millions of viewers across the nation as they rip open the plastic covering of their own microwaveable TV dinner.

As simple as this act may seem, getting to know our neighbours again is a crucial prerequisite for any of the more technical solutions that we're going to have to implement if we are to make the necessary journey to a fully localised society.

BOOZE

Whether you're going to a street party, or just have a thirst after a hard day in the sun, you may want to add some booze into the equation. Being an Irishman, I must admit to enjoying the odd pint every now and then. In my years living moneylessly, going down to the pub was one of the few things I sorely missed. That's not to say that I didn't consider it a small sacrifice worth making for the gain of all the joys of complete freedom, but I did miss it.

Not being able to go to the pub doesn't mean you can't enjoy a good pint though.

LOCAL BOOZE FOR FREE

Andy Hamilton, author of *Booze for Free*[283] and co-author (apparently he wrote the best bits too) of *The Self Sufficient-ish Bible*

Very crudely speaking, alcohol is made by a sugar fungus commonly known as yeast. The yeast will 'eat' the sugar then 'wee' alcohol and 'fart' carbon dioxide. Unfortunately, another fact is that sugar doesn't grow that abundantly here in the UK, making it hard to have real UK booze for free.

I say hard as is it isn't impossible. Indeed, the easiest booze to make for free is cider. The amount of sugars and even the yeast needed occurs naturally in the apple and on its skin. To make a drinkable cider is ridiculously easy to do too, in a few steps.

1. Crush apples
2. Ferment the juice
3. Drink
4. Fall over

I said to make drinkable cider, but if you want to make good cider then care also needs to be taken when selecting the apples. Here are a few pointers:

- Too many cooking apples makes a very sour tasting cider.
- Too many sweet dessert apples can mean a bland cider.
- Single variety ciders are not as full flavoured as a good mix.
- About three carrier bags full = 4.5 litres/1 gallon of cider.

The most efficient way to crush apples is with a cider press. They can be juiced if you have a juicer but the waste to cider ratio is rather high and I known plenty of people burn out their juicers this way, meaning it can be a rather expensive business, quite the opposite of what we are after.

A cider press is a little more appealing. In some villages people still go around with a cider press offering to crush apples in return for some cider or apples. Ask about to see if anyone does the same in your neighbourhood. Here in Bristol there are a few groups that got together to make a cider press, and each year they pick wild apples together and press enough apples for 100 litres of cider for each group. Not bad for an afternoon's work!

To crush, cut up the apples, place into a nylon bag (or pillow case) and press!

The resulting juice is then placed into a clean and sterilized demijohn. I got half of mine from Freecycle (see page 97) as retired booze makers are often glad to get rid of these bulky items to make more space, and so are frequently listed. They all came with airlocks and bungs too. These help seal in the juice/cider and protect it from any airborne contaminants whilst also letting the CO_2 out.

If Freecycle proves fruitless, you can also use a plastic 5 litre container, make a small slit in the lid and ram in an airlock.

Leave the demijohn in a place with a regular temperature of between 10-25ºC for about 6 months or until the bubbling has ceased. Siphon into bottles.

The bottles you use can be obtained from recycling bins, from saving your own or by throwing a *bring a few bottles of beer party.*

If you can get hold of a capping machine then great. You could reuse old caps, but too many times and they won't seal properly. Otherwise the swing top bottles can be reused, so perhaps try and forage some from a posh friend.

Using the same principles outlined above you can also make wine, just replace the apples for grapes.

OTHER FUN STUFF

Games

Humanity's love for board games seems to be impervious to technological regression (or as some would prefer to call it, progress). Despite the growth in computer gaming, sales of board games appear to be on the increase. Of course, there is no need to buy them – you could just make your own. You could make a scrabble board and its pieces out of cardboard in a matter of hours, or a pack of cards out of paper. Word and singing games require no resources at all.

I am planning on making an almost life-size chess board out of locally grown wooden pieces. I've seen this work in many city parks, such as in Sydney, and they become the centre of attraction for the local area, with men and women and children all sitting around watching two warriors battle it out, as they wait to get a game themselves. Combine this with a few musicians lazing around with their instruments and you have yourself one hell of a relaxing day, with no fossil fuels being burnt, no money required, nothing except the simple coming together of neighbours and future friends (aka strangers). We're planning ours to be under the shade of a tree, with park benches around it where people can debate, eat, drink and be merry. If you live in a city without a big enough garden to do this, why not speak to your council about funding a chess board area in one of your parks, or just giving permission for you to create one. Even though I can't imagine the council's administrators making the pieces themselves, they would cost next to nothing to produce and they'd provide a lifetime of free fun for the local residents. This idea worked very well in Sydney, and the people there really respected the games area, which people tend to do when they see that it has been created for (and ideally by) their own community.

For those who like more athletic games, there are all sorts of places to play, and you'll have no problem finding any necessary equipment on the likes of Freegle. Organisations such as Tennis For Free[284] in the UK are creating places where people can play tennis without any membership costs, and they've got thousands of free courts all over the country. Any park can be temporarily converted into a five-a-side football pitch.

I've also seen some kids in Africa make their own pool table out of earth, bamboo and dung. Of course it's not as perfect as one of our industrialised ones, but who cares, it's just a game, it's only meant to be fun! And there is the added benefit that their table didn't come at the cost of the destruction of an entire planet. By means of a shit (literally speaking) pool table, these kids have shown that you can strike a balance between having fun *and* a healthy inhabitable planet that respects the needs of all of the community of life we share it with.

Music, comedy and performance

Open mic nights are a great way to exhibit and enjoy the best – and worst – local talent in your area. They tend to be focused on music, but some of the best I've been to are showcases for many of the arts, such as storytelling, comedy, fooling, poetry, puppetry and any number of weird and wonderful performances that people put together. These evenings are as easy as freeskilling events to organise – you simply agree a venue, do a little promotion locally (talk to your local radio station or newspaper), and the performers will show up and perform for free. Many use it as a way to build confidence in front of a very encouraging and supportive crowd, who are always more than happy to have been gifted an evening of free entertainment.

This doesn't have to be in a bar or café, and nothing has to be consumed. The audience could bring food and drink to share if they wished, and there is nothing like the sharing of food, the discovery of unsuspected talents in each other and self-produced entertainment to make people feel good about the community they live in. You could organise an acoustic open mic night in any space that is free, whether it be your house, a park or the local social centre or squat.

Groups

Organising an interest group (a writers' circle, a nature society, a five-a-side football team), or joining an existing one, is a great way to meet like-minded people in your local community. Take a nature group for example – one week someone from the group with tree identification skills could take the rest on a tour of the local woods or city park, whilst the next someone who is an expert in wildlife could bring everyone badger spotting. This could just as easily be a weekly or monthly chess group, jogging club or willow weaving get together.

If you feel enthused to set one up, simply organise an initial event, get a core group together if you can and then use local media (such as notice-boards, newsletters or small radio stations or newspapers) to get word out about it. Once you get going, word of mouth will do the rest of the work.

Even better, why not go out committing random acts of kindness[285] to strangers (or join groups such as the Kindness Offensive[286]) whenever the feeling comes upon you, or get yourself a big piece of cardboard, write *Free Hugs* on it, and stand offering open arms to anyone walking down the High Street who looks like they would enjoy a hug. Best done with a few friendly looking friends, so you don't scare anyone not used to such behaviour. I once witnessed people getting kicked out of a shopping centre for offering free hugs, the security guards (in uniforms that were oddly similar to those of police officers) telling them that they hadn't permission to be there. Strangely, I'd been to shopping centres countless times previously to buy stuff and never once did I need prior permission to be there!

Debate evenings

I love a good debate – too much sometimes. The format it normally takes has so much potential for us to explore subjects, using often passionate and polemic speakers to share their perspectives on the big issues of the day. If there isn't a regular debate evening in your area, then take the lead on it; these things aren't going to organise themselves. Come up with a few potential subjects, contact some well-known local voices on the subject (ideally with different views – a hunter and an animal rights activist being one example), and promote it through free local networks. Not only is it a great method of communication, it gives the audience a forum to ask questions within, gets like- and unlike-minded folk together, and ideally everyone comes away understanding the other side's perspective a little more. That is if everyone goes into it with an open mind that their original point of view may not have been the most complete.

Movies

There is no need to go to the cinema if you want to watch a good movie, unless you've got an inexplicable weakness for formulaic Hollywood love stories and action movies. Hundreds of entertaining and educational documentaries are now available for free on websites such as TopDocumentary Films(.com)[287] and FilmsforAction(.org).[288]

Another idea is to invite local filmakers to showcase their work amongst locals, which can also help them get the support they need to bring it to more people. Projection equipment is often shared between members on my local Freeconomy group, so ask for a loan from your own group if you like the thought of hosting an evening yourself. For a venue, social centres such as *The Cowley Club*[289] in Brighton or *Kebele*[290] in Bristol are always more than happy to host such events for free.

Imagination

All you really need to have fun is imagination. Look around you and try to see everything in a different way to how you've seen it up to now. Think how much fun you could have with the world. Old car tyres and rope become swings, lakes become swimming pools, shopping malls and town centres become venues for flash mobs, the countryside becomes free adventures, dead wood and brush become forest hideouts, waste plastic, cord and canes become kites, parks become venues for music and comedy, logs become sculptures and everything has the potential for art.

FREE YOURSELF FROM YOUR MONETARY MASTERS

The monetary economy kills our spirit, teaching us to consume instead of play. It has bought up the entire planet – a planet that was once ours to share freely – so that it can then sell it back to us. Because of this, we fools spend all of our time doing work we derive little or no meaning or happiness from, instead of doing all the things that we love to do.

Slavery never ended in the nineteenth century, it was merely rebranded and marketed to us in a different packet. The monetary economy doesn't serve us, we serve it. It is out-of-date, obsolete, a chain around our necks. So let's change it, and together co-create stories that serve both us and the land we inhabit well.

The function of moneylessness is *not* to impose limits on your creativity. The point is to give your creativity wings. It is counter-intuitive but widely recognised that creativity blossoms within limits. As psychologist Rollo May put it, "creativity requires limits, for the creative act arises out of the struggle of human beings and against that which limits them". Ask me to invent a game and I'm stumped, but ask me to invent a game I can play with just twelve people, six sticks and a spoon and I start getting inspired! So let's set limits on ourselves that preserve a world worth living in, and then reap the joy and creativity that those limits miraculously give birth to.

CHAPTER 16

THE BEGINNING IS NIGH

> *There is one thing stronger than all the armies in the world, and that is an idea whose time has come.*
>
> Victor Hugo

We find ourselves at a fascinating point in human history. Terrible, sad, violent and confusing, without a doubt, but a place also in which the seeds of something beautiful have an unprecedented chance to grow. All around us our world is melting, both in the Arctic ice caps and in the stories of our minds. Economically as well, our structures are falling apart. The choices our forebears made are no longer working for us – even if we stopped all production today and lived off the wealth we've already created (such a scenario couldn't be more unlikely to happen), we'd still be in the process of an ecological meltdown to some degree. The Doomsday criers desperately warning that civilisation is about to collapse could not be more wrong: civilisation is already collapsing. Once we remove our gaze from the glittering chintz of our shopping bags, our collective acknowledgement of this is only a matter of time.

For many, collapse is well under way. As Terence McKenna remarked, "the apocalypse is not something which is coming. The apocalypse has arrived in major portions of the planet and it's only because we live within a bubble of incredible privilege and social insulation that we still have the luxury of anticipating the apocalypse."

That said, I'm feeling pretty upbeat about it all. Never has possibility been more potent; never have our culture's stories – so obviously not working – been more open to scrutiny. People everywhere are crawling out of the burning woodwork, gasping for air, demanding a change. And this is where our hope lies. But hope needs to put on a pair of overalls if it is to be turned into anything meaningful.

We are extraordinarily adaptable creatures. We can be any beings we want to be, if we want it badly enough. Out of the flames and smouldering embers of such a remarkable world as ours can rise a thousand phoenixes, a million transformations. Out of monetary economics can rise the gift economy; competitive relationships can transform into symbiotic ones, hoarding into sharing, stress into play, complexity into simplicity, the conditional into the unconditional, boredom into creativity and isolation into connection. We are faced with an incredibly exciting chance to create a new way of living, one that mixes the best of the old with the best of the new and undiscovered.

The way we live right now is a choice, one of many options available to us. As Graeber points out, "if democracy is to mean anything, it is the ability to arrange things in a different way".[291] We can decide how it is we want to live, and as long as that respects the natural limits of our habitat, we can create whatever lives we want. How do you want to live yours?

I know how I want to. I want to live in freedom, in a manner that also affords the rest of life the same autonomy over their lives. I want to be intimately connected to the land and the people of my habitat. I want to nurture relationships that are based on sharing and unconditional giving, relationships that uplift and inspire and affirm that people are in fact loving and kind. I want to live as I see fit regardless of whether the melting of the ice caps – and civilisation with it – is inevitable or not. I want to live a life that is present in the moment, not regretting yesterday or worrying about tomorrow. I want to share the fruits of my labour as freely as Nature shares them with me, without a taint of the notions of credit or debt on my mind. I want to delve into the depths of life and experience aspects of both it and myself that I don't even know exist yet. And when only my body remains, I want my closest friends to make things out of every spare part of my flesh and bones – shoes, belts, tools and drums. I want my beloved to then play a beautiful beat on my tanned skin that will echo across the valley, an eternal beat that every bird, every otter and every human recognises as the heartbeat of the land.

But if I want this, I have to choose it. And choice is not a passive beast, sitting in a coffee shop, drinking soya cappuccinos; choice is an active bastard, who gets off his arse and does something. If we want change, we're going to have to change. If we want significant change, we're going to have to change significantly. As David MacKay astutely pointed out, "if everyone does a little, we'll achieve only a little".[292] Our children will not care about *how good our intentions were* in fifty years time; they'll care about *how effective our actions were* and whether or not they have clean air to breathe, enough water to drink and healthy food to eat.

Similarly, what use to the Borneo pygmy elephant is grandly philosophising about Oneness if we continue to destroy their only remaining habitat in order to feed our palm oil habit? What use is it to the salmon if we sit around sadly shaking our heads as those we elect build another dam? What use is it to the Amazon rainforest if we sign a petition to save it before joyfully tucking into our beef (or veggie) burger, made possible only by the destruction of the same habitat we would, conceptually, theoretically, wouldn't-it-be-nice-if-we-could, want to save? It is of no use whatsoever. The humans and non-humans whose lives we are devastatingly destroying do not care what we think or say about things – they care about what we do to stop it. What we do, not what we say we will try to do if we can find the time, will be all that matters in the end. It is our responsibility, because it is *our* choices that are informing and feeding this destruction; it is our responsibility because the culprit is *our* culture.

We need to act. And we need to act now. Of course, this is where it gets tricky. What the hell can we do, and what if it is already too late? Howard Thurman once said, "don't ask yourself what the world needs. Ask yourself what makes you come alive and then go do that. Because what the world needs is people who have come alive." There is no right or wrong way to act – do whatever it is your soul is calling you to do, and pursue it full of courage and with an unconditional love for the whole of which you are a part.

For some of you, that will mean spending your lives developing new cultural seeds for humanity, whether that be through writing or performance or by simply enacting a more inspiring story in your every day lives. If this is your calling, do it to the fullest of your ability, for the Western world desperately needs new stories to bring it into an absolutely sustainable, non-exploitative and symbiotic economy.

To others this will mean planting those cultural seeds for the new economy, whether that means creating the first Freeshop in your area, organising a clothes swap or Freeskilling evening, or simply being a couch-surfing host. If this is you, resolve to nourish and expand the richness of these experiences every day of your life from here onwards. To do so involves no sacrifice and they will feed the world you inhabit everyday with a spirit that will uplift, inspire and empower you and those around you.

For a number of you, in the spirit of Henry David Thoreau, whose writings inspired the likes of Gandhi and Martin Luther King, this may mean chopping down some big metaphorical trees, so as to let a little sunlight into the forest floor, allowing the new cultural seeds of the gift economy to germinate and flourish, bringing back diversity and health to the whole system; in other words, this may involve breaking the law. As Thoreau wrote, "it is not desirable to cultivate a respect for the law, so much as for [rightness]. The only obligation which I have a right to assume is to do at any time what I think right … Cast your whole vote, not a strip of paper merely, but your whole influence … If the alternative is to keep all just men in prison, or give up war and slavery, the State will not hesitate which to choose. If a thousand men were not to pay their tax bills this year, that would not be a violent and bloody measure, as it would be to pay them, and enable the State to commit violence and shed innocent blood. This is, in fact, the definition of a peaceable revolution."[293]

To a few of you, this may translate as stink-bombing your nearest multinational supermarket's fridges, or fast food chain's toilets, every day until they leave town, or protecting the last fragments of the Wild by whatever means available to you, just as *Seldom Seen Smith* and *George Hayduke* once did in their own charming way.[294] Many laws are unjust, and to submit to an unjust law is unjust towards those whose lives are destroyed by them. Abide by your own laws, not those made for you by people who display care for little other than maximum financial profit and 'economic' growth, nor those who have made defending habitats illegal whilst they lawfully loot the entire planet. Ask yourself what is the most effective and loving action you can undertake, and then act in the most potent way, for "inaction is a weapon of mass destruction".[295]

We all have a role to play, so let's support each other in those roles, let's unite under that which we have in common, instead of berating each other for the little differences that inevitably exist between us.

Moving beyond the concept of money is one part act of resistance and one part creation. It simultaneously erodes old ways of living and creates new ones – as one thing decays, it gives birth to another. To believe that either of these parts by themselves will be sufficient to preserve our diverse world, and the most admirable parts of ourselves, is delusional. By creating a new way of living for yourself, one which is focused on connection and relationship rather then the accumulation of meaningless notes and coins, you will inevitably discover and create new ways of being that will be witnessed by all who come into contact with you on a daily basis. Nothing, in this respect, is more powerful than example. And the relationships you form will nourish and support the social projects you co-create with others in your local community – the plants that grow from your new philosophical seeds.

It has become almost impossible for me to finish this book. Language, pages, ink, are such imperfect containers for the feelings, ideas and passions that surge in me that it's tempting to spill over into eternal waterfalls of words in order to try and compensate. How to stop writing when the violence continues? How to stop urging when the apathy still abides? It has become almost impossible for me to shut up. So instead I will hand you over to a much wiser man than me, Patrick Whitefield, and end this book as he began his seminal work:[296]

> *All we can do in life is to make sure that we play our own part in it the best we can. Much as we would like to, we can never do more than that. Everything we do is so complex, and relies for its ultimate completion on so many different people and natural forces, that we can never take responsibility for the final outcome of our actions. We can only take responsibility for the actions themselves.*

Give action.

NOTES

1 Graeber, David (2011). *Debt: The First 5,000 Years*. Melville House Publishing. p.109.
2 Sundeen, Mark (2012). *The Man who Quit Money*. Riverhead.
3 Smith, Adam (1776). *The Wealth of Nations*. Penguin Classics: New edition, 1982.
4 Fiat money is currency that has been declared by a government to be legal tender (i.e. it must be accepted as a form of payment within the borders of a country, for both private and public debts), but which has no intrinsic value in itself and whose value is derived from people's faith in it.
5 Eisenstein, Charles (2011). *Sacred Economics: Money, Gift and Society in the Age of Transition*. Evolver Editions. p.79.
6 Boyle, Mark (2010). *The Moneyless Man: A Year of Freeconomic Living*. Oneworld: Oxford.
7 Watts, Alan (1975). *Psychotherapy East and West*. Vintage.
8 Rand, Ayn (1964). *The Virtue of Selfishness*. Signet.
9 Eisenstein, Charles (2007). *The Ascent of Humanity*. Panenthea.
10 The understanding of this process of separation is crucial to anyone seeking to understand how we arrived at where we are today. Charles Eisenstein's *The Ascent of Humanity* is a seminal work in this respect, and essential reading on this subject. It is also available on the internet in "the spirit of the gift" that Eisenstein himself puts so courageously into practice.
11 Griffiths, Jay (2000). *Pip Pip*. Flamingo. p.14.
12 Everett, Daniel (2009). *Don't Sleep, There are Snakes: Life and Language in the Amazonian Jungle*. Profile Books.
13 Eisenstein, Charles (2007). *The Ascent of Humanity*. Panenthea. p.206.
14 Eisenstein, Charles (2011). *Sacred Economics: Money, Gift and Society in the Age of Transition*. Evolver Editions.
15 Hyde, Lewis (1983). *The Gift: Imagination and the Erotic Life of Property*. Vintage: New York.
16 Prieur, Ran. http://ranprieur.com/archives/009.html
17 Atwood, Margaret (2008). *Payback: Debt and the Shadow Side of Wealth*. House of Anansi Press. 2nd edition.
18 Graeber, David (2011). *Debt: The First 5,000 Years*. Melville House Publishing. p.92.
19 For more information about DEFRA, go to www.defra.gov.uk
20 For the full article on the BBC News website, go to www.bbc.co.uk/news/magazine-17353707
21 Trainer, Ted (2007). *Renewable Energy Cannot Sustain a Consumer Society*. Springer. pp.7-8.
22 Jensen, Derrick (2006). *Endgame: The Problem of Civilisation Volume I*. Seven Stories Press, U.S. 1st edition.
23 Thoreau, Henry David (1863). 'Life without Principle'. *The Atlantic Monthly*. Vol. 12, Issue 71. pp.484-495.
24 For more information on the Dunbar number, go to www.guardian.co.uk/technology/2010/mar/14/my-brightidea-robin-dunbar
25 Graeber, David (2011). *Debt: The First 5,000 Years*. Melville House Publishing. pp.22-28.
26 To read the full study, go to www.guardian.co.uk/uk/series/reading-the-riots
27 Norberg-Hodge, Helena (1991). *Ancient Futures: Learning from Ladakh*. Sierra Club Books: San Francisco. pp.101-102.
28 Lovelock, James (2006). *The Revenge of Gaia*. Penguin. Gaia theory, a term coined by James Lovelock and named after the primordial Earth goddess from ancient Greek mythology, propounds that all organisms and their inorganic surroundings on Earth are integrated to form a self-regulating system, and includes 'both animate and inanimate parts'.
29 Eisenstein, Charles (2011). *Sacred Economics: Money, Gift and Society in the Age of Transition*. Evolver Editions. p.16.

30 Doctorow, Cory (2010). *Down and Out in the Magic Kingdom*. Harper Voyager. In this book, a Whuffie is a reputation based currency within a post-scarcity economy where everything is free.
31 Graeber, David (2011). *Debt: The First 5,000 Years*. Melville House Publishing. p.130.
32 For more information about Freeconomy, go to www.justfortheloveofit.org
33 Shuman, Michael (2000). *Going Local: Creating Self-Reliant Communities in a Global Age*. Routledge.
34 North, Peter (2010). *Local Money*. Green Books.
35 For more information about the Transition network, go to www.transitionnetwork.org
36 For more information about Timebanks, go to www.timebanking.org
37 For more information about LETS, go to www.letslinkuk.net
38 For more information about The Zeitgeist Movement, go to www.thezeitgeistmovement.com
39 For more information about The Venus Project, go to www.thevenusproject.com
40 Built-in obsolescence is a concept in which manufacturers deliberately shorten the lifespan of their products in order to ensure that their customers keep having to buy new ones.
41 For more information about the ideas and philosophies of Peter Joseph, go to www.whoispeterjoseph.com
42 For more information about The Happy Planet Index, go to www.happyplanetindex.org
43 For more information about the New Economics Foundation (NEF), go to www.neweconomics.org
44 Helena Norberg-Hodge, winner of the Right Livelihood Award, is an analyst of the impact of the global economy on the cultures of people around the world, and a pioneer of the localisation movement. She has also produced another award winning documentary, 'The Economics of Happiness', www.theeconomicsofhappiness.org
45 You can watch Helena Norberg-Hodge's film 'Ancient Futures – Learning from Ladakh' online for free at http://video.google.com/videoplay?docid=-7846941319183318053
46 For more information about Shaun Chamberlin, founder of Dark Optimism, go to www.darkoptimism.org
47 Chamberlin, Shaun (2009). *The Transition Timeline: for a local, resilient future*. Green Books.
48 Abraham Maslow, in his book titled *Motivation and Personality*, proposed a theory known as 'Maslow's Hierarchy of Needs'. Normally illustrated as a pyramid, this hierarchy suggests that people are motivated to meet their basic needs first and then increasing levels of advanced needs once the previous level of needs have been sufficiently met. At the bottom you have physiological needs such as food water and sex, and above that are layers labelled safety, love/belonging, esteem and (at the top) self-actualisation, which includes elements such as morality, creativity and spontaneity.
49 For more information about Peace Pilgrim, go to www.peacepilgrim.org
50 Suelo, Daniel. 'Zero Currency blog'. http://zerocurrency.blogspot.com
51 For more information about *Resurgence* magazine, go to www.resurgence.org
52 Kumar, Satish (2000). *No Destination: Autobiography of an Earth Pilgrim*. Green Books. 2nd revised edition.
53 Astikainen, Tomi. *The Sunhitcher* is licensed under a Creative Commons Attribution-NonCommercial 3.0 Unported License, and is free to read online at www.tomiastikainen.com
54 For more information about Jurgen Wagner, go to www.holistic-love.net
55 For more information about Forward the Revolution, go to www.forwardtherevolution.net
56 Kruse, Sonja. 'Ubuntu in Abundance blog'. www.letterdash.com/skruse
57 For more information about Adin Van Ryneveld, go to www.adin.co.za
58 For more information about Elf Pavlik and his project, go to http://moneyless.info
59 For more information on Julez Edward, go to http://worldtripforever.com
60 The phrase 'low-impact dwelling' usually refers to the minimal ecological impact of such a home on its landscape and the planet. However, I prefer to think of these dwellings as 'high-impact', in that they can provide inspirational examples of solutions to the myriad challenges we face for all those who come into contact with them.
61 According to the UN Environment Programme.
62 Johnstone, Chris (2010). *Find Your Power*. Permanent Publications. 2nd edition.

63 Macy, Joanna; Johnstone, Chris (2012). *Active Hope*. New World Library.
64 Black, D. (2007). 'A Review of Compulsive Buying Disorder'. *World Psychiatry*, Vol.6, Number 1 pp.14-18.
65 Cahill, Kevin (2002). *Who Owns Britain: The Hidden Facts Behind Landownership in the UK and Ireland*. Canongate.
66 Simon Fairlie is the editor of *The Land* magazine and founder of Chapter 7. For more information on Chapter 7, go to www.tlio.org.uk/chapter7
67 Monbiot, George (1994). 'The Tragedy of Enclosure'. www.monbiot.com/1994/01/01/the-tragedy-ofenclosure
68 Rosen, Nick (2007). *How to Live Off-grid*. Bantam. 3rd edition. p.31.
69 Author of *Low Impact Development: Planning and People in a Sustainable Countryside*.
70 Report by the Ecological Land Coop, 'Small is successful'. www.ecologicalland.coop/projects-small-successful
71 For more information about Chapter 7, go to www.tlio.org.uk/chapter7
72 For a copy of the *DIY Planning Handbook*, or free planning advice from Chapter 7, go to www.tlio.org.uk/chapter7/planningadvice
73 For more information about the Ecological Land Cooperative, go to www.ecologicalland.coop
74 For more information about Lammas, go to www.lammas.org.uk
75 Sugden, Chrissie (2011). 'How To Get Planning Permission on Non-Development Land'. www.permaculture.co.uk/articles/how-get-planning-permission-non-development-land
76 For more information about Free and Real, go to www.freeandreal.org
77 For more information on the Freeman on the Land movement, go to The People's United Community (TPUC) website at www.tpuc.org
78 For more information about Simon and Jasmine Dale's house in Lammas, go to www.simondale.net/house
79 For more information about Association Ardheia, go to http://ardheia.free.fr
80 Jensen, Derrick (2006). *Endgame: The Problem of Civilisation* Volume I. Seven Stories Press, U.S. 1st edition. p.149.
81 Gibran, Kahlil (1923). *The Prophet*. Pan. 4th edition.
82 Ray, Rebecca; Schmitt, John (2007). 'No-vacation Nation USA – a comparison of leave and holiday in OECD countries'. www.law.harvard.edu/programs/lwp/papers/No_Holidays.pdf
83 Lo, Alpha; Bevington, Alden (2008). *The Open Collaboration Encyclopedia*. Pioneer Imprints. 2.1 edition.
84 For more information about HelpX, or to join, go to www.helpx.net
85 North, Peter (2010). *Local Money*. Green Books. p.70.
86 For more information about Swapaskill, or to join, go to www.swapaskill.com
87 For more information about LocalSkillSwap, or to join, go to www.localskillswap.com
88 Derrick Jensen is the author of *Endgame* (2006, Seven Stories Press), *A Language Older Than Words* (2002, Souvenir Press), *The Culture of Make Believe* (2004, Chelsea Green) amongst many others.
89 Mears, Ray (2001). *Outdoor Survival Handbook: A Guide To The Resources And Materials Available In The Wild and How To Use Them For Food, Shelter, Warmth and Navigation*. Ebury Press.
90 Mears, Ray (2003). *Essential Bushcraft*. Hodder & Stoughton.
91 Wiseman, John Lofty (2006). *SAS Survival Handbook*. Harper Collins.
92 For more information about Will Lord, flint kanpping or his courses, go to www.beyond2000bc.co.uk
93 For more information about Freegle, or to join, go to http://uk.freecycle.org
94 For more information about Freecycle (UK), or to join, go to http://uk.freecycle.org
For Freecycle Global go to www.freecycle.org
95 For more information about Books for Free and Healthy Planet, go to www.healthyplanet.org
96 For the full article, go to www.dailyecho.co.uk/news/features/living/9428232.A__shop__giving_away_free_books_has_come_to_Southampton
97 For more information about The Really Really Free Market, go to www.reallyreallyfree.org
98 If you want to set up a Really Really Free Market, go to www.reallyreallyfree.org/index.php?l=startrrfm for advice.

99 For more information about Streetbank, or to join, go to www.streetbank.com
100 For more information about FavorTree, or to join, go to www.favortree.com
101 For more information about LetsAllShare, or to join, go to http://letsallshare.com
102 For more information about Ecomodo, or to join, go to http://ecomodo.com
103 Figures according to the Women's Environmental Network (WEN). For more information about WEN, go to www.wen.org.uk
104 For more information about Elimination Communication, go to www.nappyfreebaby.co.uk/what-is-elimination-communication
105 For more information about ReaditSwapit, or to join, go to www.readitswapit.co.uk
106 For more information about Bookmooch, or to join, go to http://bookmooch.com
107 For more information about Bookhopper, or to join, go to www.bookhopper.com
108 For more information about Bookcrossing, or to join, go to www.bookcrossing.com
109 Boyle, Mark (2010). *The Moneyless Man*. Oneworld, Oxford. pp.102-103.
110 Hugh Fearnley-Whittingstall is a broadcaster, writer and smallholder based in the UK, and is the founder of River Cottage.
111 For more information about Landshare, or to join, go to www.landshare.net
112 For more information on WWOOFing, or to join the organisation, go to www.wwoof.org
113 For more information on the New Local Government Network, go to www.nlgn.org.uk/public
114 Hope, Nick; Ellis, Victoria (2009). 'Can you dig it?' www.nlgn.org.uk/public/wp-content/uploads/can-you-dig-it
115 For the full briefing, go to www.parliament.uk/briefing-papers/SN00887.pdf
116 For the full article, go to www.lep.co.uk/news/pensioners_turn_wasteland_into_a_haven_1_70109
117 For more information about the Capital Growth project, go to www.capitalgrowth.org
118 For more information about Eastside Roots, go to www.eastsideroots.org.uk
119 For more information about Embercombe, go to www.embercombe.co.uk
120 Macartney, Tim (2007). *Finding Earth Finding Soul*. Green Books. For more information go to www.timmacmacartney.co.uk
121 An English version of Eurotopia is available at www.eurotopia.de/english.html
122 To watch a video about Lakabe, go to www.faircompanies.com/videos/view/medieval-spanish-ghost-townnow-self-sufficient-ecovillage
123 Holmgren, David (2009). *Future Scenarios*. Green Books.
124 Holmgren, David (2011). *Permaculture: Principles and Pathways Beyond Sustainability*. Permanent Publications.
125 Mollison, Bill; Holmgren, David (1978). *Permaculture One*. Corgi.
126 For the scope of permaculture design solutions see Mollison, Bill (1988). *Permaculture: A Designers' Manual*. Tagari.
127 For an explanation of systems thinking and design principles of permaculture see Holmgren, David (2002). *Permaculture: Principles and Pathways Beyond Sustainability*. Permanent Publications. For a summary of the book download *The Essence of Permaculture* from www.holmgren.com.au/html/Writings/Writings.html
128 Barclay, Christopher (2012). 'Allotments'. p.5. www.parliament.uk/briefing-papers/SN00887.pdf
129 This quote was taken from the following article in *The Independent*. www.independent.co.uk/life-style/houseand-home/gardening/the-big-question-should-landowners-be-forced-to-give-up-space-for-allotments-1787352.html
130 Figures according to research by the American Water Works Association.
131 Fore more information about Power Off weekends, go to www.guardian.co.uk/environment/green-livingblog/2010/mar/16/power-off
132 Fore more information about Slow Sundays, go to www.resurgence.org/take-part/slow-sunday.html
133 Fore more information about how to make a bicycle powered smoothie maker, go to www.instructables.com/id/How-to-create-a-human-powered-bike-blender-for-les
134 For more information about Transition Heathrow, go to www.transitionheathrow.com
135 This quote was taken from the Grow Heathrow website. For more information, go to www.transitionheathrow.com/grow-heathrow

136 For more information about the Advisory Service for Squatters, go to www.squatter.org.uk
137 Kahn, Lloyd; Easton, B. (2000). *Shelter*. Shelter Publications Inc.,U.S.; 2nd revised edition.
138 Kahn, Lloyd (2004). *Home Work: Handbuilt Shelter*. Shelter Publications Inc., U.S. Illustrated edition.
139 Kahn, Lloyd (2012). *Tiny Homes: Simple Shelter*. Shelter Publications Inc., U.S.; 1st edition.
140 For more information about Earthships, go to http://earthship.com
141 For more information about Earth bag construction, go to www.earthbagstructures.com/basics/stepbystep.htm
142 Jones, Barbara (2009). *Building with Straw Bales: A Practical Guide for the UK and Ireland*. Green Books.
143 Oehler, Mike (1982). *The $50 and Up Underground House Book*. Mole Publishing Co.
144 Pearson, David (2001). *Circle Houses: Yurts, Tipis and Benders*. Chelsea Green.
145 Horning, Jonathan (2009). *Simple Shelters: Tents, Tipis, Yurts, Domes and Other Ancient Homes*. Wooden Books.
146 To learn more about how to build a bender, go to www.stewardwood.org/resources/DIYbender.htm
147 Wrench, Tony (2008). *Building a Low Impact Roundhouse*. Permanent Publications.
148 Steinfeld, Carol (2010). *Liquid Gold: The Lore and Logic of Using Urine to Grow Plants*. Green Books. 2nd revised edition. p.3.
149 The word 'humility' comes from the same semantic root as 'humus', interestingly, which is exactly what thermophilic composting should create from raw humanure.
150 Scott, Nicky (2010). *How to Make and Use Compost: The Ultimate Guide*. Green Books.
151 Dick Kitto is the author of *Composting: The Organic Natural Way* (1988, Thorsons), as well as many other books on organic gardening, education and compost.
152 Jenkins, Joseph (2006). *The Humanure Handbook: A Guide to Composting Human Manure*. Jenkins Publishing, U.S. 3rd revised edition. For more information, go to http://humanurehandbook.com
153 To read *The Humanure Handbook* online for free, go to http://humanurehandbook.com/contents.html
154 Pilkington, George (2005). *Composting with Worms: Why Waste Your Waste*. Eco-logic Books.
155 McConnell, Campbell R.; Brue, Stanley L. (2005). *Economics: Principles, Problems and Policies*. McGraw-Hill Irwin. p.3.
156 For more information about Fergus Drennan and his foraging courses, go to www.wildmanwildfood.co.uk
157 Kennedy, David (1993). *Leaf Concentrate: A Field Guide for Small Scale Programmes*. It is available free online at: www.leafforlife.org/PDFS/english/Leafconm.pdf
158 Figures according to The Mammals Trust.
159 Snyder, Gary (1990). *The Practice of the Wild*. Counterpoint. p.10.
160 Jared Diamond is the author of many books including *Guns, Germs and Steel: A Short History of Everybody for the Last 13,000 Years* (1998, Vintage) and *Collapse: How Societies Choose to Fail or Succeed* (2011, Penguin). He is also Professor of Geography and Physiology at UCLA.
161 Diamond, Jared. 'The Worst Mistake in the History of the Human Race'. www.ditext.com/diamond/mistake.html
162 Strickland, Sue (2001). *Back Garden Seed Saving: Keeping Our Vegetable Heritage Alive*. Eco-logic Books.
163 Hamilton, Dave (2011). *Grow your Food for Free (well almost)*. Green Books.
164 Dowding, Charles (2009). *Organic Gardening: The Natural No-dig Way*. Green Books. p.166.
165 Whitefield, Patrick (2004). *The Earth Care Manual*. Permanent Publications. pp.197-198.
166 To learn more about how to grow food through the hungry gap, read Charles Dowding's *How to Grow Winter Vegetables* (2011, Green Books).
167 Crawford, Martin (2012). *How to Grow Perennial Vegetables: Low-maintenance, Low-impact Vegetable Gardening*. Green Books
168 For more information about Steph Hafferty and her work, go to www.stephaniehafferty.co.uk

169 Martin Crawford is the director of the Agroforestry Research Trust. He also runs courses, a demonstration site, a larger research forest garden, and a mail order business for plants that are useful for forest gardening.
170 Crawford, Martin (2010). *Creating a Forest Garden: Working with Nature to Grow Edible Crops*. Green Books. p.60.
171 For more information about The Agroforestry Research Trust, go to www.agroforestry.co.uk
172 Crawford, Martin (2010). *Creating a Forest Garden: Working with Nature to Grow Edible Crops*. Green Books.
173 Dowding, Charles (2011). *How to Grow Winter Vegetables*. Green Books. For more information about Charles Dowding, go to www.charlesdowding.co.uk
174 For more information about guerrilla gardening go to www.guerrillagardening.org/ggwar.html
175 For more facts about levels of food waste, go to Tristram Stuart's (author of *Waste: Uncovering the Global Food Scandal*) website at: www.tristramstuart.co.uk
176 For more information on this case and the legal issues around 'skipping', go to www.bbc.co.uk/news/magazine-13037808
177 For more information on the British Hen Welfare Trust, go to www.bhwt.org.uk
178 Organisations such as Margaret Green Animal Rescue will help you rehome cockerels and other birds such as ducks. For more information, go to www.animalsanctuaryuk.com/adopt-sponsor/adopt-birds.html
179 Thear, Katie (1999). *Starting with Chickens: A Beginners Guide*. Broad Leys Publishing Limited. Reprint edition.
180 These statistics from the Centre for Ecology and Hydrology were reported in the following article: www.guardian.co.uk/environment/2010/jun/22/chemicals-bees-decline-major-study
181 To learn how to build a horizontal bee-hive perfect for beginners, go to http://permaculture.org.au/2010/06/21/home-made-bee-hives/
182 For more information about natural bee-keeping, go to www.biobees.com
183 Warren, Piers (2003). *How to Store your Garden Produce*. Green Books.
184 Clifford, Sue; King, Angela (2011). *Community Orchards Handbook*. Green Books. 2nd revised edition.
185 For more information about the Abundance project in Manchester, go to http://abundancemanchester.wordpress.com/contact
186 *The Abundance Handbook: A Guide to Urban Fruit Harvesting* can be found at www.growsheffield.com/pages/groshefhandb.html
187 If you would like to see a bicycle powered water pump extract water from a 90ft well at a rate of ten gallons per minute, go to https://www.youtube.com/watch?v=5ux5YsqFXsw
188 Bee, Becky (2001). *You Can Make The Best Hot Tub Ever*. Groundworks.
189 McVicar, Jekka (1994). *The Complete Herb Book*. Kyle Cathie Limited. p.178.
190 Crawford, Martin (2010). *Creating a Forest Garden: Working with Nature to Grow Edible Crops*. Green Books. pp. 190-191
191 McGuire, Thomas (1972). *The Tooth Trip*. Random House – Bookworks. 1st edition.
192 Anderberg, Kirsten (2011). *Oral Health, Naturally*. Kirsten Anderberg.
193 For more detailed information on *Sapindus drummondii*, go to the Plants for a Future website at www.pfaf.org
194 For more information about Steph Hafferty and her work, go to www.stephaniehafferty.co.uk
195 Hobbes, Thomas (1651). *Leviathan*. Oxford Paperbacks. Reissue edition, 2008.
196 For more information about Malcolm Handoll, or Five Senses, go to www.allfivesenses.com
197 To learn how to make your own flip-flops from old carpet, blown tyres and used shopping bags, go to www.instructables.com/id/Blown-Tire-Shoes
198 Abbey, Edward (1994). *Desert Solitaire*. Ballantine Books Inc. Reprint edition.
199 Boyle, Mark (2010). *The Moneyless Man*. Oneworld: Oxford. p.83.
200 For the full article, go to http://news.bbc.co.uk/1/hi/uk_politics/4953922.stm
201 For more information about Instructables, go to www.instructables.com
202 For more information about Green Tyres, go to www.greentyre.co.uk
203 Murphy, Tom (2011). 'MPG of a Human.' http://physics.ucsd.edu/do-the-math/2011/11/mpg-of-a-human

204 For more information about The Splinter Bike, go to www.splinterbike.co.uk
205 For more information about The Eco-shed, go to www.rammed-earth.org
206 For more information about Liftshare, or to join, go to https://www.liftshare.com/uk
207 For more information about National Car Share, or to join, go to www.nationalcarshare.co.uk
208 For more information about Freewheelers, or to join, go to www.freewheelers.com
209 For more information about Freebus, go to www.freebus.org.uk
210 For more information about Couch-surfing, or to join, go to www.couchsurfing.org
211 For more information about WarmShowers, or to join, go to www.warmshowers.org
212 For more information about Hospitality Club, go to www.hospitalityclub.org
213 For more information about Global Freeloaders, or to join, go to http://globalfreeloaders.com
214 For more information about Servas, or to join, go to http://servas.org
215 For more information about Esperanto, go to www.esperanto.net
216 For more information about Stay4Free, or to join, go to http://stay4free.com/
217 Kemp, William (2009). *The Renewable Energy Handbook: The Updated Comprehensive Guide to Renewable Energy and Independent Living*. Aztext Press.
218 Piggott, Hugh (2011). *Wind Power Workshop: Building Your Own Wind Turbine*. Centre for Alternative Technology Publications. Revised edition.
219 For more information about Open Source Ecology, go to http://opensourceecology.org
220 For more information about how to make your own beeswax candles, go to http://idiotsguides.com/static/quickguides/homegarden/how_to_make_beeswax_candles.html
221 For the full report, go to www.greenpeace.org.uk/MultimediaFiles/Live/FullReport/7154.pdf
222 Boyle, Mark (2010). *The Moneyless Man*. Oneworld: Oxford. pp.35-36.
223 Ferguson, Sue. 'Make your own slow cooker.' *Permaculture* magazine, Issue 21. pp.22-23.
224 Denzer, Kiko (2007). *Build Your Own Earth Oven*. Hand Print Press.
225 To find a model of gas bottle wood-burner that suits your needs, search the Instructables website at www.instructables.com
226 Whitefield, Patrick (2004). *The Earth Care Manual*. Permanent Publications. p.153.
227 Ibid.
228 Congreve, Lady Celia. The Firewood Poem. Believed to have first appeared in the March 2nd 1930 edition of *The Times*.
229 Rosen, Nick (2007). *How to Live Off-grid*. Bantam Books. p.313.
230 For more information about the The Global Village Construction Set (GVCS) go to http://open-sourceecology.org/gvcs.php
231 For more information about Skype, or to get a free account, go to www.skype.com
232 For more information about Open-office, go to www.openoffice.org
233 For more information about Libre Office, go to www.libreoffice.org
234 For more information about DuckDuckGo, go to http://duckduckgo.com
235 To learn more about filter bubbles, see Eli Pariser's TED talk at www.thefilterbubble.com/ted-talk
236 For more information about using Startpage as an alternative to Google, go to https://startpage.com
237 For more information about Hushmail, go to www.hushmail.com
238 For more information about Truecrypt, go to www.truecrypt.org
239 Louv, Richard (2010). *Last Child in the Woods: Saving Our Children from Nature-deficit Disorder*. Atlantic Books.
240 Holt, John (1964). *How Children Fail*. DaCapo Press. Revised edition, 1995.
241 Holt, John (1967). *How Children Learn*. Penguin. New edition, 1991.
242 Illich, Ivan (1971). *Deschooling Society*. Marion Boyars Publishers Ltd. New edition, 1995.
243 Mountney, Ross. 'Ross Mountney's Notebook'. http://rossmountney.wordpress.com
244 Mountney, Ross (2008). *Learning Without School*. Home Education. JKP.
245 For more information about how Freeskilling works, go to www.freeskilling.org.uk
246 For more information about The Khan Academy, go to www.khanacademy.org
247 To see a talk given by Salman Khan for TED, go to www.ted.com/talks/salman_khan_let_s_use_video_to_reinvent_education.html

248 For more information about Instructables, go to www.instructables.com
249 A cantenna is simply a beer can 'MacGyvered' onto your internet wireless box to increase the signal you receive.
250 To see a talk given by Bunker Roy about The Barefoot College for TED, go to www.ted.com/talks/bunker_roy.html
251 For more information about The Barefoot College, go to www.barefootcollege.org
252 For more information about Steiner Waldorf schools, go to www.steinerwaldorf.org
253 For more information about the Montessori method, go to www.montessori.org.uk
254 For more information about The Small School, go to www.thesmallschool.org.uk
255 For more information about Schumacher College, go to www.schumachercollege.org.uk
256 For more information about Summerhill School, go to www.summerhillschool.co.uk
257 Jensen, Derrick (2006). *Endgame: The Problem of Civilisation* Volume I. Seven Stories Press, U.S. 1st edition. p.129.
258 Illich, Ivan (1974). *Medical Nemesis: The Expropriation of Health*. Marion Boyars. Paperback edition. p.16.
259 CIA (2012). 'The World Factbook'. https://www.cia.gov/library/publications/the-worldfactbook/rankorder/2102rank.html
260 To view the source of this information, go to www.guardian.co.uk/environment/interactive/2011/oct/24/howbig-worlds-population-born
261 Hawes, Zoe. www.zoehawes.co.uk/Welcome.html
262 For more information about the Ruskin Apothecary, go to www.ruskinapothecary.org.uk
263 Hawes, Zoe (2010). *Wild Drugs: A Foragers Guide to Healing Plants*. Gaia Books.
264 For more information about Zoe Hawes, go to www.zoehawes.co.uk
265 For more information about the research and studies carried out, go to www.umm.edu/altmed/articles/feverfew-000243.htm
266 According to scientists at the Center for Health and Global Environment in Harvard Medical School.
267 Wong, James (2009). *Grow Your Own Drugs: Easy Recipes for Natural Remedies and Beauty Treats*. Collins.
268 McVicar, Jekka (2009). *Jekka's Complete Herb Book: In Association with the Royal Horticultural Society*. Kyle Cathie.
269 Figures according to www.mooncup.co.uk
270 Hering, Sabine; Maierhof, Gudrun (2002). *Die unpäßliche Frau: Sozialgeschichte der Menstruation und Hygiene*. Mabuse-Verlag GmbH.
271 Research by The Environment Agency, for example, has shown that one third of male fish in British rivers are in the process of changing sex due to hormones, produced by the female reproductive pill, being in such high quantities in sewage.
272 Pollan, Michael (2002). *The Botany of Desire: A Plant's-eye View of the World*. Bloomsbury.
273 Eisenstein, Charles. 'Rituals for Lover Earth.' www.realitysandwich.com/rituals_lover_earth
274 Morris, Desmond (1967). *The Naked Ape: A Zoologist's Study of the Human Animal*. McGraw-Hill. 6th edition.
275 Cherrett, Nia et al. 'Ecological Footprint and Water Analysis of Cotton, Hemp and Polyester'. Download report at www.sei-international.org/publications?pid=1694
276 For more information about Swishing, go to http://swishing.com
277 For more information about Stich 'n Bitch, go to http://stitchnbitch.org
278 Richards, Matt (2004). *Deerskins into Buckskins: How to Tan with Brain, Soap or Eggs*. Backcountry Publications.
279 For full instructions on how to make a peg loom for use with sheep's wool, read John Adams' article 'How To Weave A Woollen Underblanket' in *Permaculture* magazine (issue 47) or at: www.permaculture.co.uk/articles/how-weave-woollen-underblanket
280 Askew, Katherine. 'From Plant to Paintbox'. *Permaculture* magazine, Issue 38. pp. 6-8.
281 For more information about Streets Alive, go to www.streetsalive.org.uk
282 For more information about how to organise a street party, go to www.streetparty.org.uk

283 Hamilton, Andy (2011). *Booze for Free*. Eden Project Books.
284 For more information about Tennis For Free, go to http://tennisforfree.com
285 For more information about Random Acts of Kindness, go to www.randomactsofkindness.org
286 For more information about the Kindness Offensive, go to http://thekindnessoffensive.com
287 For hundreds of top documentaries free online, go to http://topdocumentaryfilms.com/watch-online
288 For over '300 documentaries hand-picked to change the world', go to www.filmsforaction.org/walloffilms
289 For more information about The Cowley Club, go to www.cowleyclub.org.uk
290 For more information about Kebele, go to www.kebelecoop.org
291 Graeber, David (2011). *Debt: The First 5,000 Years*. Melville House Publishing. p.390.
292 MacKay, David J.C (2008). *Sustainable Energy: Without the Hot Air*. UIT.
293 Thoreau, Henry David (1849). *Civil Disobedience*. Public Domain Books, 1993.
294 Seldom Seen Smith and Hayduke are characters from Edward Abbey's classic, *The Monkey Wrench Gang*.
295 Armstrong, Rollo et al. This quote is taken from a song by Faithless titled 'Mass Destruction'.
296 Whitefield, Patrick (2004). *The Earth Care Manual*. Permanent Publication.

INDEX

Inspiration for Creating a Better World

Permaculture magazine helps you live a more natural, healthy and environmentally friendly life.

Permaculture magazine offers tried and tested ways of creating flexible, low cost approaches to sustainable living, helping you to:

- Make informed ethical choices
- Grow and source organic food
- Put more into your local community
- Build energy efficiency into your home
- Find courses, contacts and opportunities
- Live in harmony with people and planet

Permaculture magazine is published quarterly for enquiring minds and original thinkers everywhere. Each issue gives you practical, thought provoking articles written by leading experts as well as fantastic ecofriendly tips from readers!

permaculture, ecovillages, ecobuilding, organic gardening, agroforestry, sustainable agriculture, appropriate technology, downshifting, community development, human-scale economy ... and much more!

Permaculture magazine gives you access to a unique network of people and introduces you to pioneering projects in Britain and around the world. Subscribe today and enrich your life without overburdening the planet!

PERMANENT PUBLICATIONS
The Sustainability Centre, East Meon, Hampshire GU32 1HR, UK
Tel: 01730 823 311 Fax: 01730 823 322 (Overseas: int code +44-1730)
Email: info@permaculture.co.uk

To subscribe and for daily updates, vist our exciting and dynamic website:

www.permaculture.co.uk